CITIZEN LAWMAKERS
The Ballot Initiative Revolution

Preface and Acknowledgments

During the late 1960s, radical protesters adopted the slogan "Power to the People," but the real power of government remained in the hands of politicians and political parties. Beginning in the early 1970s, however, "Power to the People" became a reality through a tremendous upsurge in the use of Initiative and Referendum, the people's power to propose and enact (or reject) laws by citizen petition and popular vote. Between 1968 and 1982, the number of such voter-initiated propositions on state ballots nationwide increased by more than 600 percent, and their focus moved from the purely local to such national issues as the Tax Revolt (heralded by California's "Proposition 13") and the Nuclear Weapons Freeze. The Nuclear Freeze votes of 1982 were the closest approximation to a national referendum in the history of the United States.

Just as the American Revolution shifted ultimate authority from the agents of a distant Crown to locally elected representatives, the Ballot Initiative Revolution is shifting ultimate authority from representatives in state legislatures, city councils, and even Congress to the people themselves. This trend toward participatory democracy is deeply disturbing to some observers, who distrust the capacity of the electorate to make intelligent decisions on complex issues. To others, however, from the late Howard Jarvis, originator of Proposition 13, to consumer advocate Ralph Nader, greater use of ballot Initiatives is a major advance toward a government truly of, by, and for the people.

What are the historical origins and results of the ballot Initiative? Are there local and regional variations? And who *are* these citizen lawmakers who, like Prometheus, have stolen the lawmaking fire from the political gods who once monopolized it?

The underlying causes of the Ballot Initiative Revolution of the 1970s and 1980s are difficult to pinpoint. No national crisis or grand crusade for reform impelled it onward. Although there have been some identifiable leaders like California's late Ed Koupal and Howard Jarvis, who trained and inspired imitators, local ballot Initiative campaigns have sprung up by the dozens under the leadership of individuals who knew little or nothing about these leaders.

In *No Sense of Place: The Impact of Electronic Media on Social Behavior,* Joshua Meyrowitz suggests that television has become the great leveler in all social relations, including political ones.[1] Whereas the highest levels of government were once insulated from public scrutiny, television has now taken voters behind the scenes into legislative halls, political party conventions, and the White House. It used to be said that the making of laws, like the making of sausage, should not be viewed by the public lest they be disgusted by what they saw. But television, beginning in the 1950s and accelerating in the 1960s and 1970s, has ignored this taboo, and not only in the political realm. The consequence, according to Meyrowitz, is that experts and authorities in every field are shown to be just ordinary humans.

Since the mid-1960s the nation's political authorities have again and again revealed their human failings on nationwide television. Yet as television brought the politicians down to human size, it offered the voters no mechanism to correct their misdeeds. In fact, it made them even less accountable by magnifying the importance of looks, style, and money at the expense of issue-based information, which had been the chief currency of political campaigns when the printed news media were dominant.

Not surprisingly, disillusionment set in. Polls show that citizens' trust in authorities of all kinds dropped steadily from the late 1960s onward, and voter turnout dropped as well. As frustration led to disillusionment with traditional forms of political action, however, it encouraged experimentation with new ones. Creative political activists, having decided that the major political parties and politicians were all alike, sought alternative channels of influence.

"The Who," a British rock and roll group, summed up the political attitudes of young people of the Vietnam era in their 1970 song, "Won't Get Fooled Again": "Meet the new boss / Same as the old boss / Won't get fooled again!" The alternative for those who did not want to give up on democracy was political self-reliance, institutionalized in the Initiative and Referendum.

This attitude of political self-reliance spread rapidly in the 1970s, spawning the Ballot Initiative Revolution, keeping it a durable, dynamic institution in the 1980s, and making citizens receptive to the efforts of a new breed of activists: citizen lawmakers. Very few of the citizen lawmakers profiled in this book were ever elected or appointed to any major political office, nor were most of them interested in running. Ronald Reagan, elected governor of California for two terms on a platform of tax reduction, failed to fulfill these promises. But Howard Jarvis, as an ordinary citizen, made it possible for the *people* to do the job themselves, through his campaign to put Proposition 13 on the ballot.

The new public conviction that ordinary people are just as able to decide public policy as the politicians did not automatically induce thousands to take up Initiative petitions of their own accord. As the profiles of citizen lawmakers show, it took years of painstaking organizing. The overriding lesson that they learned, and the lesson of the Ballot Initiative Revolution for all Americans, is that ordinary individuals, even in this age of monstrous bureaucracies and larger-than-life celebrities, can change this nation's laws to make government more accountable.

This book is divided into three sections. The first chapter deals with the historical origins of the Initiative and Referendum process from its beginnings in Switzerland, through the Populist and Progressive movements, to its decline at mid-twentieth century. Chapter 2 covers arguments for and against the Initiative powers. The second section, comprising Chapters 3 through 8, focuses on a series of case studies of Initiative campaigns in the 1970s and 1980s: first those sponsored by liberal activists and environmentalists, later the conservative tax cut Initiatives pioneered by Howard Jarvis in California, and the Nuclear Freeze movement, which was aimed explicitly at changing national policy through a national Initiative. The section ends with a look at recent efforts to put the right to make laws through Initiative into the federal Constitution. In this chapter (Chapter 8) a case is made for a ballot Initiative process at the federal level as an essential complement and corrective to the American system of lawmaking by elected representatives.

The third section, consisting of Chapter 9 and four appendices, should be of special interest to activists in that it not only gives instructions on how to put an Initiative on the ballot and plan an effective campaign, but details the history of I&R, and the differing requirements for them, at both state and local levels in all 50 states.

Readers who wish to keep up with the latest Initiative and Referendum developments should contact the Initiative Resource Center, a nonprofit, nonpartisan clearinghouse for information on ballot-box lawmaking, and request a free copy of the IRC newsletter, *Initiative and Referendum: The Power of the People!* The center also has additional publications on Initiative and Referendum politics. Write to IRC,

235 Douglass St., San Francisco, California 94114, or call
(415) 431–4765.

I am grateful first of all to John Forster and Roger
Telschow of Washington, D.C., co-founders of my newsletter
on ballot Initiative campaigns and procedures nationwide,
who gave me the idea of this book in 1980 and encouraged
my earliest efforts on it.

Secondly, I am deeply indebted to Ralph Nader and John
Richard of the Center for Study of Responsive Law for their
endorsement and support of my work from 1985 through
1987.

Thirdly, I am thankful for the invaluable editing assistance of Mary B. Skinner, Senior Lecturer in Politics at
the University of Buckingham in England, and for the word
processing skills of Linda Andrew of Richmond, California,
who performed the arduous task of transferring the manu-
script from paper to computer disk.

And finally, I am grateful to the Citizen Lawmakers
whose stories I have recorded in this book, whose courage,
determination, and political skills have renewed my faith,
time and again, that democracy *does* work in America,
through the people's power to propose and enact laws at the
ballot box—the Initiative process.

CITIZEN LAWMAKERS

The Ballot Initiative Revolution

1
History

The word "initiative" today means many things to many people. In state and local American politics for the past century, it has had a specific meaning: a new law or resolution proposed and placed on the ballot by citizen petition, and enacted directly by popular vote. Through an Initiative, the people *initiate* legislation; through its less frequently used complement, the Referendum, voters *refer* a newly enacted law, by petition, from the legislature to the ballot for final approval.

Both Initiative and Referendum ballot propositions, as well as other propositions placed on ballots by legislatures, are included in the more general term "referendum" (note lower case "r").

These various forms of legislation by popular vote have made the American ideal of "government of, by, and for the people" a reality since colonial times. Since the seventeenth century, voters in hundreds of New England towns have exercised their lawmaking powers in annual town meetings, using a method similar to the Initiative: citizens place proposed ordinances or other questions on the agenda by petition, meet and discuss the proposals, and then vote to accept or reject them. Beyond colonial New England, however, Americans have had to struggle continually to secure their rights as citizen lawmakers.

The first significant advances came during the American Revolution, when some of the first independent state constitutional conventions introduced the idea of voter ratification of state constitutions. Thomas Jefferson, in his proposed 1775 Virginia state constitution, included a requirement for voter approval by statewide referendum. (Unfortunately, Jefferson was hundreds of miles from Virginia at the time, attending the Continental Congress. By the time the Virginia delegates received his proposal, the convention was over.)[1]

In 1776 Georgia delegates gathered in Savannah to draft their state's constitution. The document included a provision (apparently never invoked) that would allow amendments whenever a majority of voters in each county signed petitions calling for a convention.[2] In 1778 the Massachusetts legislature held the first statewide referendum in the United States when it submitted its constitution to the voters for ratification. The citizens promptly rejected it by a five to one margin, forcing the legislature to rewrite its proposal.[3] Since then, all constitutional amendments in that state have been subject to voter approval. In 1792 New Hampshire became the next state to institutionalize the voters' power to ratify or reject state constitutional provisions.[4] Between 1818 and 1824 Connecticut, Maine, New York, and Rhode Island followed their example.[5] In the South the people's power movement began in 1830, when western Virginians successfully demanded voters' veto power over amendments to their state constitution.[6] By 1834 Alabama, Mississippi, Georgia, and North Carolina residents had also won such rights.[7]

The trend quickly became tradition. All but three of the states that joined the Union after 1830 required voter approval of their constitutions. Congress required referendums to approve state constitutions after 1857, and by 1900 only Delaware had no such stipulation.[8] By then, other states had begun debating the expansion of voter powers to include Initiative and Referendum (I&R): the right not just to block constitutional amendments, but to propose and enact new laws, and block enactments of the legislature, by citizen petition and popular vote.

THE ADVENT OF INITIATIVE, 1885–1917

Rapid changes brought about by the Industrial Revolution—explosive urban growth, industrial expansion, the railroads, political corruption, labor strikes, and land evictions—led to increasing demands for social and political reforms in the late 1800s.

In 1885 Father Robert W. Haire, a priest and labor activist from Aberdeen, South Dakota, and Benjamin Urner, a newspaper publisher and unsuccessful Greenback Party congressional candidate from Elizabeth, New Jersey, became the first reformers to propose Initiative and Referendum (I&R) in the United States.[9] Shortly thereafter, the Initiative process began to attract serious attention when the news spread that the same system was already operating in Switzerland. The Swiss system of Initiative and Referendum had been introduced in Zurich in the 1860s, largely through the efforts of socialists under the leadership of Karl Bürkli.[10] Impelled, like their counterparts in the United States, by the effects of the Industrial Revolution, the Swiss reformers drew inspiration and justification from the ancient rural Swiss tradition of the *Landsgemeinde*—annual open-air meetings where all the men in a canton would vote on the policies of local government. By the 1800s this form of direct democracy, a striking parallel to the rural New England town meeting, survived in only a handful of the most thinly populated mountain cantons.

The parallels between the Swiss and American movements are more than just historical coincidence. In 1888 the New York City labor theorist James W. Sullivan went to Switzerland to study how the I&R system worked and how it might be adapted for use in the United States. Upon returning home, Sullivan became a tireless promoter of the I&R cause. He wrote *Direct Legislation Through the Initiative and Referendum* (1892) and published it privately, setting the type himself (he was a printer by trade).[11] Then he organized the People's Power League, a group dedicated to persuading the national political parties to include I&R in their platforms. The league sent delegates to the 1892 conventions of several political parties, and won approval of I&R resolutions in the platforms of the Socialist Labor Party and the Populist Party.[12]

Failing to win such approval at the Democratic and Republican party conventions, the group reorganized as the "Direct Legislation League of New Jersey" and embarked on a new strategy: to amend the New Jersey constitution to include an I&R provision. Sullivan and league leaders such as Henry A. Beckmeyer of Newark recruited a broadly based group of influential supporters: professors, ministers, elected officials, and journalists. The league's five elected officers included members of four political parties.[13]

Sullivan's work soon attracted the attention and enthusiasm of Samuel Gompers, life-long president of the American Federation of Labor, the forerunner of the AFL-CIO. Gompers viewed I&R as a peaceful way to achieve union objectives, vastly preferable to costly, potentially bloody strikes. In the early 1890s Gompers promoted I&R in speeches, testified in favor of the New Jersey constitutional amendment, and made I&R the first political plank in the AFL's platform.[14]

Gompers' support was crucial. By the turn of the century, the AFL claimed half a million members; by 1914, with 2 million members, the federation was well established as the country's leading representative of unionized workers.[15] Under Gompers' leadership, state AFL offices became centers of I&R agitation, and the eventual successes of the movement throughout the country owe much to his outspoken and unrelenting support.

The New Jersey league failed to secure an I&R provision in the state constitution, but the group's campaign caught fire around the country. Sullivan's book sold between 10,000 and 15,000 copies each year from 1892 to 1895. In 1894 Eltweed Pomeroy of Newark began publishing the *Direct Legislation Record,* a quarterly periodical that promoted I&R. His efforts led to the founding of the National Direct Legislation League in 1896, whose more than 50 "vice presidents" included such well-known reformers as Benjamin Orange Flower, crusading journalist and publisher of the reform-minded *Arena* magazine; Eugene V. Debs, labor leader, Socialist Party organizer, and future presidential candidate; William Jennings Bryan, Democratic presidential candidate in 1896 and 1900; Edward Bellamy, author of *Looking Backward: 2000–1887;* and Ignatius Donnelly, principal author of the Populist Party's 1892 platform.[16]

The National League was founded in conjunction with the Populist Party convention in 1896 and united the reform impulses of the urban labor movement with those of rural Populist farmers, bringing a new momentum to the I&R cause.[17] From the Populist strongholds of the midwestern farmlands came the movement's first important victories. In 1897 Nebraska passed a state law allowing cities to include I&R in their charters, and in 1898 South Dakota passed a statewide I&R amendment.

"Direct legislation by the people became almost an obsession with the Populists," wrote John D. Hicks in his definitive study *The Populist Revolt.*[18] Farmers, who made up a majority of midwestern voters, believed that I&R would result in policies of benefit to them. Moreover, I&R appealed to their frontier spirit of independence and self-sufficiency.

The Populists believed that both the state legislatures and the judicial system were corrupt, and that new mechanisms were needed to restore control of government to the people. Though the Populist Party faded, its goal of promoting popular government through I&R continued to spread nationwide. In 1899 the Oregon legislature approved an amendment providing statewide I&R rights, the result of a seven-year organizing effort by the Populist leader William Simon U'Ren. Voters passed it in 1902 by a margin of 11 to 1.[19] Then, on 6 June 1904, Oregonians made history by voting on—and approving—the first two Initiatives ever to appear on a state ballot. The first gave voters the right to choose candidates for state office in primary elections (instead of in party conventions); the second gave counties the right to ban liquor sales. Oregon demonstrated to the rest of the country that the initiative process worked, an example I&R advocates lost no time in publicizing.[20]

Two years later Oregonians signed enough petitions to put 10 Initiatives on the 4 June 1906 ballot. Voters passed seven of them—three laws and four constitutional amendments. These four amendments, the first ever to be passed by Initiative in any state, included a provision granting I&R to all municipalities and another requiring voter approval for any law calling for a constitutional convention (to discourage the legislature from abolishing I&R).

Reformers across the country trumpeted Oregon's advances for democracy, and the I&R movement accelerated.[21] Montana's legislature passed an I&R amendment, which voters ratified in 1906 five to one. The same year Delaware voters approved a nonbinding referendum asking for statewide I&R provisions. When Oklahoma joined the Union in 1907, it was the first state with an I&R provision in its original constitution. In 1908 both Maine and Michigan passed I&R amendments. These state efforts were bolstered by numerous successful campaigns to install I&R provisions at the level of local government—in places like San Francisco,

Grand Rapids, Des Moines, and Wilmington, Delaware—during the same period.[22]

The I&R movement's early successes coincided with the explosive growth of the AFL, and they were fueled by the Progressive movement. The Progressives, who adopted most of the Populists' reform agenda as their own, drew their strength and leadership from young, prosperous members of the urban middle class.[23] They saw the corruption of the cities as a challenge and provided an eager audience for "muckraking," investigative journalism aimed at exposing social problems and government and corporate wrongdoing. The muckrakers showed Americans what needed to be fixed, and Progressive activists seized upon Initiative and Referendum to do the job. They adopted a broad range of goals: election reforms, regulation of corporations, government efficiency, and public ownership of utilities. Swept to victory on the rising tide of Progressivism, reformers secured passage of I&R provisions in legislatures and constitutional conventions in 18 states between 1910 and 1914.

Third parties, such as the Socialists and Prohibitionists, used I&R to thrust their own reform goals to the forefront of local, state, and national political agendas. Although third parties rarely won enough elective offices to govern a city or state, they served another important role: "to agitate, educate, generate new ideas and supply the dynamic element in our political life"[24]—rather like the effects of I&R.

As Progressivism reached its high-water mark, national leaders endorsed the cause. After years of indecision, Theodore Roosevelt declared himself an I&R advocate. In his 1912 "Charter of Democracy" speech, delivered to the Ohio constitutional convention, he said: "I believe in the Initiative and Referendum, which should be used not to destroy representative government, but to correct it whenever it becomes misrepresentative."[25]

Woodrow Wilson also became a convert during his term as governor of New Jersey. "The immediate thing we have got to do is resume popular government," Wilson said. "We are cleaning house and in order to clean house the one thing we need is a good broom. Initiative and Referendum are good brooms."[26]

Hiram Johnson made I&R a priority following his election as governor of California in November 1910. "I most strongly urge, that the first step in our design to preserve and perpetuate popular government shall be the adoption of the Initiative, the Referendum, and the Recall," he said in his inaugural speech on 4 January 1911. By October of that year, all three of these reforms had been ratified by the voters as amendments to the California constitution.

By mid-1917 World War I had brought both Progressivism and the expansion of I&R to an end. Many gains had been made—only three states were without provision for I&R on at least one level of government. But the victory was far from complete. By the war's end in November 1918, 28 states still lacked statewide initiative provisions, and the quality of local I&R laws varied widely.[27]

WHY THE WEST WAS WON (BUT THE EAST WAS NOT)

A map of the states with statewide I&R provisions (see Map 1-1) reveals an interesting pattern. Despite the nationwide strength of the Progressive movement, about four-fifths of the Initiative states are west of the Mississippi. While the obstacles facing I&R advocates varied from state to state, regional political culture and history supplied important common factors.

First, the Progressive movement in the Northeast, unlike Progressivism in the West, did not build on a Populist foundation. In the elections of 1892 and 1894—the most successful years for Populism—Populist candidates garnered less than 5 percent of the vote in all states east of Indiana and north of Virginia. Populists did better in at least one of these elections in all other states.[28]

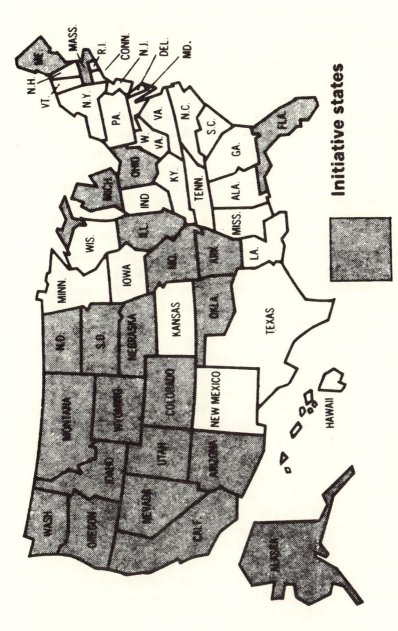

Map 1-1. Initiative states, 1989. Voters can propose new state laws or state constitutional amendments by citizen petition, and enact them directly by popular vote. Gray = Initiative states.

Initiative states

Second, the Progressive movement in the East was mild and soft-spoken. "[Its] goal was not a sharp change in the social structure, but rather the formation of a responsible elite, which was to take charge of the popular impulse toward change and direct it into moderate and, as they would have said 'constructive' channels," wrote Richard Hofstadter in *The Age of Reform*.[29] In profound contrast with the egalitarian outlook of the West, Progressivism in the East was rooted in elitism. "Their ideal leader was a well-to-do, well-educated, high-minded citizen."[30]

A third factor that hindered the establishment of I&R in the Northeast was the high proportion of immigrants in the cities. In 1890 first-generation newcomers made up an incredible four-fifths of New York City's population. Immigration peaked at nearly 9 million entrants in the decade between 1900 and 1910, with most arriving from southern and eastern Europe. They were poorer and less educated than their northern European predecessors, and the political differences between the two groups were immense.[31] The outnumbered white Anglo-Saxon Protestants feared the immigrants' potential voting power and doubted their ability to read, much less comprehend, ballot questions. Further, the immigrants provided the voting strength that elected the urban machine bosses, the reformers' enemies.[32]

Racism added to the I&R advocates' difficulties. Professor Ellwood P. Cubberley of Stanford University voiced a common nativist belief of the early 1900s when he labeled immigrants "illiterate, docile, lacking in self-reliance and initiative, and not possessing the Anglo-Teutonic conceptions of law, order, and government."[33] Compounding these difficulties was the tendency of rural white politicians in the East and South to oppose I&R, fearing that the urban masses, once empowered by I&R, would overrule the decisions of malapportioned legislatures dominated by rural interests. Throughout those regions, I&R activists typically had to settle for "half a loaf," in that the legislatures generally allowed I&R in the cities but not statewide. Even here there is a distinction between East and West. The majority of residents in the boom towns of the West were white native U.S. citizens who had moved in from other states, not from other countries, and therefore did not represent the same kind of threat.[34]

In the South I&R advocates faced even greater obstacles. The less industrialized South had a weaker labor movement than the North, and therefore felt less pressure for I&R from the AFL's labor activists. A 1908 confrontation between union I&R advocates and Gov. M. R. Patterson of Tennessee is indicative of the southern outlook of the time. Upon hearing the union men plead for expanded voting powers, the governor reportedly flew into a rage and thundered: "Government by the people is impossible. We never did and never will have government by the people!"[35]

In contrast with the self-reliant egalitarianism of the West, southern politics was still steeped in aristocratic—and racist—traditions. Not that the westerners were not racist—it was simply that the victims of western racism were not numerous enough to outvote the native U.S. citizens. Southern Progressivism drew its voting strength from poor rural whites, as had southern Populism.[36] Their first priority as reformers was to oust the aristocrats. Once this was done, they saw nothing to gain from I&R, which might lead to black political power. In 1911 the national I&R periodical *Equity* printed, under the headline "Alabama": "Many conscientious Southerners oppose direct legislation because they fear that this process of government would increase the power of the Negro, and therefore increase the danger of Negro domination."[37]

The fact that Mississippi reformers succeeded in achieving statewide I&R in 1914 is probably a testimony to the state's near-total political "blackout." Blacks could no longer vote in sufficient numbers to pose a threat to white political power. Even so, the Mississippi Supreme Court abolished I&R on a legal technicality in 1922, and the legislature never reinstated it. After that the statewide Initiative process was entirely absent south of the Mason-Dixon line and east of the Mississippi River. (By the time Florida adopted statewide initiative provisions in 1968, its population, swelled by northern retirees, no longer fitted the traditional southern model.)

Another hindrance to I&R in the South was widespread illiteracy: like many European immigrants in the Northeast, southern illiterates were unable to participate in I&R. The reform was not particularly useful to them; nor was it useful to the literate until they could end the rampant ballot-box stuffing that was practiced whenever the power of the ruling Democratic aristocrats was threatened.[38]

The lagging southern economy also obstructed I&R because it discouraged the positive outlook characteristic of the Progressive movement. Unlike the West, where rapid growth confirmed Progressive optimism, the predominant atmosphere of the South was one of decline, despair, and nostalgia for the antebellum Golden Age.

THE DECLINE OF PROGRESSIVISM

Among the most powerful opponents of I&R throughout the nation were the big-business interests and their conservative Republican allies, big-city political bosses and their machines, and the liquor industry (which feared prohibitionist Initiatives).[39] After 1918, with the decline of the Progressive movement, all these dominant forces (with the exception of the liquor industry) were strengthened in areas where statewide I&R had not been successful. The war-generated wave of patriotism and fear of Russia's Bolshevik Revolution caused the reformers' criticisms to be regarded as unpatriotic or, in the case of the Socialist Party, downright treasonous. but the Progressives' impact was permanent. Many of their reforms, including I&R, have become such accepted practices that their existence rarely faces any serious challenge. In I&R the Progressives created a perpetual reform machine that not only continues to be a vehicle for political change, but is increasing in its usefulness to reformers more than three-quarters of a century after it first gained widespread acceptance.

Table 1-1 shows the results of popular votes to add I&R provisions to state constitutions. These votes ratified I&R amendments that had already been approved by state legislatures or constitutional conventions.

EARLY INITIATIVE VOTING TRENDS, 1904–1944

Progressive and New Deal era reformers primarily succeeded in passing ballot Initiatives aimed at making government more honest, efficient, and responsive. Nationwide, voters in over a dozen states approved 58 Initiatives in the areas of political reform and governmental reorganization. Among these were Initiatives to establish nomination of candidates through primary elections (Ark., Maine, Mont., Oreg., S.D.); establishment of presidential primaries (Mont., Oreg.); direct election of U.S. senators (Oreg., Mont., Okla.); strengthening the initiative process (Ariz., Ark., N.D.); procedures for the recall of public officials by citizen petition (Colo., Oreg.); home rule for municipalities (Colo., Oreg.); and permanent voter registration instead of requiring voters to re-register every election (Calif., Wash.). One of the most far-reaching reforms by Initiative was the "Executive Budget" amendment to the California state constitution, which voters approved by a greater than two to one margin in 1922. This strengthened the powers of the office of governor by giving governors "line-item veto power," which allows reducing or eliminating any item in the state budget bill passed by the legislature. A 1912 Arizona initiative required reapportionment of the lower house of the state legislature based on population, more than half a century before the U.S. Supreme Court ruled this method of reapportionment mandatory. Five other states also passed reapportionment initiatives (Ariz., Ark., Calif., Colo., Wash.). An early Montana Ini-

Table 1-1
Chronology: Popular Votes on State Bills/Amendments
to Get Initiative Process

State	Year	Pass/Fail	Margin	Yes	No
South Dakota	1898	Passed	3–2	23,816	16,483
Utah	1900	Passed	5–2	19,219	7,786
Oregon	1902	Passed	11–1	62,024	5,688
Illinois[a]	1902	Passed	5–1	428,469	87,654
Missouri	1904	Failed	2–3	115,741	169,281
Nevada[b]	1905	Passed	5–1	4,393	792
Montana	1906	Passed	5–1	36,374	6,616
Delaware[c]	1906	Passed	6–1	17,405	2,135
Oklahoma	1907	Passed	5–2	180,333	73,059
Missouri	1908	Passed	55–45	177,615	147,290
Maine	1908	Passed	2–1	51,991	23,712
Michigan[d,e]	1908	Passed	2–1	244,705	130,783
Illinois[a]	1910	Passed	3–1	443,505	127,751
Colorado	1910	Passed	3–1	89,141	28,698
Arkansas	1910	Passed	2–1	91,363	39,680
California	1911	Passed	3–1	138,181	44,850
Arizona[e]	1911	Passed	3–1	12,534	3,920
New Mexico[f]	1911	Passed	5–2	31,724	13,399
Nebraska[g]	1912	Passed	13–1	189,200	15,315
Idaho[h]	1912	Passed	8–3	38,918	15,195 (I)
			3–1	43,658	13,490 (R)
Nevada[b]	1912	Passed	10–1	9,956	1,027
Ohio	1912	Passed	3–2	312,592	231,312
Washington	1912	Passed	5–2	110,110	43,905
Wyoming[i]	1912	Failed	6–1	20,579	3,446
Mississippi[j]	1912	Failed	2–1	25,153	13,383
Michigan[d]	1913	Passed	5–4	204,796	162,392 (C)
	1913	Passed	3–2	219,057	152,388 (S)
Mississippi[j]	1914	Passed	2–1	19,118	8,718
North Dakota[k]	1914	Passed	2–1	43,111	21,815 (C)
			5–2	48,783	19,964 (S)
Minnesota[l]	1914	Failed	3–1	162,951	47,906
Wisconsin	1914	Failed	2–1	84,934	148,536
Texas	1914	Failed	48–52	62,371	66,785
Maryland[m]	1915	Passed	3–1	33,150	10,022
Minnesota[l]	1916	Failed	4–1	187,713	51,546
Massachusetts	1918	Passed	51–49	170,646	162,103
North Dakota[k]	1918	Passed	3–2	47,447	32,598
Alaska[e]	1956	Passed	2–1	17,447	8,180
Florida[e]	1968	Passed	55–45	645,233	518,940
Wyoming	1968	Passed	3–1	72,009	24,299

State	Year	Pass/Fail	Margin	Yes	No
Illinois[a]	1970	Passed	57–43	1,122,425	838,168
Dist. of Columbia	1977	Passed	4–1	27,094	5,627
Minnesota[1]	1980	Failed	53–47	970,407	854,164
Rhode Island	1986	Failed	48–52	129,309	139,294

[a]Illinois's 1902 and 1910 votes were advisory—not binding on the legislature. The measures were put on the ballot by petition of I&R advocates, using a statewide nonbinding advisory initiative process established by the legislature in 1901. The legislature never followed the people's mandate. A constitutional convention passed the 1970 provision.

[b]Nevada's 1905 amendment secured only the Referendum—that is, the right to veto by petition and popular vote a law that has just passed the legislature. The Initiative—the right to pass *new* laws by petition and popular vote—was secured by Nevada's 1912 amendment.

[c]Delaware voted on an advisory referendum put on the ballot by the legislature, asking voters whether they wanted the Initiative process. Their reply was overwhelmingly "yes," as shown here, but the legislature never followed that mandate.

[d]The Initiative procedures put in place in Michigan in 1908 proved so difficult that citizens were unable to put Initiatives on the ballot. Reformers got the legislature to approve less restrictive procedures, which were placed on the ballot in 1913 and ratified by the voters. There were two separate Initiative amendments on that ballot, one giving voters power to propose and enact Initiative statutes (laws), the other giving voters power to propose and enact Initiative amendments to the state constitution.

[e]Voters in Arizona approved their new constitution, including I&R, in a single vote—the I&R question was not separate, as in most states. The same route to approval of I&R was taken in Alaska, Florida, and (in 1908 only) Michigan.

[f]New Mexico's new constitution—like Arizona's, ratified by the people in a single vote, not provision by provision—included the Referendum power, but not the Initiative.

[g]Nebraska's 13–1 victory margin for I&R is somewhat misleading, since blank ballots were counted as "yes" votes. The highest actual approval margin for I&R was thus, most likely, Oregon's 11–1.

[h]In Idaho, there were separate amendments for Initiative and Referendum.

[i]Wyoming's I&R amendment failed because the state constitution required approval by a majority of "all those voting in the election" rather than "those voting on the (I&R) question." The former system in effect counts blank ballots as "no" votes—so the I&R amendment would have lost even with 100 percent approval if half the voters ignored the I&R ballot question.

[j]Mississippi had the same voter approval requirement as Wyoming—a majority of "all those voting in the election." In 1912, a presidential election

Table 1-1 (*continued*)

year, the "no" votes plus blanks on the I&R question were in the majority. The fact that a two to one majority of those *voting on the question* favored I&R made no difference. In 1914, however, "no" votes plus blanks were just shy of a majority—which allowed the I&R amendment to squeak through.
ᵏThe I&R amendment passed by the legislature in North Dakota, and ratified by the voters in 1914, had such strict procedures that no Initiatives qualified for the ballot in the following election, so I&R advocates put an Initiative on the 1918 ballot to ease the procedures. Like Michigan, one Initiative amendment applied to statutes (laws) and one applied to the state constitution.
ˡMinnesota's I&R amendment failed all three times it was on the ballot because of the "majority of all those voting in the election" requirement— the same rule that had defeated I&R in Wyoming and Mississippi in 1912.
ᵐMaryland's amendment provided for the right of statewide Referendum, but not Initiative.

tiative limited campaign spending by candidates, while in North Dakota, when the Depression reached its nadir in 1932, voters passed eight Initiatives designed to cut government costs, mostly by cutting the salaries or expenses of high-level public officials, such as judges. Perhaps the most daring reform initiative was Nebraska's 1934 constitutional amendment to establish a unicameral legislature.

Labor issues, too, were high on the Initiative ballot agenda. By 1924 labor unions had won passage of an Arkansas Initiative restricting child labor; an Oregon Initiative on job safety, workmen's compensation, and a ban on the hiring of prison inmates; Arizona Initiatives prohibiting the black-listing of union members and discouraging the employment of non–U.S. citizens (in this case Mexicans willing to work for low wages); and three 1912 Colorado Initiatives limiting the work day to eight hours for women, public works employees, and workers in underground mines and smelters. During the Depression, however, labor unions' success in passing Initiatives declined. The only three to win in this era were measures to increase workmen's compensation in Arkansas and Colorado and to expand public employees' benefits in Missouri. At the same time, employers began sponsoring anti-union Initiatives: Oregonians approved a restriction on picketing and boycotts, and in 1944 Arkansans approved the first "Right to Work" Initiative, prohibiting labor unions from requiring all workers at a work site to be union members, and thus weakening the unions' bargaining power.

Well in advance of the New Deal, Progressive reformers pioneered government aid programs for the poor, disabled, and elderly. Arizonans passed a pension Initiative to benefit widowed mothers and senior citizens in 1914; Coloradans passed four separate Initiatives to aid mothers, children, the blind, and the insane. By the end of World War II, voters in various states had passed 13 more pension or welfare Initiatives. Other government services established or expanded by successful Initiatives included education (Ariz., Calif., Mont., N.D.), road building (Colo., Mo., Mont., N.D.), and public power and water supply systems (Ariz., Nebr., Oreg.). A controversial 1918 North Dakota farm-aid Initiative passed by the voters was perhaps the most innovative government program of its day; it established a state bank for loans to farmers, a state-owned grain elevator, and a farm tax to insure crops against weather damage.

In the area of civil rights, successful 1912 women's suffrage Initiatives in Arizona and Oregon helped prepare the way for passage of the national suffrage amendment nine years later. Voters in three states banned poll taxes (Calif., Oreg., Wash.); Coloradans established a juvenile court system.

Progressive reformers in Oregon and Montana won passage of Initiatives to raise taxes on undertaxed big businesses. One Oregon Initiative taxed companies that operated sleeping, refrigerator, and oil-carrying railroad cars; the second taxed express, telephone, and telegraph companies. Montanans raised taxes on large metal mines, the state's richest industry. During the Depression, however, hard-pressed citizens launched Initiatives to lower their own taxes: eight Initiatives limiting property taxes passed in five states, and Ohioans abolished the state sales tax on food.

During the Progressive era, prohibitionists won passage of initiatives to ban liquor sales in seven states, thus gaining momentum for passage of the federal Prohibition amendment in 1919. When public opinion turned against Prohibition in the late 1920s and early 1930s, however, voters in five states (Colo., Mass., Mont., N.D., Oreg.) passed Initiatives intended to legalize liquor, which led to repeal of national Prohibition in 1933.

There were also a few successful business regulation (or deregulation) Initiatives. Oregonians abolished the "blue laws" that had kept stores closed on Sundays; Californians passed an anti-usury law, and North Dakotans passed Initiatives to ban crop mortgages and corporate buyouts of family farms.

The first successful conservation Initiative was Oregon's 1910 law banning the use of nets and other fish-harvesting techniques in the Rogue River, but allowing the use of hooks and lines. Each of the three west coast states passed additional Initiatives to control fishing, and voters in four states passed Initiatives during the 1930s and early 1940s to establish state fish and game commissions (Ark., Idaho, Mo., Wash.). Oregonians, once again in the environmental forefront, in 1938 passed an Initiative to clean up the badly polluted Willamette River.

During its first decade (1904–1914), Initiative use skyrocketed from its lowest historical level (2 per year) to its all-time high of 90. However, as Americans focused their energies on World War I, Initiative use plunged to 34 (in 1918). The postwar "return to normalcy" brought Initiative use back up briefly, but nowhere near the 1914 record. The Depression year of 1932 brought Initiative use to another peak of 75, and it stayed relatively high until the outbreak of World War II, which once again distracted Americans from local issues: the number of Initiatives on state ballots dropped from 50 in 1940 to 13 in 1942.[40]

IS INITIATIVE OBSOLETE?
THE DECLINE OF INITIATIVE USE,
1946–1968

Just after World War II, the number of Initiatives on state ballots rose sharply, again mirroring a return to domestic concerns. But the peak year of this period, 1948, saw only 40 state Initiatives, less than half the all-time record of 90 set in 1914. By 1954 the number of statewide Initiatives was halved again to a paltry 18. As in the post–World War I decade, the patriotic, conservative mood of the late forties and fifties muted calls for reform.

In addition, petition thresholds—the number of signatures required to put Initiatives on state ballots—rose sharply with the growth in population. Many western states experienced wartime and postwar population booms: between 1940 and 1950, populations jumped 50 percent in Arizona, 54 percent in California, 45 percent in Nevada, and 40 percent in Oregon. Low-budget citizen groups now found petition circulation doubly difficult. Despite the reawakening of reform pressures such as the Civil Rights Movement, fewer and fewer Initiatives qualified for ballots, and this was especially true of those sponsored by liberal reformers—the philosophical heirs of the Progressives.

One factor remained constant: as in prewar eras, voters throughout the country remained distrustful of politicians. The people passed more Initiatives on government reform than on any other issue, 27 in all. Reapportionment was again a major concern, and Initiatives implementing various redistricting schemes passed in Oregon, Arkansas, Washington, and Colorado between 1952 and 1962. Voters established or expanded the civil service systems to ensure bureaucratic integrity in Arizona, Utah, and Washington between 1948 and 1960. Initiatives to expand or restructure government services again gained much voter support. Citizens in six states passed 10 education measures, mostly increasing government funding (Ariz.: 1958, 1964; Ark.: 1964; Calif.: 1946, 1952; N.D.: 1955; Okla.: two in 1946; and Oreg.:

two in 1948). Other Initiatives expanded pension benefits to senior citizens (Calif., Colo., Oreg., and Wash.), increased pensions for public employees (Mass.), and extended compensation or bonuses to veterans (Mont., Oreg., and Wash.).

Business interests used the Initiative process aggressively to promote "Right to Work" measures once the Taft-Hartley Act of 1947 let states decide on this issue. By 1954 three more states had passed "Right to Work" provisions by popular vote (Ariz., Nebr., and Nev.; voters rejected such legislation between 1948 and 1958 in Calif., Idaho, Mass., Ohio, and Wash.). Between 1964 and 1966 railroad companies successfully sponsored Initiatives in three states (Ariz., N.D., and Wash.) to repeal state laws that required the employment of superfluous crew members on trains, a practice known as "featherbedding."

In the field of business regulation, consumers in Oregon united against the politically potent dairy industry and passed an Initiative to end state control of milk prices in 1954. In another move against the wishes of the dairy industry, between 1949 and 1952 voters in Ohio, Michigan, and Washington passed Initiatives to permit the sale of colored margarine. (Until then, in these states and others, state laws required that margarine be sold in colorless form because the dairy industry wanted it to be as unappealing as possible.) Initiatives between 1948 and 1964 loosened liquor restrictions in Washington, Oregon, and North Dakota by approving sale of liquor "by the drink"—that is, in bars and restaurants.

Voters across the country approved 10 statewide tax Initiatives from 1948 to 1968, but there was no discernible pattern to the measures, which ranged from a 1946 Arkansas Initiative allowing local voters to impose taxes for new libraries to a 1966 law eliminating the property tax in Nebraska. Initiatives adopted in Arizona and Michigan required larger portions of the sales tax revenue to go to the cities, to counteract the decisions of malapportioned legislatures dominated by rural lawmakers.

Conservation remained a concern in the Northwest. Oregonians approved limitations on fishing in 1948 and 1956; Washington voters approved an anti-dam measure to save salmon runs in 1960 and an Initiative to set aside coastal lands for recreation in 1964; and Idahoans bucked the state's powerful mining industry to pass by nearly six to one a 1954 Initiative to stop dredge mining in riverbeds, which had been wiping out fish through siltation.

Nevertheless, during the late 1950s and throughout the 1960s, some states went for a decade or longer without a single voter-initiated ballot measure. Even the Initiative bastions of the west coast saw sharp drops in ballot activity. In 1966, for the first time in 62 years, Oregon voters did not place a single Initiative on the ballot, and California had only one. Washington's crop of three was one-quarter of the national total. In 1968 the number of Initiatives on statewide ballots across the country sank to 10[41] as the divisive turmoil of the Vietnam War protests, political assassinations, and black power reached its height (see Figure 1-1 on next page). The children of the postwar "baby boom," now reaching their teens and twenties, were more politically active than previous generations, but their concerns were national and international, not local.

However, one tiny group with a state cause, the Recall Reagan Campaign, was beginning to mobilize in California. When it could not collect even half the nearly a million petition signatures needed to force a recall election on Gov. Ronald Reagan, political observers saw this failure as a confirmation of Reagan's dismissal of the group as inconsequential. But the experts were wrong. The Recall Reagan Campaign was the seed of a movement that would transform state, local, and national politics for the next two decades.

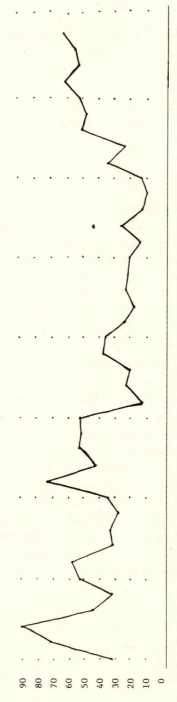

Figure 1-1. Frequency of Initiative Use, 1910–1988: Number of Statewide Initiatives on the Ballot in the United States

Note: Each point on the graphs represents a two-year period. Each even year listed includes the initiatives on the ballot in the previous odd year, i.e., 1980's total of 52 initiatives includes 7 that were on state ballots in 1979.

2

Arguments For and Against

In the 23 states and countless local jurisdictions where citizens already enjoy the right of Initiative, lawmaking by popular vote is as sacrosanct as any other voting right. But in the other 27 states, the debate over whether to add Initiative to existing statewide voting rights has at times risen to a furious pitch as each side attempts to attach the "special interest" label to the other. Although this occurs in any political debate, it is absurd when applied to the Initiative process, a reform that allows the public itself to decide what constitutes the public interest.

THE BENEFITS OF INITIATIVE

The Initiative process is not a cure-all, but it does result in increased government responsiveness to the will of the people, greater citizen participation and a better-informed electorate. It is a safeguard against the concentration of political power in the hands of a few, and it provides a means of putting new ideas on the political agenda.

More Accountable Government. Since the turn of the century, in the 23 states with statewide Initiative provisions, voters have passed over 600 state laws or state constitutional amendments. The use of Initiative has put elected representatives on notice that they must be responsive, or they will be overruled by the electorate. Kelly Jenkins, a Helena, Montana, attorney and author of a successful statewide Initiative requiring disclosure of lobbying expenses put it this way: "Now [the legislators are] listening better. They don't want the voters to make them look bad with another Initiative. Groups like Common Cause [sponsor of the 1980 Initiative] have a lot more credibility in the legislature now."[1]

Frequently, just the filing of an Initiative petition will spur legislators into action. Laws passed under the pressure of an Initiative petition include Massachusetts' laws to reduce the air pollution that causes acid rain (1985) and ban the experimental use of cats and dogs from pounds (1983); Arizona's laws abolishing the state sales tax on food (1980), making funding available for Medicaid (1982), and restricting water pollution caused by toxic chemicals (1986); and Wyoming's law to maintain stream flows adequate for fish and wildlife (1986).

This increase in government accountability represents a quantum leap in the power of self-government. Without Initiative, self-government all too often boils down to giving the voters a choice between the lesser of two evils once every two to four years. With the Initiative process, however, the voters can control specific policies of government, and even change its structure.

Greater Citizen Participation. In an age when political activity is more and more dominated by big-money fundraising and 30-second television ads, Initiative campaigns are one sector of politics where the efforts of ordinary individuals still make a difference.

Every election year since 1976, about half a million people, mostly volunteers, have circulated Initiative petitions, and over 25 million voters have signed these petitions to put Initiatives on state and local ballots. Each of the hundreds of campaigns activates dozens, hundreds, or even thousands of volunteers to participate in campaign work. In one particularly contentious instance (the 1982 California handgun control Initiative), a single opposing committee recruited 30,000 volunteers.[2]

Citizens tend to participate if they believe their involvement makes a difference. Initiative campaigns, much more than candidate campaigns, produce tangible results proving that their involvement *does* matter. It is clear that a law passed by Initiative is more likely to take effect than a law *promised* by a politician during an election campaign. A hypothetical rational voter, looking at the nationwide results of the 1986 campaigns for the U.S. House of Representatives, in which only 2 percent of 394 incumbents were defeated, would not be likely to get involved in future electoral challenges to House incumbents. But the same voter might well be attracted by the 46 percent success rate of state-level Initiative campaigns in 1985–1986.

Increased citizen participation through ballot measure campaigns has a "spillover effect" on candidate campaigns: those who turn out specifically to vote on the Initiatives usually vote for candidates as well, thereby raising overall voter participation. In five straight election years beginning in 1976, turnout was higher in states with Initiatives on the ballot. In 1982, the peak year for Initiatives in the period from 1934 to 1987, turnout was a full one-sixth higher in states with Initiatives on the ballot (Table 2-1).

A Better-Informed Electorate. Each Initiative campaign raises a lively public debate, which in turn increases voters' awareness of substantive issues. This is especially needed in

Table 2-1
Voter Turnout in Elections With and Without Ballot
Initiatives (as percentage of population over 18)

	1976	1978	1980	1982	1984
States with Initiatives on ballots	59.0	44.7	59.8	46.8	54.5
States without Initiatives on ballots	56.0	39.4	55.0	39.8	53.0
Difference	3.0	5.3	4.8	7.0	1.5

the age of television, which has made the looks and person-
alities of candidates more prominent factors in the outcome
of elections than the candidates' stands on issues. Again,
there is a spillover effect on campaigns for office. When an
Initiative is on the ballot, voters are more likely to demand
that candidates take a stand on an issue. During the 1976
presidential primary race, for instance, Jimmy Carter avoided the question of his stance on nuclear power in state after
state—until he reached Oregon, where persistent questioning by sponsors of an anti–nuclear power Initiative induced
him to state that he favored nuclear power only as a "last
resort."[3]

Initiative campaigns also give candidates an opportunity
to make an issue-based appeal to voters that goes beyond
campaign promises. In 1974 California gubernatorial candidate Jerry Brown built his primary campaign around the
theme of "clean government" and to emphasize his point
backed an Initiative to restrict lobbying expenditures and
require pre-election disclosure of campaign spending and
funding sources. Similarly, Democratic Sen. Alan Cranston
(running for re-election) and Los Angeles Mayor Tom Bradley (candidate for governor of California) tied their electoral
appeal for votes to "Proposition 65," a 1986 statewide Initiative to prevent toxic chemical pollution. Voters re-elected
Cranston, defeated Bradley, and passed the Initiative
(thereby fulfilling a Bradley campaign "promise," despite
the fact that he was not elected)!

Initiative spillover may go far beyond the boundaries of the original state. California followers of Lyndon LaRouche sponsored Initiatives on the state ballot in November 1986 and June 1988 to quarantine carriers of the AIDS virus. The measures were soundly defeated, but the campaign debate raised voter understanding of both the AIDS epidemic and the extremist tactics and ideology of LaRouche. Multistate Initiative campaigns have an even broader educational impact. Initiatives on nuclear power (1976), taxes (1978–1986), and the nuclear weapons freeze (1982) all generated substantial news media coverage of national issues and raised voter awareness nationwide.

A Safeguard Against the Concentration of Political Power in the Hands of the Few. American political history is rife with instances of corruption and misrule, but even under an honest government, political power in a given city or state can fall into the hands of an individual, a small group, or a single party. With the Initiative process, however, the people retain ultimate authority, thus preventing any monopoly on political power, even when an individual or party controls the legislative, executive, and judicial branches of government. Political bossism and one-party rule have disappeared, for the most part, in states with the Initiative and Recall processes, but they have proved particularly difficult to root out in jurisdictions that lack direct democracy—like Chicago or the Deep South. It is notable that this nation's most notorious flirtation with dictatorship in the twentieth century occurred during the rule of Huey Long in Louisiana, a state without the voting rights of Initiative, Referendum, or Recall. Long was retired not by the voters, but by an assassin.

Had the United States had a national Initiative process in the late 1960s and early 1970s, the course of the Vietnam War and protests against it might have been different. The Initiative process is effective not only in *venting* popular discontent, but in *channeling it constructively* to make the necessary changes.

A Means for Putting New Ideas on the Political Agenda. With the Initiative process, state, local, and national political agendas are shaped by the people. It gives them a role alongside the news media, politicians, and judges who otherwise control policy innovation. Major "new ideas" introduced or promoted by ballot Initiative in the 1980s include toxic pollution prevention (California, 1986), the nuclear weapons freeze (nationwide 1982), and "Motor Voter" laws that register people to vote when they get or renew driver's licenses (Arizona, 1982; Colorado, 1984).[4]

Initiative campaigns capture the attention of the news media, which is a prerequisite for effective political action. Grassroots citizen groups are finding ballot Initiatives to be far more effective in bringing issues to public consciousness than such traditional political activities as protest marches, letter-writing campaigns, and lending support to sympathetic candidates.

THE TROUBLE WITH LEGISLATURES

The purpose of elected legislatures and councils is to represent the will of the people in making laws. While state legislatures typically pass hundreds of laws in each session, these laws do not always reflect the needs or desires of the people. There are several reasons why legislatures should never be entrusted with sole lawmaking authority.

Campaign Spending and PACs. Common Cause's analysis of the spending in the congressional campaigns of 1978 and 1982 shows that the bigger spenders won in 86 percent of their campaigns.[5] In California, according to the state chapter of Common Cause, state senate incumbents outspent their 1986 challengers by 75 to 1; state assembly incumbents outspent challengers by 39 to 1. In November 1986 every single incumbent who sought re-election to the state legislature won it. An ever-increasing proportion of campaign money on both local and national levels comes from

PACs (political action committees), most of which represent business and labor interests. Since incumbents get the lion's share of the PAC money, there is little chance that any legislature will enact spending or contribution limits. Although this money does not buy votes directly, it does help monied interests get what they want—often to the detriment of the more general interest.

Unequal Lobbying and Off-Year Campaign Contributions. In 1985, in California alone, lobbyists reported spending over $73 million. (This does not include an additional $25 million that legislators and other elected officials collected in campaign contributions in this nonelection year.)[6] Again, this money does not usually buy votes directly, but it helps the spenders get what they want.

A case in point is the 1981 lobbying campaign by the investment firm E. F. Hutton. The firm's executives traveled from state to state, successfully persuading 18 state legislatures to create authorities empowered to float tax-subsidized farm-loan bonds. This was a lucrative proposition for bond-brokers like E. F. Hutton, but the program was not designed to help the struggling farmers who needed the most help, since the loans were only for new equipment and expansion.[7]

Some legislatures stack the deck against citizen lobbyists with unpublicized committee meetings and sudden schedule changes. A *Washington Post* article in 1983 described the "mass confusion that passes for Virginia's legislative process. . . . [With] abrupt cancellation and rescheduling of subcommittee meetings, frequently with no public notice; agendas that are hard to come by and rarely posted, and late-night or early-morning meetings in which bills are killed with little input from citizens."[8]

Gerrymandering. In many states, elected representatives in state legislatures are responsible for drawing up their own district boundaries, presenting the majority party with an irresistible temptation to draw them so as to ensure the re-election of its own incumbents. The leaders of the legislatures are in a perfect position to ensure their own re-election through gerrymandering, which gives them the seniority to further strengthen their control over the legislature. Gerrymandered "safe" seats discourage qualified opponents from running for office and deny voters a real choice by discouraging potential contributors to challengers. (Gerrymandering can also be used to get rid of a maverick—as the anti-war activist and one-term congressman Allard Lowenstein discovered to his dismay in 1972.)

Legislators' Committee Assignments. Leaders of the legislature "stack" key committees with members who can be trusted to vote as the leaders wish. Bills opposed by the leaders can then be sent to these "graveyard" committees for burial. Conversely, reform-minded maverick legislators can be relegated to committees where they can accomplish little, thereby reducing their chances of re-election.

Logrolling and Pork Barrel Legislation. Logrolling is vote trading, as in: "If you vote for my bill, I'll vote for yours." Such transactions are often made in ignorance of or without regard for the merits of the bills in question. Pork Barrelling refers to the passage of a number of spending proposals, each of which favors just one district and, considered alone and on its own merits, would not pass. Legislators create a single bill combining as many as possible and favoring as many districts as is needed to ensure passage. The public pays for the unnecessary projects in higher taxes.

Unrepresentative Representatives. Most elected legislators at the state level and in Congress are white, middle-aged male attorneys. Although the number of women and minorities is increasing, legislatures do not reflect the makeup of the general population and will not in the foreseeable future.

"Cats and Dogs." Bills of dubious merit may be brought up for votes in the frantic closing hours of a legislative session. Sponsors can sometimes slip through their pet proposals—known as "cats and dogs"—in the confusion.

Legislators' Arrogance. Sometimes legislators let the enjoyment of their power take precedence over their judgment. An eyewitness described the scene that took place in Virginia's legislature in 1984:

> It was the night of the long knives. Good bills, bad bills, almost 200 of them rolled through the Virginia General Assembly's House Courts of Justice Committee. . . .
>
> With cries of "PBI" (pass by indefinitely) ringing through the air—a euphemism for kill the bill—the 20-member execution committee performed its tasks with great relish. And as the night progressed and patience wore thin, the panel's thirst for sending legislation to the graveyard increased.
>
> The mood grew mischievous. The members—attorneys all—exulted in their quick decisions, their knowledge of the law and their power to do pretty much as they pleased.
>
> . . . And as the repartee and pace quickened through the night, it helped a little to be a Democrat, and a well-liked one. "I've been down here 17 years and I'm still baffled by what they do," said Fairfax Republican Delegate Vincent F. Callahan, Jr. . . . "Nobody else understands the bills. Even the lawyers don't understand them."[9]

Many Ways To Kill Bills. There are several ways to kill a bill that allow legislators to avoid answering to the electorate—politicians are very creative in this regard. The New Jersey state senate in 1981 and 1983 passed bills nearly unanimously to amend the state constitution to provide for a statewide Initiative process. Many of the legislators actually opposed Initiative, but voted for it because they knew that it would be blocked in an assembly committee. This arrangement allowed the senators to report to constituents that they had voted for Initiative, and allowed the assembly members—with the exception of the handful who voted to block I&R in committee—to report to constituents that they too favored I&R, but did not get a chance to vote on it. Although this analysis may sound cynical, it is supported by I&R's repeated failure to pass in 1984, 1985, 1986, 1987 and 1988—as it should have if majorities in both houses of the legislature actually supported it.

The point of focusing on this and all the other failings of the legislatures is not to argue that they should be abolished, but to demonstrate that the people they serve should have the power of Initiative to correct them when necessary.

ANSWERING THE OBJECTIONS

Here are the 10 objections most commonly cited by those who oppose extension of Initiative rights to the states that do not already have them—along with the answers to those objections.

1. "Initiatives are poorly written and often unconstitutional." Initiatives are usually drafted more carefully than bills in legislatures because sponsors cannot (except in Massachusetts) make any changes once their petition drive begins. Sponsors have a strong incentive to draft Initiatives well because any flaw becomes ammunition for an opposition campaign and thus lessens the likelihood that the Initiative will gain voter approval. While a few Initiatives that pass are later invalidated by the courts on constitutional grounds, these are the exceptions. For example, of the 40 state-level Initiatives passed by voters in 1980–1982, only two were ruled wholly unconstitutional (Washington State's 1980 ban on importing nuclear waste and Alaska's 1982 "Tundra Rebellion" Initiative; Washington State's 1981 "Don't Bankrupt Washington" Initiative on energy bond approval was judged to be unconstitutional in part). The rest took effect as written.

2. *"The side that spends the most money wins."* Of the 189 state-level Initiative campaigns during the years 1976–1984 for which spending data are available (about three-quarters of all campaigns during this period), campaign spending can be judged the decisive factor in only about 23—one-eighth of the total.

In these 23 campaigns, voters rejected Initiatives after campaigns in which opponents outspent proponents by at least a two to one ratio—that is, overwhelming "Vote No" campaigns.[10] The conclusion that money was the decisive factor is based on analysis of three categories of spending: overwhelming "Vote No," overwhelming "Vote Yes," and negligible or roughly equivalent spending. As shown in Table 2-2 slightly more than half of the Initiatives in the "Vote Yes" and negligible/roughly equivalent categories won voter approval, which indicates that campaign spending in these races had little impact on the final outcome. In the "Vote No" category, however, only 25 percent of the Initiatives won voter approval. If campaign spending had no impact, the approval rate for these Initiatives should have been comparable to that for the other categories—52 to 55 percent—that is, 23 additional Initiatives in the overwhelming "Vote No" category should have been approved. These

Table 2-2
Campaign Spending, 1976–1984

	Won		Lost	
	No.	%	No.	%
Overwhelming "Vote No" spending	21	25	62	75
Overwhelming "Vote Yes" spending	17	55	14	45
Negligible/roughly equivalent spending	39	52	36	48
All Initiatives (includes Initiatives with unknown spending)	91	39.9	15	60.1
Initiatives with unknown spending	15	38	24	62

Initiatives represent one-eighth of the total of 189 Initiatives. Money, or the lack of it, is certainly a factor in the outcome of all Initiative campaigns, but other factors—like the strength of initial public support for the Initiative, the credibility of opponent and proponent groups, and advertising strategy—are usually more decisive than money alone.

In local-level Initiative campaigns, the assertion that "money wins" is even more questionable. Although no comprehensive study of local Initiative campaign spending has yet been done, the results of urban growth restriction and land use Initiatives and Referendums in California from 1976 through early 1986 show that, at least on this issue, money is definitely *not* the deciding factor. Out of 72 city or county ballot measure campaigns that pitted poorly funded local residents and environmentalists against the overwhelming spending of developers, the developers *lost* two-thirds!

The thresholds of what constitutes "overwhelming" spending were set as follows. First, the spending on one side was more than double that on the other side *and* the amounts involved on the heavier-spending side exceeded $250,000 in 1976–1981 campaigns and $500,000 in 1982–1984 campaigns in California; $100,000 in 1976–1981 campaigns and $250,000 in 1982–1984 campaigns in Ohio; $100,000 in Illinois, Michigan, and Florida in 1976–1984; and $50,000 for all other states.

The California 1976–1981 thresholds were chosen to match the thresholds set by Daniel Lowenstein in "Campaign Spending and Ballot Propositions: Recent Experience, Public Choice Theory, and the First Amendment," 29 *UCLA Law Review,* 505 (1982). The thresholds in other states were adjusted to approximate these California figures.

Figures for these campaigns are taken from *Initiative News Report* 6:8 (3 May 1985), 6:7 (19 April 1985), 4:23 (2 December 1983), 3:10 (17 May 1982), and 3:8 (19 April 1982). Researchers interested in obtaining these figures for all of the 1976–1984 Initiative campaigns should contact the author (see address in Preface).

3. "Initiatives are a tool of special interests/the Right/the Left" (choose one). The "special interest" label is ambiguous; one person's "special interest group" is another's "public interest group." And while Initiatives and their sponsors can usually be classified as leaning Right or Left, it would be wrong to reject the Initiative voting right because one side is more successful at any given time—this is like arguing that there should be no right to vote for president because Republicans have won that office in four out of the last five elections.

In fact, Initiative politics has been remarkably balanced between Left and Right in recent years. In 1977–1986 liberal, environmentalist, or left-leaning groups secured ballot placement for 96 state-level Initiatives, and voters approved 43 of them. During the same period, conservative-oriented groups put 91 Initiatives on state ballots, and voters approved 41 of them.

Ultimately, Initiatives are controlled neither by Right, Left, nor special interests, but by the people. The people exercise their control not only by voting, but also by signing (or refusing to sign) petitions to put Initiative questions on the ballot, and by circulating these petitions. Although it is legal to pay petition circulators, fully two-thirds of all Initiatives on state ballots in 1980–1984 were put there entirely through the efforts of volunteers. Paid petition circulators are employed routinely only in the states with the largest signature requirements: California, Ohio, and Florida. This is a result of necessity: it is extremely difficult to collect over 300,000 signatures purely through volunteer effort.

4. "Initiatives enhance minority rule because many voters do not vote on them." Voter participation levels on Initiatives are consistently high, compared with candidate races. In the general elections of 1976, 1978, 1980, and 1982, the number of people voting on statewide Initiatives averaged 93 percent of the number casting ballots for the highest office on the ballot (governor, U.S. senator, president). Studies comparing participation in Initiatives with participation in state legislative races have found Initiative turnout to be just as high or higher.[11] (Turnout for both Initiatives and candidate races is lower in primary and off-year elections.)

5. "Voter-initiated ballot propositions cause ballot clutter." During the past decade, in the states that provide for I&R, an average of just two voter-initiated measures per state, per general election, have qualified for ballots. In 1982 and 1984, which were typical of recent election years, four times as many ballot propositions were placed on ballots by state legislatures—mostly minor constitutional changes or bond issues that require voter approval under state constitutions. And the number of candidates on state and local ballots is even greater.

6. "Initiatives create tyranny of the majority." "Tyranny" is defined by Webster's Ninth New Collegiate Dictionary as "oppressive power" or "a government in which absolute power is vested in a single ruler." To apply such a label to lawmaking by popular vote under U.S. state and national constitutions is absurd, since the Initiative power is not absolute, and since it provides an additional check on tyrannical tendencies (like bossism) which crop up periodically in American local politics. Even state constitutional Initiatives are subject to judicial review—that is, they must conform to the federal constitution, as interpreted by the federal courts. Initiatives can no more be labeled "tyranny" than enactments of state legislatures, which are subject to the same restriction.

7. "If the people can make laws by Initiative, why have a legislature?" The Initiative process complements—but does not replace—legislatures. Legislatures remain necessary to handle the hundreds of bills introduced in each state every year. Even where Initiative use is highest, laws passed by Initiative represent less than 1 percent of the total number enacted. The electorate, through the Initiative process, passes on average less than one state law per state per election year.

8. *"The voters selfishly 'vote their pocketbooks.'"* Between 1978 and 1984, voters throughout the nation cast ballots on 19 state Initiatives proposing major tax cuts, but passed only 3 of them. Voters resisted the temptation to "vote their pocketbooks" in all but these 3 cases, where the case for a tax cut was particularly strong (Table 2-3 demonstrates voters' restraint on major tax cut Initiatives during the height of the nationwide Tax Revolt; see also Chapter 6).

9. *"Proposition 13 in California and Proposition 2½ in Massachusetts have been disastrous."* It has been said that democracy is the political system that allows the people to make their own mistakes. The people of California and Massachusetts, however, do not agree that Proposition 13 and Proposition 2½ (the property tax cut Initiatives approved by

Table 2-3
Outcomes of Major Tax Cut Initiatives, 1978–1984

Year	State	Outcome	Year	State	Outcome
1978	Calif.	Passed	1980	S.D.	Failed
1978	Idaho	Passed	1980	Utah	Failed
1978	Mich.	Failed	1982	Oreg.	Failed
1978	Oreg.	Failed	1983	Ohio	Failed
1980	Calif.	Failed	1983	Ohio	Failed
1980	Ariz.	Failed	1984	Calif.	Failed
1980	Mass.	Passed	1984	Mich.	Failed
1980	Mich.	Failed	1984	Oreg.	Failed
1980	Nev.	Failed	1984	Nev.	Failed
1980	Oreg.	Failed			

voters in 1978 and 1980) were mistakes. Polls in the mid-1980s showed that majorities of voters continued to support them, and attempts to repeal or substantially change them have, as of 1988, consistently failed. Moreover, the "disasters" predicted by opponents have not happened.

10. *"The people cannot be trusted to vote intelligently on complex issues."* In 1787 Thomas Jefferson took the then-radical position that "the will of the majority should always prevail." In 1820 he still stood by the philosophy of direct democracy: "I know of no safe repository of the ultimate power of society but the people, and if we think them not enlightened enough, the remedy is not to take the power from them, but to inform them by education."[12]

The late George Gallup, Sr., after more than 50 years in the public opinion polling business, said in 1984; "The judgment of the American people is extraordinarily sound. The public is always ahead of its leaders." Gallup had such faith in the electorate's intelligence that he even supported citizen-initiated lawmaking by popular vote at the national level:

> I think the country would have been a hell of a lot better governed over the past 50 years if we had national Initiative. . . .
> On most major issues we've dealt with in the past 50 years, the public was more likely to be right—based on the judgment of history—than the legislatures or Congress.[13]

In fact, voters in the 23 states that provide for I&R have been voting intelligently on complex issues for nearly a century. Woodrow Wilson, an early opponent of I&R, changed his mind in 1911 after having seen I&R in use for seven years: "For 15 years I taught my classes that the Initiative and Referendum wouldn't work. I can prove it now—but the trouble is *they do!*"[14]

3

The Story of Ed Koupal and People's Lobby

Edwin A. Koupal was an unlikely candidate for militant activism. Born in Oregon in 1927, he moved to Sacramento, California, as a young adult, married Joyce Nash, and settled into a conventional life.[1] By the early 1960s Ed and Joyce Koupal had three school-age children, and Ed had become a successful Ford dealer.[2] His lack of interest in politics was such that he had never registered to vote.[3]

Koupal's political conversion began shortly after the family moved to a big new house with a swimming pool in a suburban subdivision east of Sacramento. A member of the district's sewer board called on the Koupals to help thwart a plan by other board members to charge local residents higher rates to allow residents of a newer subdivision nearby to get free sewer service. Outraged, the Koupals started a petition drive to recall the board directors who were supporting the deal. They collected enough signatures to force a recall vote, at which point the directors canceled the proposal. Now

41

attracted to further activism, the Koupals continued to investigate, believing that they had uncovered what Joyce called "a web of corruption" throughout the Placer County government. They dogged the wrongdoers, speaking up at county government meetings and hearings.[4] At this point, political action was still a sideline for the Koupals, but after the inauguration of Ronald Reagan as governor of California in 1967, it became a full-time—though unpaid—career.

THE RECALL REAGAN CAMPAIGN

Ronald Reagan made a lot of enemies during his first year as governor. His cuts in education funding alienated public school teachers and state college faculties; his reduction of the mental health budget offended families of mental patients and the state's social services community; his support for the Vietnam War and advocacy of police and military force to quell campus unrest angered students.[5]

Unlike most state constitutions, California's allows a recall of the governor at mid-term if enough voters sign petitions. At that time about 780,000 signatures were required, 12 percent of the ballots cast in the preceding gubernatorial election.[6] Allowing for illegible or invalid signatures, recall advocates needed approximately one million.[7]

The Koupals took on the challenge. They calculated that a recall election stood a good chance of success if the number of citizens personally hurt by Reagan's policies exceeded 50 percent of the population. In late 1967 Joyce and Ed began clipping newspapers to tally the extent of the hardships, and in March 1968 they started the recall drive. Ed Koupal stopped selling cars and started selling people on the concept of political power through petition circulation.[8]

He traveled up and down the state recruiting volunteers and collecting thousands of signatures himself. It was during this period that he hit upon a method that revolutionized petition campaign strategy. Experimenting with techniques to get the maximum number of signatures in the shortest time, he found that individual petition circulators were inefficient. Going door to door meant that too much time was spent trying to convince each skeptic. Working crowds with a clipboard also resulted in too many one-on-one confrontations. Furthermore, individual volunteer petitioners working alone were notoriously unreliable (they'd promise to go out petitioning for a certain number of hours, but all too often would find something else to do). His solution to these problems was "tabling": the method whereby two (or more) volunteers set petitions on a folding table, and one person shows people where to sign while the other approaches pedestrians and directs them to the table. (For a more detailed description of tabling, see Chapter 9.) Thanks to Koupal, the petition table became standard equipment for Initiative and Referendum petition circulators throughout the United States. Experienced volunteers can collect up to a hundred signatures per hour using this method.[9]

Although there was widespread dissatisfaction with Reagan's policies, no one in the state's political establishment, even Democrats, would contribute to the recall campaign. Yet despite the lack of financial support, recall advocates claimed to have collected 500,000 signatures by 29 May 1968 and vowed to get the additional half-million required by the 31 July deadline.[10]

A successful recall petition might well have been seen as a threat to Governor Reagan's candidacy for the 1968 Republican presidential nomination. Although the governor took no formal note of the Koupals' campaign,[11] his calm was not shared by all of his supporters, and a number of violent incidents were perpetrated against the recall organizers. One night in mid-July, vandals broke windows and painted swastikas on the walls of the Southern California recall office, along with the slogan "Communist Jews Get Out." The Koupals believed that the vandalism was meant to intimidate the many Jewish volunteers in the recall effort. In another incident, a recall volunteer was allegedly assaulted while staffing a petition booth at the Orange

County Fair; the assailants tore up the recall petitions they found there.[12]

Ironically, Koupal was offering an alternative to the violent protests taking place across the country that year. He was trying to show people that they could bring about social change by legal, peaceful means through the petition process, even while they remained outside the halls of the official decision-makers.

On 31 July 1968 the recall volunteers turned their petitions in to county registrars throughout the state. To the disappointment of the petitioners, they had achieved a total of 491,000 signatures, just under 50 percent of what they needed. Apparently, many volunteers had promised Koupal a lot more signatures than they delivered. Governor Reagan held a press conference at the Republican convention in Miami to proclaim the recall effort "a colossal failure."[13]

The Koupals suffered a certain amount of harassment after the campaign. Two Republican state assemblymen alleged that the Koupals had illegally taken money from the recall committee fund. Although they could not track down the source of the allegation, the harassment served only to strengthen the Koupals' determination. They increased their political involvement at the cost of their comfortable suburban life. They left Sacramento and moved into a ramshackle house in Los Angeles,[14] California's biggest population center, seeking access to the highest concentration of potential petition signers in the state.[15]

PEOPLE'S LOBBY AND THE CLEAN ENVIRONMENT INITIATIVE CAMPAIGN

Though their drive to recall Reagan had fallen short, the Koupals realized that the number of petition signatures they had collected would be more than sufficient to put a statewide Initiative on the ballot. They had already noticed an issue on which nearly everybody in Southern California agreed: the smog problem.[16] In late 1968 they began meeting with local environmental groups to gather support for an anti-pollution ballot campaign. They recruited Roger Jon Diamond, a young attorney and member of the local environmental group "Stamp Out Smog." He and several other members had been trying, without success, to persuade their board of directors to undertake an anti-smog Initiative petition drive. He was pleased to draft the proposal for the Koupals' newly incorporated citizens' group, People's Lobby.[17]

On 28 August 1969 People's Lobby launched a double petition drive: one petition for an anti-pollution amendment to the state constitution and a companion Initiative to enact an anti-pollution statute.[18] The Koupals were once again mapping virgin political terrain in California, and the ambitious undertaking presented the organizers with new problems. Explaining to voters why they needed to sign *two* petitions proved more time-consuming than asking for one signature in the Recall Reagan Campaign had been. A further complication arose when a firm hired by the Koupals to affix precinct numbers to each signature to confirm the voters' registration inexplicably failed to complete the task.[19] In late January 1970 the petition deadline ended the drive before enough signatures could be collected.

Despite this failure, Ed Koupal used his sales background and exceptional organizational ability to convince People's Lobby volunteers that they had almost succeeded. He pointed out that had the drive consisted of a single petition and had they done the precinct verification themselves, their Initiative would have qualified for the ballot. The group decided to combine the two Initiatives into one and start again later that year. Meanwhile, People's Lobby bolstered their effort by focusing public attention on smog problems in two lawsuits brought against Standard Oil of California and several state air-pollution-control districts.[20] The former suit charged that Standard Oil's advertisements misled viewers about the supposed environmental benefits of its new gasoline additive, "F-310." The ads featured astronaut Scott Carpenter standing next to two idling cars, which filled huge, transparent balloons with their exhaust. One balloon filled with dense, black smoke; the other—thanks to F-310—remained clear. Koupal ridiculed the ad by challenging Carpenter to stand *inside* the balloon of clear exhaust to prove the additive's anti-pollution claims.[21] (In 1974 the Federal Trade Commission ruled that the F-310 ads were indeed deceptive and misleading—long after the ads had stopped being broadcast.)

The activists achieved their most important victory of 1970 in a third lawsuit. The California Supreme Court upheld citizens' right to circulate Initiative petitions in privately owned shopping malls (*Diamond* v. *Bland,* 3 Cal.d 653). The ruling was crucial because the "table method" of petition circulation had proven more effective in a mall setting than anywhere else.[22]

Buoyed by the ruling, the Koupals and their cadre of volunteers, mainly students and housewives, kicked off their third statewide petition drive—this time for the "Clean Environment Act"—on 7 December 1970. The Koupals gave 50 dedicated workers the responsibility of gathering 10,000 signatures each, either by recruiting new volunteers or working with experienced ones. The "Fanatic Fifty," as the Koupals dubbed them, collected over 400,000 signatures during the five-month drive.[23] Joyce Koupal, her teenaged children, and the volunteers worked late each night, poring over voter registration lists to identify the precinct of each signer. County and state officials checked the signatures and found 14,000 more than the minimum required to put the Initiative on the state ballot.[24] For the first time since 1938, citizens had put an Initiative on the statewide California ballot wholly by volunteer effort.[25]

The entire drive cost only $8,000, at a time when professional petition managers were charging up to $1 million for Initiative campaigns. Of the $8,000, Joyce Koupal had contributed $1,000 from her salary—she had taken a full-time job at a nursing home to support the family while Ed devoted all his energy to People's Lobby.[26] Ed Koupal said during a particularly lean period that he would "rather put social justice in the bank than money."[27]

Although the Initiative had qualified for the June 1972 primary ballot, money was still needed to run the election campaign. A teenaged volunteer, Peter di Donato, came up with one of People's Lobby's most successful fundraising gimmicks: the "Bike for Life." Di Donato mapped out a 30-mile bicycle course, set a date for a mass ride, and distributed leaflets in schools telling students how they could raise money for the Clean Environment Act. Riders would solicit pledges from parents, relatives, or any other willing party for each mile covered. Most pledges were in nickels, dimes, and quarters, but they added up. Ed and Joyce Koupal were skeptical—until more than a thousand riders took part in the first "Bike for Life." In the year prior to the June 1972 election, People's Lobby raised some $174,000 through bike rides.[28]

Meanwhile, industry and labor leaders were working behind the scenes to put together a high-powered publicity campaign to defeat the Initiative. The bank accounts these forces tapped were virtually limitless. The state's powerful agribusiness lobby opposed the Initiative's provision banning such pesticides as DDT. Business groups were afraid that the Initiative's restrictions on lead in gasoline and sulfur in diesel fuel would drive up transportation costs. Oil companies faced the prospect of multimillion-dollar fines for air pollution from refineries. Utility companies opposed the Initiative's five-year moratorium on nuclear power plant construction, and trade unions were afraid of job losses.[29]

The campaign against the Initiative became public in late 1971 with the emergence of a committee called "Citizens Against the Pollution Initiative" (CAPI). It was co-chaired by four men with impressive credentials: Dr. Emil Mrak, chancellor emeritus of the University of California at Davis and director of a DDT study; Joseph J. Diviny, first vice president of the Teamsters Union; Dr. J. E. McKee, professor of environmental engineering and former member of the

Atomic Energy Commission's Advisory Committee on Reactor Safeguards; and Myron W. Doornbos, president of the Southern Council of Conservation Clubs.[30] Doornbos was clearly chosen to give the impression that environmentalists opposed the Initiative. His organization, however, consisted largely of hunters and motorized-sports enthusiasts. People's Lobby had in fact secured the endorsement of most of the state's ecology groups, with the important exception of the Sierra Club, which took a neutral position after rejecting a moratorium on nuclear power plant construction.

By the end of 1971, reporters and officers of every imaginable organization had received press kits from CAPI outlining its case against the Initiative. In a slick circular entitled "How the Pollution Initiative Affects You," CAPI predicted a number of disasters: "Hundreds of thousands of people [will] lose their jobs. . . . You may have to go back to the scrub board and laundry tub for washing clothes. . . . Your very life will be endangered [by] epidemic diseases such as typhoid fever, malaria, yellow fever, and encephalitis."

The Koupals got their chance to strike back in early 1972 when they received from an anonymous source documents revealing that Standard Oil of California was playing a key role in the opposition campaign. In March 1972 People's Lobby reprinted the two most damaging documents and distributed them by the thousands in a sensationally titled booklet, "Standard Oil's Secret Plan to Defeat the Clean Environment Act."

One of the documents was a memo from Standard Oil's chief lobbyist to the chairman of the board detailing a proposed campaign plan. It was dated 4 June 1971—a full year before the election. The other was a campaign plan submitted to Standard Oil on 1 June 1971 by Whitaker and Baxter, a long-established San Francisco political campaign consulting firm. The scheme set up a "front" organization (the model for CAPI) to give the appearance of broad-based citizen opposition to the Initiative. In reality, however, the campaign would be controlled by the utilities and oil companies. The link between CAPI and Whitaker and Baxter was clear—they even had the same San Francisco address.[31]

The Koupals thought that they could destroy CAPI's credibility by exposing it as a puppet organization controlled and funded by big polluters. They were unsuccessful, however. Voters did not respond to People's Lobby's implicit argument that everyone should vote "yes" merely because the oil companies and utilities opposed the Initiative. So CAPI's scientists and other experts maintained their credibility, despite Standard Oil's backing. In those days of 33-cent-a-gallon gasoline, oil companies were not generally regarded as villains. Moreover, People's Lobby had its own problems with credibility. New to the political scene, it was unknown to most voters, and an environmental Initiative not supported by the Sierra Club was viewed with suspicion by many pro-environmentalists.

People's Lobby wasted a lot of time and effort attacking CAPI. Given its limited funds, the organization found itself unable to disseminate the case for the Initiative on its own merits and the arguments of the group's own pollution experts.

For three weeks before the election, CAPI flooded the airwaves with "Vote No" radio and television ads showing haunting images of cities darkened by power outages, unemployment lines, empty supermarket shelves, and exhausted women scrubbing laundry by hand. Then, in the last week before the election, People's Lobby's "Vote Yes" ads were finally broadcast. One television spot featured the actress Candace Bergen making an earnest plea to stop air pollution, followed by a chemist explaining why the Initiative's provisions were reasonable. Another was a clever psychedelic cartoon in which a man in a business suit walked through a dull, gray landscape to a voting booth, cast a ballot for the Initiative, and emerged (clad in colorful clothes) into a world of flowers, trees, and smiling deer.[32]

But the opposition's advertising dominated the airwaves. Faced with a choice between a polluted yet livable environment and a return to the Dark Ages, Californians opted to retain the status quo, rejecting the Initiative by a two to one vote. People's Lobby had spent approximately $225,000 on the campaign; CAPI and its supporters had put out some $1.7 million, more than half of it contributed by the petroleum, chemical, and utility industries.[33] With this investment, these interests successfully blocked the most stringent anti-pollution law to be considered in the 1970s.

Over the next several years, however, many of the provisions contained in the Initiative became law. The federal Environmental Protection Agency banned DDT and other poisons named in the Initiative, and state laws passed in 1976 prevented construction of additional nuclear plants. And, gradually, state and federal rules phased out leaded gasoline.[34]

Moreover, California voters soon had another chance to strike a blow for environmental protection. In the election of November 1972, they approved an Initiative that severely limited urban and industrial land development in a 1,000-yard-wide coastal zone stretching the length of the state. The Sierra Club stood solidly behind this proposal, and People's Lobby gave the effort a crucial boost by training club volunteers in the table method, which undoubtedly pushed the Initiative onto the ballot.

The Coastal Conservation Initiative, designated "Proposition 20" on the November 1972 ballot, was bitterly opposed by many of the same formidable interests that had defeated the Clean Environment Act—oil companies, utilities, labor unions—plus some new ones, such as real estate developers. Again, Whitaker and Baxter ran the opposition campaign. The "Vote No" effort spent $1.16 million, compared with $295,000 spent by the proponents, but the Initiative got a 55 percent favorable vote.[35] A decade later observers hailed the California Coastal Commission, the regulatory agency created by the Initiative, as the toughest government environmental agency in the United States.

Still, People's Lobby did not recover easily from the defeat of the Clean Environment Initiative. Koupal had run the group as a virtual dictator. In late 1972, in a move to regain momentum, he created a "steering board" to be the policy-making body of the organization, with the Fanatic Fifty as its original members. Even under the new arrangement, however, he clearly commanded the organization: "Between campaigns this is a democracy," he told the board. "But once we've decided on a course of action, I'm in charge."[36]

The board agreed to pursue another Initiative for the June 1974 state ballot. This time, rather than drafting the Initiative first and then soliciting endorsements from other groups, Koupal invited all the state's environmental and political reform groups to participate in the drafting. By late 1972 three separate proposals had emerged. One would limit campaign spending to eliminate the huge advantages held by wealthy interests, like the ones that had defeated the Clean Environment Initiative, in ballot campaigns. Another Initiative would require nuclear power companies to take full financial responsibility for power plant accidents (utility companies' liability for nuclear accidents was, and still is, limited by the federal Price-Anderson Act). The third Initiative would reduce pollution and ban harmful pesticides.[37] It was the proposal on campaign spending that became the major focus for the next Initiative drive.

THE POLITICAL REFORM INITIATIVE OF 1974

The idea for an Initiative to limit campaign spending grew into a wide-ranging anti-corruption measure that attacked secret expenditures by lobbyists, conflicts of interest among governmental officials, and incumbent politicians' advantageous position at the top of the ballot.[38]

Early drafts of the proposal borrowed heavily from a political ethics Initiative passed by voters in Washington State in 1972; additional provisions were taken from ethics bills proposed in both Congress and the California legislature. People's Lobby completed its first draft in January 1973 and circulated it to legislators and citizen groups for suggestions.[39]

Upon receipt of the draft, Secretary of State Edmund G. ("Jerry") Brown immediately informed the Koupals that he was drafting his own political ethics Initiative for the June 1974 ballot.[40] Brown, then 33 years old, was running for the Democratic gubernatorial nomination, which was to be decided at the same election. He planned to make his Initiative the central plank in his "clean government" platform. Brown needed to ally himself with People's Lobby for two reasons: to counteract charges that his Initiative was merely an election gimmick inspired by the Watergate scandal, and to harness the manpower needed to collect the required half-million signatures.

Soon after Brown teamed up with the People's Lobby, Common Cause joined the coalition, followed by the Sierra Club and California chapters of the National Association for the Advancement of Colored People, the National Women's Political Caucus, the Ripon Society (a Republican group), and Ralph Nader's Citizen Action Group. The alliance dubbed itself the Coalition for Political Reform. Its first task was to draft an Initiative acceptable to all members. It was agreed that People's Lobby, Jerry Brown, and Common Cause would hammer out the specifics. A curious relationship developed among the three drafting parties. They distrusted each other, yet recognized their mutual dependence. In particular, People's Lobby demanded strict limits on campaign spending, while Common Cause, using First Amendment arguments, tried to weaken or eliminate them. Ed Koupal stubbornly refused to yield and repeatedly stomped out of meetings, threatening to pull People's Lobby out of the coalition. (He was cunning enough to leave a Lobby representative in the room, however, to prevent the others from out-maneuvering him.)[41]

Eventually, People's Lobby won the strict spending-limit provisions (although some of these were later struck down by the California Supreme Court as unconstitutional *Citizens for Jobs and Energy* v. *Fair Political Practices Commission,* 16 Cal. 3d 671, 547 P. 2d 1386 [1976]). In addition, the final wording included a little-noticed section designed to improve the Initiative process. The provision abolished the requirement to identify the election precinct of each signer, a monumental task. According to Joyce Koupal, the new rule would "eliminate half the work in qualifying an Initiative for the ballot." It also applied conflict-of-interest standards to every elected official and high-level state or local bureaucrat, required disclosure of all campaign contributions over 50 dollars to either candidates or promoters of ballot measures, and limited the amount lobbyists could spend on legislators to 10 dollars a month—sufficient for "two hamburgers and a coke" each week, as Jerry Brown put it.[42]

People's Lobby and Common Cause kicked off the petition drive in September 1973, but during the 12 weeks of the drive, neither group would inform the other of its running signature totals. In the end, People's Lobby volunteers had collected 325,000 signatures; Common Cause, 195,000. The measure qualified easily for the ballot as "Proposition 9."[43]

Organized opposition to the Initiative had begun to stir before the petition drive ended. In October 1973 Martin B. Dyer, director of the California Manufacturers Association (CMA), invited lobbyists to a meeting to review the Initiative and hear a presentation by a lobbyist from the Pacific Gas and Electric Company, California's largest energy utility and a major opponent of the 1972 Clean Environment Initiative. Someone leaked Dyer's invitation to People's Lobby, and Ed Koupal gleefully prepared copies for distribution with the comment: "The campaign to defeat the people has started; . . . [it is] conceived, and orchestrated by *big business!*"[44]

The statement was the sort of bluster that California political observers had come to expect of Koupal and People's Lobby. This time, however, Koupal pursued a new strategy. The first step had already been accomplished—forging a broad support coalition before the opposition could mobilize. His next step was to attack potential opponents early and individually to discourage joint organizing efforts. As the Koupals later wrote:

> Early in the campaign it was shown that key opinion leaders were supporting Political Reform, and that public opposition would be exposed, and perceived as supporting corruption in government. [After People's Lobby exposed the CMA memo,] the embarrassment forced them into early retirement. They refused to comment and not another word came from them during the whole campaign.[45]

The next Initiative opponent to feel the heat from a People's Lobby blast was State Sen. Clark L. Bradley (R–San Jose). Unlike most legislators, Bradley was outspoken in his opposition to the Initiative. He authored the argument against it that was printed in the state's official ballot information booklet and sent to each voter on the eve of the election. The reprisal was swift. People's Lobby discovered, and announced at a Sacramento news conference, that Bradley's state-paid district office secretary was doing work for his private law firm during office hours. The unfavorable publicity in the San Jose papers contributed to Bradley's defeat in the November election, ending his two decades in the state senate.[46]

John F. Henning, the chief lobbyist for the state AFL-CIO and head of the union political arm, the Committee on Political Education (COPE), was next. Probably the most important labor leader in the state, Henning had asked the state

AFL-CIO executive committee to pass a unanimous resolution opposing the Initiative in March 1974.[47] People's Lobby investigated Henning's records in the state capitol and found that he had not complied with the letter of the existing law requiring registration of lobbyists and disclosure of their expenses. The group filed a lawsuit in Sacramento Superior Court, asking the court to revoke Henning's certification as a lobbyist if he was proven to have violated the law.[48]

Meanwhile, Ed Koupal repeated a tactic from the Recall Reagan drive and started walking—this time from San Diego to the state capitol in Sacramento. He was accompanied by a few People's Lobby diehards who walked the whole way, and joined by large numbers of local supporters as he passed through their towns. In the major cities People's Lobby organizers recruited walkers in advance, requiring them to get pledges of donations for each mile they walked. As he walked, Koupal repeated his slogan, "While the politicians talk, the people will walk—actions speak louder than words."[49]

Those reporters who walked alongside him for any distance found out that he had many more colorful, though unprintable, words for the politicians. In fact, he mixed ribald stories with a steady stream of profane vilification of the lawmakers. The reporters loved it, even if they could not report it. One of his printable stories that year ironically linked the oil shortage of early 1974 with his sponsorship of the defeated Clean Environment Initiative two years earlier: "They [the oil companies] told me that if I voted for the Initiative, it would cause energy shortages. They told me that if I voted for the Initiative, gasoline prices would skyrocket, jobs would be lost. Well, I voted for the Initiative, and sure enough, it all came true."[50]

Later, the Koupals learned that they had more cause to distrust the oil companies: in 1970 Standard Oil's attorneys had hired private detectives to spy on the Koupal family. When they found out about it in January 1975, the Koupals promptly sued Standard Oil, the attorneys, and the detective agency for invasion of privacy, asking $63 million in damages.[51]

While Koupal's spring of 1974 walk was in progress, the AFL-CIO was threatening to drop the union endorsement of any candidate who refused to disavow support for the Initiative. The main implication of the threat was the potential loss of AFL-CIO campaign contributions. Several candidates who had publicly supported the Initiative recanted at the April AFL-CIO state convention. Among them was State Sen. Mervyn Dymally (then running for lieutenant governor, and later elected to Congress), who rescinded his endorsement of Proposition 9, despite the fact that he had offered to become a co-chairperson of the "Yes on 9" Campaign steering committee just two months earlier.[52]

Candidates who continued in their vigorous support for the Initiative, such as gubernatorial candidates Jerry Brown and Congressman Jerome Waldie, suffered the consequences. On 14 May the executive committee of the AFL-CIO met in San Francisco behind closed doors, with Brown present, to give him a chance to state his case before they withdrew their endorsement. The vote went overwhelmingly against him. Afterward Brown told reporters that he could not understand the AFL-CIO's opposition to the Initiative, since it was "pro-labor and anti-corruption." He also claimed to have telegrams from labor unions throughout the state supporting his stand.[53]

Labor's disunity on the Political Reform Initiative was good news for People's Lobby: their most active opponent thus far was facing dissension from within its own ranks. But it was bad news for the opposition, especially the firm of Whitaker and Baxter.

For weeks Clem Whitaker, Jr., principal of the campaign management firm, had been trying to unify the opposition, holding numerous meetings with lobbyists in Sacramento. Ed Koupal knew that Whitaker was involved in anti-9 efforts, and he held a press conference in mid-May to accuse Whitaker and Baxter of having broken the law by failing to file statements of disclosure with the state by the legal deadline. The charge forced Whitaker to reveal his hitherto-secret organizing activities. The most experienced ballot measure campaign manager in the state claimed that there had been no campaign before the deadline—"the pieces just fell together this weekend," three weeks before election day. Whitaker and Baxter may have been suffering from the scars inflicted on their reputation by People's Lobby and other environmentalist groups during the 1972 Clean Environment and Coastal Conservation campaigns.[54] The firm, noted the *Sacramento Bee,* on 14 May 1974, "has been tied to special-interest causes and often taken on campaigns against environmentalists. . . . For this reason, say lobbyists in Sacramento, there was a marked reluctance to hire a company whose name could become an issue in the campaign to defeat a measure that would tightly control lobbyists."

Still, Whitaker and Baxter got not only the job, but the support of most of the state's most powerful lobbying groups. In addition to the AFL-CIO and the CMA, the "Vote No" coalition included the Teamsters Union and the United Auto Workers, and the California Chamber of Commerce, Bankers' Association, Medical Association, and Farm Bureau Federation.[55] These financial giants spent a paltry $183,000—compared with the hefty $537,000 raised by the citizen groups supporting the Initiative.[56] A half-million dollars even then was not a large sum as California Initiative campaigns go, but it was sufficient to get the "Vote Yes" message to a substantial portion of the voters. The industry-backed "media blitz" that supporters expected from the opposition in the final days of the campaign never materialized. The leaders of these groups must have sensed that they had little chance to defeat the Initiative, or they would have contributed more money to the opposition campaign.

On 4 June California voters turned in a 70 percent landslide favoring the Initiative.[57] A gloating Ed Koupal sent the following telegram to Clem Whitaker, Jr.: "Dear Clem:

The people have won. Couldn't have done it without you. Thanks."[58] It was Whitaker and Baxter's last attempt to direct a statewide Initiative campaign, after 40 years in the business.

Jerry Brown won his primary and went on to win the governorship in November 1974. Tom Quinn, Brown's 1974 campaign manager, who was later appointed by him to head the state's Air Resources Board, commented: "The success of Proposition 9 was a microcosm of how our system works. It began in the streets and emerged as a classic document. Who could believe that the Koupals, in their funny little house, could help shape the destiny of this state?"[59]

"DREAM BIGGER!"

The Koupals continued to produce political causes for the now famous People's Lobby: a proposed city Initiative for a municipal buy-out of PG&E's facilities in San Francisco,[60] a lawsuit to stop payment of Lieut. Gov. Ed Reinecke's salary after his conviction for perjury,[61] a lawsuit charging San Francisco Mayor Joseph Alioto with conflict of interest and seeking his removal from office,[62] and a complaint filed with the state attorney general against Assembly Speaker Bob Moretti regarding possible laundering of campaign funds.[63] They even bestowed an "Arrogant Lobbyist of the Year" award upon AFL-CIO leader Henning for his opposition to the Coastal Conservation and Political Reform Initiatives and to a pension reform bill under consideration by the legislature in the same year, 1974.[64]

In the midst of all this activity, Ed Koupal launched his biggest campaign of all: the National Initiative Amendment. In early September 1974 the Koupals announced that a national Initiative process was to be People's Lobby's contribution to the coming Bicentennial celebration.[65] As Ed Koupal himself explained it:

Marking a ballot every couple of years is absentee management.[66]

On the 200th anniversary of America, we'll have both a President and a Vice President who were not elected by the people [Ford and Rockefeller]. We are going to rewrite the involvement of you and me into the federal constitution![67]

Predictably, Congress turned a deaf ear to the proposal.[68] The Koupals, meanwhile, had chosen the environmentalist issue of nuclear power to spearhead the National Initiative cause. The first objective was to be a California Initiative petition designed to stop the expansion of nuclear power and possibly shut it down completely in the Golden State. The next goal was to turn the statewide petition drive, already in progress by late 1974, into a coordinated multistate drive, thus demonstrating the feasibility of a National Initiative.[69] It had never been done before. Once again, the Koupals were breaking new political ground.

The national campaign was christened "Western Bloc" after the geographical bloc of 18 western states where state constitutions allow voters to pass laws by Initiative.[70] Koupal outlined the plan to Ralph Nader, and they agreed to include the five states east of the Mississippi that allow citizen Initiatives at the state level.[71] A year later, with the Western Bloc campaign well under way, Nader invited Koupal to address the anti–nuclear power activists at his 1975 "Critical Mass" convention. Like a party chairman counting votes at a national nominating convention, Koupal called on a representative from each of the various states to report their progress: Californians and Oregonians had successfully completed their petition drives; petitions were circulating in Montana, Colorado, Maine, and Massachusetts; and plans were being made to start petitions in 12 additional states. "You could feel the place vibrating with the political power that everyone was realizing they had: this ability to mount a nationwide Initiative drive," said one participant.[72]

People's Lobby had other ambitious plans in the works for California: a constitutional Initiative to make it as easy for the legislature to raise corporate taxes as to raise individual taxes (this was put on the June 1976 ballot by the legislature soon after People's Lobby started a petition drive), and an Initiative proposal to create a unicameral legislature, backed by former governor Edmund G. ("Pat") Brown, Sr., and State Treasurer Jesse Unruh.[73] Sadly, Ed Koupal did not live to see the election. One day in late 1975, he entered a hospital for tests and received the devastating news that he had cancer of the colon. Despite his illness he continued to keep in touch with Western Bloc organizers scattered throughout the continental United States. In his last conference call, in March 1976, Koupal stressed the importance of the National Initiative.[74]

He died on 29 March at the age of 48.[75] Though he never lived to see the vote on the anti-nuclear Initiatives that qualified for the ballot, his influence was felt throughout the nation.[76] Thanks in large measure to his tenacity and drive, Americans rediscovered their right to greater self-government via the Initiative petition and popular vote. It was Ed Koupal who, with his wife, Joyce, had the boundless optimism to believe that a voter petition could be the means to a renewal of democratic institutions in an era when bureaucracy and centralized decision making vied with rioting and assassination for the role of the decade's most salient political characteristics.[77]

In his eulogy Ralph Nader called Ed Koupal a "citizens' citizen" who "revitalized the use of the Initiative, Referendum, and Recall and put these vital citizen tools back into the mainstream of state politics."[78] Ed Koupal's most fitting epitaph, however, is his own admonition to the steering board of People's Lobby. Koupal shook his audience to open themselves to their unrealized potential: "Dream bigger. Think bigger, and things will get bigger. No room in a strong organization for devil's advocacy. We need positivism."[79]

Following Ed Koupal's death, People's Lobby was never again a major force in state politics, though the group continued to provide training for hundreds of volunteer Initiative petition circulators, under the direction of Joyce Koupal. Among those trainees was a retiree obsessed with property tax reduction, Howard Jarvis, with whom we shall deal later.

4

Energy Crises

In the 1960s most established environmental organizations favored nuclear power, believing the nuclear and electric utility industries' claims that it would provide a cheap, virtually nonpolluting, inexhaustible source of electrical energy. One of the first environmentalists to question this conventional wisdom was David Pesonen, a resident of the San Francisco Bay Area who began a one-man campaign against the construction of a nuclear power plant in the late 1950s. PG&E, California's largest energy utility, planned to locate the plant at Bodega Bay, an untouched rural site on the coast about 50 miles north of San Francisco. In 1962 PG&E abandoned construction work after the discovery of an earthquake fault running directly underneath the power plant site.

The People's Lobby's unsuccessful 1972 Clean Environment Initiative represented the environmental movement's first attack on the nuclear industry as a whole, in contrast to efforts against specific plants at specific sites. Although it had proposed a five-year moratorium on nuclear plant construction as a sort of after thought to provisions dealing with other pollution problems, the campaign was a turning point in California environmentalists' perceptions of nuclear power. After 1972 mainstream environmentalists took a closer look at nuclear power's dark side: the deadly, long-lived nuclear waste, the untested safety systems, and the federal government's limit on the nuclear industry's financial liability in case of accidents.

Another turning point came on 24 November 1973, when Californians woke up to find front-page headlines about another earthquake fault, this one only two miles away from the nuclear construction site at Diablo Canyon on the California coast, where PG&E was building two reactors.[1] Barely a decade after the debacle at Bodega Bay, PG&E had made the same costly mistake!

That winter the Arab Oil Embargo forced oil prices sky-high. The utilities' answer to the "energy crisis" was to plan a network of a thousand nuclear power plants by the year 2000, including 35 in California alone. (Only about 50 plants were operating nationwide in 1974.) Environmentalists wanted nuclear power phased out, and solar energy and conservation technologies phased in. A clash was inevitable.

THE RISE AND FALL OF
THE WESTERN BLOC

By 1973 Ralph Nader had become the nation's most prominent critic of nuclear power. Nader's point man in California was Richard B. Spohn, director of the California Citizen Action Group and a former Nader's Raider. In late 1973 and early 1974, Spohn drafted an anti–nuclear power Initiative that represented a compromise between his group, People's Lobby, the Sierra Club, and Friends of the Earth.[2] This was the Initiative that Ed and Joyce Koupal had chosen as the basis for the Western Bloc National Initiative movement, and it made California a major focus of that campaign.

The proposal was weighted in favor of those who wanted to see nuclear power shut down everywhere. It proposed to allow nuclear power "only if it can be proven safe." Under the Initiative, nuclear plants would be phased out over a 10-year period unless the following conditions were met: (1) the nuclear industry would take full financial responsibility for nuclear accidents; (2) the legislature would agree by a two-thirds majority that safety systems had been adequately tested; and (3) some means would be devised to store nuclear waste safely over the millennia it would remain dangerous.

The Initiative was given scientific respectability by the endorsement of the Federation of American Scientists, and several celebrities joined the campaign, among them the actor Jack Lemmon.[3] Lemmon had a grudge to settle: he and David Pesonen had collaborated on a television documentary critical of nuclear power in 1972, but PG&E's lawyers had so intimidated television station managers that it was never broadcast. Lemmon got even not only by backing the Initiative, but later, by co-starring with Jane Fonda in the 1979 nuclear meltdown drama, *The China Syndrome*. The plot involved a fictional nuclear power plant on the California coast, strikingly similar to the actual plant then under construction at Diablo Canyon.

The environmentalists began their petition drive in late 1974 and struggled for several months to get the half-million signatures needed to put their Initiative on the June 1976 state primary ballot. With the enlistment of the Creative Initiative Foundation, a Palo Alto–based human potential group whose liberal and relatively affluent members took on the task of petition circulation with religious intensity, they succeeded.[4]

In March 1976 three Creative Initiative Foundation members kicked the campaign off by resigning in protest from their jobs as nuclear engineers at General Electric's San Jose nuclear power office. A few days later an engineer working for the federal Nuclear Regulatory Commission resigned. All four cited concerns about the safety of nuclear power.[5]

Meanwhile, both sides had begun raising funds for their campaigns to pass or defeat "Proposition 15," promoted as the "Nuclear Safeguards Initiative" by backers, and condemned as the "Nuclear Shutdown Initiative" by pronuclear critics. California's utility companies called on utility companies and allied industries throughout the nation— including nuclear power plant contractors and builders like General Electric and Bechtel, the multinational construction firm based in San Francisco—to contribute to the "Vote No" campaign. Proponents raised money for the "Vote Yes" campaign by holding rock concerts featuring such performers as Linda Ronstadt, John Denver, Jackson Browne, and the Eagles.[6]

The utilities formed a "Vote No" committee known as "Citizens for Jobs and Energy," chaired by former governor Pat Brown and directed by the Southern California public relations consultants Charles Winner and Ethan Wagner of Winner/Wagner Associates, who were retained more than a year in advance of the election.[7] The three principal environmental groups backing the Initiative consolidated to form "Californians for Nuclear Safeguards (Yes on 15)," but disagreed on campaign strategy and engaged in repeated internecine struggles.

For example, the November-December 1975 newsletter of the Southern California–based People's Lobby included a foldout chart showing the personal and political links between California's top politicians and the nuclear/utility industries; included in this "Nuclear Web" of enemies were Gov. Jerry Brown and some of his appointees who had been allies of People's Lobby in the 1974 Political Reform Initiative campaign. The Northern California "Yes on 15" staffers, for their part, talked of People's Lobby's "paranoid politics" and joked among themselves, "Don't get caught in the 'nuclear web.'" People's Lobby in turn derided the San Francisco office as "People for Spoof," a reference to the northern committee's original name, "People for Proof" (that is, proof of the safety of nuclear power). And both of these low-budget citizen groups bristled at the well-groomed leadership-seminar graduates from the Creative Initiative Foundation.[8]

While proponents squabbled, Winner/Wagner's "Vote No" ads reached the voters early and often, predicting power shortages, economic stagnation, lower living standards, and higher energy costs—$7,500 per family over the next 20 years—should the Initiative be approved. The federal government's Department of Energy supported the "Vote No" effort, not only by providing inflated and excessive cost estimates,[9] but by rushing 78,000 copies of a pro-nuclear booklet to California for distribution.[10]

Leaflets distributed by "Yes on 15" forces refuted these claims point by point, but Initiative proponents decided to use their limited broadcasting funds for last-minute ads that glossed over the details and presented the issue as "the People versus Big Money," listing "Vote No" campaign contributions, such as PG&E's $297,000 and Bechtel's $231,000, to undercut the credibility of the "Vote No" advertising.[11]

In the legislature, three bills to restrict future development of nuclear power progressed slowly toward enactment, pushed along by hints from Governor Jerry Brown that he would be forced to support the Initiative if the legislature failed to act. Preferring the legislature's bills as the lesser of two evils, utility lobbyists let them go through, and they were signed into law by Brown just five days before the Initiative vote, thereby allowing him to take credit for the passage of "the toughest nuclear power safety legislation in the nation" during his 1976 campaign for the Democratic presidential nomination.[12]

California voters rejected the Initiative by a two to one margin, but Initiative proponents, who had anticipated defeat, had reserved enough cash to carry on the anti-nuclear effort. These funds went to hire San Francisco "Yes on 15" staffers Dwight Cocke and Ken Masterton as directors of an ongoing lobbying campaign against nuclear power. In 1978 Southern California utilities' plans to build the largest nuclear power complex in the world at a site in Kern County would be derailed by a county-wide referendum, directed by Cocke, in which 70 percent of the voters rejected the nuclear power plan. Over the next decade not a single new nuclear power plant began construction in California, nor, as of 1988, were there plans to build any.[13]

California's campaign was the spearhead of Western Bloc, but it stood apart from the structure designed to tie the movement together. The responsibility for organizing the early phases of the Western Bloc campaigns elsewhere fell primarily on two young activists, John Forster and Roger Telschow. In some cases, Forster or Telschow would arrive in a state with nothing more than the Friends of the Earth mailing list and the phone numbers of a handful of local activists. They would track down these people and try to persuade them to lead the Western Bloc petition drive in their state. A couple of months in each state might have been adequate for the job, but Telschow and Forster could afford to spend only a couple of weeks.[14] In states where no established environmental group was willing to take on the petition drive, Telschow or Forster had to build organizations from the ground up. Month after month, they zealously pushed themselves up the daunting mountain of obstacles.

In Oklahoma, an eager but inexperienced anti-nuclear group drafted an Initiative proposal and collected several thousand signatures to put it on the ballot, only to discover a flaw in the wording of the petition that forced them to begin again. In Massachusetts, the state's established environmental groups were already pushing two energy-related Initiative petitions and were not willing to take on another. In early November 1975, with only a month to go before Massachusetts' deadline for completing Initiative petitions, Joyce Koupal and John Forster begged the leaders of the Cambridge-based anti-nuclear Union of Concerned Scientists to make it their issue, but to no avail.[15]

Telschow had more success in Michigan, where he had made plenty of contacts as chairperson of Michigan's Public Interest Research Group (PIRG) during his college years. He stayed five months, leaving only after Michigan activists had obtained 100,000 signatures (about 40 percent of their statewide requirement). Then, certain that the necessary momentum to meet the deadline had been achieved, he boarded a plane for Seattle, his ticket paid for by anti-nuclear activists there who were growing increasingly worried that they would fail to collect the additional 100,000 signatures needed before *their* deadline. Fifty days later, Washington State had 110,000 more signatures, and that Initiative qualified for the November 1976 ballot. Michigan's Initiative failed, however: the petition drive ground to a halt soon after Telschow left the state.[16]

In Ohio Forster's first move was to sit down in a law library and read all the applicable laws, including the footnotes that dealt with related court decisions. There, deep in the fine print, he read that by circulating a single Initiative petition, sponsors could place any number of *unrelated* propositions on the ballot. Thus, a single signature could have the force of two, or three, or four, or even more. The discovery electrified Forster: here was a chance to make history, for no other state had such a procedure, and no Ohioan had ever taken advantage of this one.[17]

The Ohioans decided to place four Initiatives on the ballot: one anti-nuclear, patterned after the Initiatives in other states; one reducing utility bills for small users; a third establishing a Residential Utility Consumer Action Group, or RUCAG; and a fourth reducing the number of signatures needed to put Initiatives on the ballot. The petition requirement of nearly 400,000 signatures was second only to California's half a million, and a nearly impossible goal for grassroots citizen groups employing only volunteer petition circulators.[18]

With just a month to go before the deadline, People's Lobby rushed Roger Telschow from Washington to Ohio. He had just finished 50 straight days of soliciting signatures in front of K-Marts in the Seattle-Tacoma area and had no time to recuperate. Like marathoners reaching their final mile, Telschow, Forster, and Columbus, Ohio, activists Sandra and Stephen Sterrett pushed themselves and their volunteers beyond their limits, gathering 10,000 signatures each day in the last 10 days before the deadline,[19] for a total of 472,000 names.[20]

Beyond the finish line, however, the Ohioans still had to run the gauntlet of utility company lawyers' last-ditch efforts to keep the Initiatives off the ballot by invoking legal technicalities. First, the utility lawyers claimed that there was no law that allowed a single petition to put more than one Initiative on the ballot. The state supreme court on 22 September, just 44 days before the election, agreed with Forster's analysis that the procedure was permitted under a 1931 court ruling (16 *State ex rel. Hubbell* v. *Bettman,* 124 Ohio St. 24, 176 N.E. 664). Other legal objections raised by the utility lawyers met the same end.[21]

Meanwhile, radio ads paid for by the utilities were flooding the state with deep-voiced advice to "Vote No on Issues 4, 5, 6, and 7." According to the ads, the Initiatives "can only increase utility rates, create energy problems, threaten jobs, and radically alter our State Constitution. Don't hurt Ohio— Don't hurt yourself."[22]

The Initiative to reduce utility rates for small users would indeed raise rates for larger users, and the one to make it more difficult to build new nuclear power plants *might* cause energy problems and threaten jobs, *if* more nuclear plants were really needed in the coming years. But the utility claims with regard to the other two Initiatives were pure blarney. The RUCAG, a consumer advocacy group funded entirely by voluntary contributions, could not conceivably cause such dire problems; and the proposed reduction (from 308,000 to 250,000) in the signature requirement for Initiatives would hardly "radically alter" the state constitution. According to the utilities, "We, the taxpayers, could be faced with 30 to 40 Special Issues [Initiatives] at every election, at $150,000 per issue." All these figures are implausible. The state had had only 44 Initiatives on its ballot in the previous 64 years. As for the $150,000, a Common Cause/ Ohio news release observed: "The weight of this argument can be put into perspective by simple division. The cost equals one-and-one-half cents per Ohioan. The opponents must therefore conclude that direct democracy isn't worth two cents!"[23]

The utilities styled their "Vote No" organization as "Citizens for Safe, Lower Cost Electricity," and hired Eugene ("Pete") O'Grady, a campaign consultant and former chairman of the Ohio Democratic Party, to be its director. Backers of the Initiatives derisively pronounced the group's acronym, CSLCE, as "Slickee," a reference to O'Grady's slick mass media campaign.[24]

O'Grady in person was not as slick as his ad campaign. Whereas his ads had been proclaiming that Issue Number 4, the "life-line" utility discount for small users, would mean higher rates for the majority of Ohioans, he admitted under questioning that this was not true for residential consumers.[25] Those who would pay more if the issue passed, however, included all of Ohio's major businesses, which therefore contributed generously to the utilities' "Vote No" campaign. Joining the business community in opposition to the Initiatives was the state's political and labor leadership, with the exception of a few mavericks who joined the "Vote Yes for Lower Utilities" committee: Cleveland's Dennis J. Kucinich, who would soon be mayor of that city; congressional candidate Mary Rose Oakar; Congressmen Charles Vanik, Louis Stokes, and Ron Motl; the United Auto Workers; and the United Mine Workers.[26]

In addition to radio, television, and newspaper ads, "Slickee" utilized its extensive business and labor network to distribute glossy foldout brochures that stated confidently: "There is only one real answer to the higher costs of electricity. That's nuclear power. . . . Nuclear power development is the single answer."[27] The brochures made no reference to ominous front-page stories that had appeared in the state's newspapers just a couple of months earlier describing "1,488 problems with the safety-related electrical wiring" at the nearly complete Davis-Besse nuclear power plant 70 miles west of Cleveland.[28] That news should have prompted contractors like Babcock and Wilcox, designers of the Three Mile Island plant that would become famous for its near-catastrophic accident three years later, to take a hard critical look at their work. Instead of facing up to its shortcomings, however, B&W joined the rest of the nuclear industry in branding Initiative proponents irrational, and donated $52,000 in Ohio alone to defeat them.[29]

"Slickee" propaganda was everywhere in Ohio that October—"Vote No" leaflets even appeared in bills sent by the state's largest oil company, Sohio, to gasoline credit card holders. Against this media barrage, "Vote Yes for Lower Utilities" had only one weapon: a television ad showing a man in a sheep suit telling people to "Vote No for lower utilities." Suddenly, a skeptic enters the picture, rips off the sheep's head, revealing a wolf beneath it, and asks, "How can *you* be for lower utilities? You *are* the utilities!"[30] The single ad, however, was too little and too late. By the end of the campaign, "Slickee" had outspent the "Vote Yes" committee by a ratio of 66 to 1. Ohioans rejected all four Initiatives by margins of roughly two to one. The unevenness of the battle was epitomized by a post-election dinner given by the Cleveland Electric Illuminating Company for a thousand employees who had worked on the "Vote No" campaign. It cost more than half the amount Initiative proponents had spent on their entire effort.[31]

Similarly lopsided campaigns were going on simultaneously in Arizona, Oregon, Washington, Montana, and Colorado, and clear majorities of voters in each of these states also rejected Western Bloc's anti-nuclear Initiatives. Only in Missouri was there a success.

IF AT FIRST YOU DON'T SUCCEED . . .

Before the November 1976 election, publications of the Atomic Industrial Forum, the nuclear industry trade association, referred to the "seven" anti-nuclear Initiatives that were to appear on state ballots. After the election, the group's literature claimed that "all six" had been defeated. The Missouri Initiative, which had won voter approval two to one, had been dropped from the list.[32] This law struck a heavy blow to nuclear power's financial foundation by banning a financing scheme known as "CWIP"—Construction Work in Progress. With CWIP, citizens had to pay for the construction costs of nuclear power plants *before* the plants produced any electricity. The utilities in various states had burdened ratepayers with CWIP surcharges because they could not pay for constructing nuclear power plants through their normal billing procedures.

In Missouri, even people who had given little thought to the issue of nuclear safety were hopping mad about CWIP. A St. Louis environmentalist, Dee Aylward, organized a petition drive to put a "Ban CWIP" Initiative on the ballot even though she had never been an activist leader.[33] The utilities spent about a million dollars fruitlessly trying to persuade Missourians to reject the Initiative—28 times as much as proponents. Four months after voters passed the Initiative, Missouri's Union Electric Company abruptly halted construction on its Callaway Nuclear Unit 2, never to start again.[34]

Seeing the effectiveness of the CWIP ban, Oregonians put a similar Initiative on their state ballot in 1978–and passed it by an even bigger margin than Missourians. In Montana, meanwhile, three Western Bloc campaign veterans came up with a new strategy. Matt Jordan, Edward M. Dobson, and Mike A. Males analyzed their 1976 defeat and decided that a major weakness of their Initiative was the label assigned to it by the state's attorney general, who was in charge of putting titles on ballot propositions. He had titled it a "ban" on nuclear power, and this label had been picked up by the nuclear industry's "Vote No" ad campaign.[35]

For 1978 Males, Dobson, and Jordan designed a new Initiative that had all the features of the 1976 version—that is, it required that the state not allow construction of a new nuclear plant unless a series of strict safety conditions had been met, and it forced builders and owners to take full financial responsibility in case of an accident—with the added provision that the voters would have the final say on any proposed nuclear plant, even if the state government approved it. This time the attorney general wrote a more favorable ballot title describing the Initiative as "giving Montana voters power to approve or reject any proposed major nuclear power facility and establishing nuclear safety and liability standards." Nuclear industry lawyers challenged that ballot title in the Montana State Supreme Court, but lost their case (*Wenzel* v. *Murray,* 1978).[36]

The utility and nuclear industries, campaigning as "Montanans for Jobs and Energy," spent twice as much money as they had in 1976 to advertise their assertion that the 1978 Initiative was a harmful "ban" on nuclear power. In the last three days before the election, the "Vote No" committee ran eight or more ads in each daily newspaper in the state and, in certain regions, four to five radio and television ads per station every *hour.* This time, the voters did not believe it, and approved the measure by a nearly two to one margin.[37]

After the near meltdown at Three Mile Island in March 1979, environmentalists in states with a nuclear plant already under construction or in operation wanted more drastic action. A Maine group under the leadership of Ray

Shadis, who lived close to the nuclear plant at Wiscasset, ran a successful petition drive to put on the ballot an Initiative to simply ban nuclear power. In Missouri, where the Callaway Unit 1 nuclear plant was in an advanced state of construction, environmentalists sponsored an Initiative to allow the plant to operate only if there was a functioning facility for the long-term safe storage of radioactive waste, an impossible technological requirement for at least a dozen years to come. In both states utility-backed campaigns predicted blackouts and brownouts (reduced power to all customers) as well as job losses and economic stagnation if the Initiatives should pass, the same dreary litany that had been broadcast to voters in the seven states with anti-nuclear Initiatives in 1976. The results in Maine and Missouri in 1980 were almost the same: despite Three Mile Island, voters were still prepared to accept the safety risks of nuclear power to avoid economic catastrophe predicted by the utilities' "Vote No" campaigns. The Initiatives were overwhelmingly defeated.[38]

In Oregon, however, environmentalists took a more moderate route and based their 1980 Initiative on the 1978 Montana measure. South Dakota's anti-nuclear Black Hills Alliance also used the Montana 1978 Initiative as a model, proposing a ballot measure to give the state's voters veto power over any nuclear power operation, including waste dumping and uranium mining. In Montana, Ed Dobson of Billings sponsored his third anti-nuclear Initiative. This one would ban nuclear waste dumping and make uranium mining uneconomical by prohibiting the dumping of uranium mill tailings.[39]

Predictably, the nuclear industry launched a "Vote No" advertising blitz in all three states in the weeks just prior to the election. In Oregon the utilities broadcast a television ad showing the person most hated by Americans at that time, the Ayatollah Khomeini. The ad asked whether Oregonians wanted such a man controlling their future, a question based on the assumption that without nuclear power, Oregon would have to rely on Iranian oil to generate electricity. But the majority of voters did not buy it. And proponents were able to turn the economic argument *against* the utilities this time: nuclear power construction was getting so expensive that more nuclear plants would mean massive rate hikes, industrial flight, and job losses. On 4 November 1980, Oregonians approved the Initiative by a 53 percent margin.[40]

In South Dakota and Montana, where the central issue was uranium mining, the "Vote No" campaign was funded by a different segment of the nuclear industry: mining firms and oil firms with mining or nuclear fuel processing subsidiaries, including Gulf Oil, Anaconda Copper, Exxon, Amoco, and Standard Oil of California. In Montana, one television ad showed a fleet of model ships and urged people to "Vote Against [the anti–nuclear waste Initiative] because our enemies would probably vote for it." Opponents outspent backers by a ratio of 57 to 1, but the Initiative squeaked through to a narrow 500-vote victory, out of over 340,000 votes cast. In South Dakota, by contrast, opponents focused on the job losses that would result from banning uranium mining, even though the Initiative would not ban mining, but merely give citizens a chance to vote on whether to allow a specific mining operation. Union Carbide and Anaconda dramatically announced that they were suspending uranium exploration until the vote. After the election, however, a Carbide spokesman admitted that the decision had been made because of reduced demand for uranium.[41]

The "Vote No" campaign in South Dakota spent nearly a quarter of a million dollars, making it a big spender by that state's standards. Proponents raised only $8,500, were outspent by a ratio of 28 to 1, and still attracted 48.4 percent of the vote—not enough to win, but a good showing.

Liberals nationwide raised $2.8 million to support the unsuccessful re-election campaign of South Dakota Sen. George McGovern.[42] Had McGovern given just 1 percent of his campaign kitty—$28,000—to the Black Hills Alliance, the Initiative might well have passed. In fact, some members of the alliance, encouraged by the vote in 1980, put the nuclear issue on the ballot again in 1984. This time the voters approved the Initiative by a 62 percent margin.

CLOSEUP OF A STATEWIDE INITIATIVE CAMPAIGN: HOW THEY WHIPPED "WHOOPS" IN WASHINGTON STATE

Washington State's Initiative 394, on the ballot in November 1981, was opposed by an array of financial giants: the nuclear power industry, Wall Street investment firms, labor unions, even the state government. Yet Initiative proponents defeated these Goliaths in a landslide electoral victory.

The issue involved a state agency known as "Whoops," the derisive pronunciation of the acronym for the Washington Public Power Supply System, or WPPSS. As early as 1973, when WPPSS began construction on a series of five planned nuclear power plants, local environmentalists pointed to the irony of allowing an agency named "Whoops" to build power plants with a potential for catastrophic accidents. Later, as cost overruns on the project mounted, the irony deepened.

Washington State environmentalists first used the Initiative process in an attempt to stop WPPSS when, with the help of Western Bloc organizer Roger Telschow, they put the "Nuclear Safeguards Initiative" on the state's November 1976 state ballot. This Initiative was defeated by a two to one margin, and its proponents, discouraged by nationwide anti-nuclear losses, disbanded their organization. For one activist, however, the 1976 campaign was merely an initiation into a new brand of political action. This was Steve Zemke, who later became founder and leader of the group that sponsored Initiative 394. In 1978 Zemke, a graduate student in biology at the University of Washington, had interrupted his studies to organize a petition drive to put a

"Bottle Bill" Initiative on the state's 1979 ballot. This Initiative was defeated, with 57 percent voting against it, but Zemke was still not discouraged.[43]

Even as the ill-fated Bottle Bill campaign was in progress, anti–nuclear power activists were discussing plans for a new Initiative. The nuclear accident at Three Mile Island had sensitized the nation to the safety problems involved in the use of nuclear power. The cost of nuclear power plants had also become an issue: The price tag for WPPSS's five plants had mushroomed from $4.1 billion in 1973 to $15.9 billion in 1979. The WPPSS nuclear construction program was to become the most costly state-sponsored construction venture in the nation.[44]

Framing the Issues

The Washington activists believed that public opposition to nuclear power could be mobilized around two issues: the dumping of nuclear waste from many other states in Washington and the costly mismanagement of WPPSS. They divided on the question of which problem to focus on. One faction argued for an Initiative to ban importation of nuclear waste into the state. The other faction argued for an Initiative requiring public approval, by referendum vote, for bond issues to finance WPPSS's nuclear projects. The latter approach, which provided the basis for Initiative 394, had several advantages. First, the concept of voter approval for government bonds was already a familiar and accepted procedure of state and local government. Second, an Initiative to require referendum approval for nuclear plants had passed in 1978 in Montana, proving the popularity of the voter-approval concept. And third, because the proposal focused on the popular and understandable issue of cost control, rather than the complex technical issue of nuclear power safety, a confusing technical debate could be avoided during the campaign.[45]

The hard-line activists sided with the nuclear waste ban faction, and the leaders of the two factions refused to cooperate with one another.[46] They made no attempt to stop any of their followers who chose to circulate both petitions in the spring of 1980, as Zemke did, but split and competing for volunteers, the campaigns' prospects were dim. Prospects grew dimmer when Mount St. Helens exploded on 18 May 1980, covering the eastern half of the state with a blanket of volcanic ash and clouds so thick that street lights had to be kept on all day. Although the heavily populated Seattle area was unaffected, petition circulators' morale throughout the state sagged. Western volunteers knew that their own signature quotas would have to be raised to make up for the shortfall in ash-covered areas where petitions could not be circulated.[47]

As the petition deadline drew near, sponsors of the antinuclear measures could see that only the nuclear waste ban had a chance to qualify for the ballot. Volunteers were assigned to set up petition tables in shopping malls for a final push. But Zemke feared that their efforts might not be enough. With a nine-to-five job, he could devote only two hours a day to petition circulation. The solution was a Zemke innovation: the unstaffed petition table. Having personally asked thousands of voters to sign Initiative petitions over the previous several years, Zemke had noticed that some people were repelled by petition circulators soliciting passersby. Thousands of people may have avoided signing simply because they did not like the high-pressure approach. Acting on this insight, Zemke and another Seattle Initiative veteran, Bill Harrington, set up folding tables all over town, each with petitions taped securely on top. At the end of the day, they drove around to retrieve the tables. In five days they collected 1,500 signatures in this manner. The secretary of state released the official total for the drive a month later. It was close but successful—1,100 signatures over the required minimum of 123,711.[48]

To the surprise of Initiative proponents, the nuclear industry mounted only token opposition to the measure, nicknamed "Don't Waste Washington," and it passed with 74 percent voting in favor.[49] But it was a hollow victory. The measure was voided as unconstitutional by a federal court before it went into effect, on the grounds of federal preemption of nuclear waste regulation and interstate commerce. Even as a publicity effort the Initiative was only slightly successful, since the lack of opposition meant that it had attained only minimal public visibility.[50]

Regrouping

In late 1980 Zemke called a meeting of the 12 most active veterans of the abortive spring petition drive and told them, "I'm going to work to put an Initiative on the ballot in 1981, and the only question for each of you is to decide whether you're going to be part of the campaign."[51]

He named the group "Don't Bankrupt Washington" in an attempt to capitalize on the popularity of the "Don't Waste Washington" Initiative, and he took over as chairperson and campaign manager. He then sent out a questionnaire to about 300 state activists, including legislators and other public officials, asking for their comments on the 1980 version of the measure, and for any suggested changes. As a result, the Initiative's spending control provisions were extended to cover cities, counties, and public utility districts, as well as joint operating agencies like WPPSS. New criteria for evaluating energy projects were added, among them the requirement that a cost-effectiveness study be done on each power plant. Amazingly, WPPSS had never done a study to determine whether any of its five nuclear plants were economically viable.[52]

The final version retained the essential feature of the earlier proposal: it would require voter approval before bonds could be issued by public agencies to build major power plants. "Major" plants were defined as those designed to generate 250 megawatts or more—about enough to supply 250,000 homes. That number was chosen because plants of this size were already required to get siting approval from the state. Since each of WPPSS's five nuclear plants was to generate about 1,000 megawatts, all would come under the restrictions of the Initiative.[53]

In February 1981 the secretary of state's office affixed its official descriptive summary, title, and number to the proposal. The "Don't Bankrupt Washington" Committee kicked off its petition drive in early March, after the legislature failed to enact a bill similar to the Initiative. During the same session, the legislature released a study that blamed WPPSS's rising costs on mismanagement and raised the price tag for the five nuclear plants to $17.3 billion. After the legislature adjourned, however, WPPSS released its own new cost estimate: a horrendous $23.9 billion (the state budget for two years was only $12 billion). These developments, which received extensive coverage in the Washington State media, aided the petitioners by keeping the WPPSS issue in the public eye and gave voters an added incentive to sign and circulate the petition. And whenever Initiative proponents were interviewed for news stories, they never failed to bring in the fact that the newest cost estimate was "a 600 percent increase over 1973."[54]

The spring season that year was exceptionally rainy, even for a state where T-shirts jokingly advertise the "Seattle Rain Festival: September–June." The weather restricted petition circulators to a few indoor shopping malls. By the first week of May, they had collected only 40,000 signatures toward a goal of 170,000. More signatures were needed than in the previous year's "Don't Waste Washington" drive, because petition requirements are based on a percentage of turnout in the most recent gubernatorial election. Since more people had voted in 1980 than in 1976, the number of signatures needed to put an Initiative on the ballot in 1981 rose by almost 15,000.[55]

At this point Zemke set up a "phone bank" to activate more petition circulators. Volunteers staffing an array of telephones called everyone on the mailing lists of supporters of previous environmental Initiatives. People were asked to sign, circulate, and return the petitions that had already been mailed to them, donate money, and volunteer time to staff petition tables. The magnitude of the effort is indicated by the size of Zemke's mailing list of supporters: by the end of the campaign, it had grown to 10,000 names, more than double the number of members in the state's largest ecology group, the Sierra Club.[56]

In early June the rain finally let up, and the citizens of Washington State emerged into the sunlight to find Initiative 394 petition circulators in malls and on street corners across the state. Volunteers urged passersby to sign and "put a lid on WPPSS's spending." Zemke publicized his own calculation, using WPPSS's latest cost estimates, that the WPPSS debt amounted to $30,000 for each household in the state.[57] By the petition deadline in the first week of July, "Don't Bankrupt Washington" had collected 186,000 signatures—enough to qualify for the November ballot.[58]

The Opposition

The interests that were profiting from WPPSS's cost overruns were not about to sit idle while their multibillion-dollar golden goose was killed by the state's taxpayers. While WPPSS, as a government agency, could not spend money on an Initiative campaign, the contractors building its nuclear plants were under no such restriction. For them, spending a million dollars to save $24 billion worth of contracts was a small investment. Nuclear industry leaders mapped out a strategy for an opposition campaign and began raising funds under the aegis of the Western Environmental Trade Association. This industry group, although sporting the green "e" symbol of the ecology movement on its letterhead, was actually an alliance made up of most of the state's biggest businesses: Weyerhauser, Georgia Pacific, Seattle First National Bank, Alcoa, Kaiser Aluminum, and others.[59]

The Initiative opponents' first move was to hire Winner/Wagner Associates of Los Angeles to manage their campaign. Charles Winner and Ethan Wagner had first impressed utility executives in 1976, when they ran the nuclear industry's successful campaign against California's anti–nuclear power Initiative. In the years that followed, Winner/Wagner developed a specialty in defeating utility-regulation Initiatives. It is a lucrative business, since individual utility companies are willing to spend millions of dollars to save a nuclear plant from the threat of shutdown. The firm was by no means invulnerable: opponents of California's tax-cutting Proposition 13 hired Winner/Wagner in 1978, and the anti-tax crusaders Howard Jarvis and Paul Gann gave the firm a thorough basting. Yet Winner/Wagner had never lost a campaign on a utility issue.[60]

One reason for Winner/Wagner's success was its overwhelming funding advantage in every case. Environmentalists supporting utility Initiatives were typically outspent by factors of 10 to 1 or greater. Winner's motivation is not merely monetary, however: opposition to Initiatives is part of his political philosophy. By 1982 he had been involved in more than 50 ballot measure campaigns in 13 states, working almost exclusively in opposition to proposed Initiatives. He has equated Initiatives with "mob rule" and characterized the upsurge in their use as a "dangerous trend" that "may strike at the very heart of representative democracy."[61]

What's in a Name? —a Lot

The opposition's next task, after hiring Winner/Wagner, was to choose a name for the "No on 394" committee. The function of the name is not necessarily to describe the committee, as one might expect, but to help create a favorable image of the "Vote No" cause. Campaign management firms like Winner/Wagner spend thousands of dollars on public opinion polls to test the appeal of various names.

No one was more aware of the importance of a name than Steve Zemke, manager of the "Yes on 394" campaign. "Don't Bankrupt Washington" had a commanding lead in the name recognition competition. But Zemke had an impish inspiration to harass the opposition by legally stealing their name. In late July, when they announced that the "No on 394" committee would be called "Citizens for an Adequate Energy Supply," they neglected to rush someone to the state capitol in Olympia to officially register the name (as is required by law before any money can be spent). When they did attempt to register the name, they learned that someone from the pro-Initiative side had already been there and filed the same name. They hurriedly came up with another one and held a press conference the next day, renaming themselves the "Committee Against Shutdown of Energy." But Zemke's people noted that the acronym "CASE" was already on file in Olympia. Finally, the anti-Initiative forces understood what was happening and sent someone to Olympia to file their next name before they announced it: "Citizens Against Unfair Taxes, the No on 394 Committee."

Zemke's view is that the skirmish over names did more than frustrate the opposition and make them spend more money. In this case, the succession of name changes focused media attention on the "No on 394" side before it had developed a unified theme for the campaign. The result was a series of conflicting statements about the effects of the Initiative, which lowered their credibility. "We flushed them out before they were ready to fight," he said.[62]

In mid-August the "No on 394" committee further weakened its credibility by accepting a loan of $200,000, plus a contribution of $25,000, from Morrison-Knudsen, Inc., a major engineering contractor involved in building the WPPSS nuclear plants. The company's interest was obvious: if voters approved the Initiative, Morrison-Knudsen's profits might be cut. While legal, the loan transaction suggested scandal to the news media. It was the largest sum ever to change hands in a Washington State political campaign, and this became a major issue. Moreover, according to the legislature's report, Morrison-Knudsen was one of the worst offenders in terms of cost overruns: its cement-pouring contract, originally for $40 million, had skyrocketed to $214 million in eight years. Once the media realized that the Morrison-Knudsen story was big news, they focused on the "No on 394" committee and other

WPPSS contractors who were contributing to the anti-Initiative campaign. One newspaper story listed the contractors along with the contribution each one had made and the exact amount of cost overrun attributable to it. Other stories played up the financial underdog status of the "Don't Bankrupt Washington" Committee.[63] By 10 September 1981 the state Public Disclosure Commission records showed that the "No on 394" side had spent $403,675, almost 10 times as much as "Don't Bankrupt Washington."

Paid Versus Free Media

While the "No on 394" money could not buy favorable news coverage, it could advertise the "Vote No" message incessantly. In most Initiative campaigns, both sides concentrate their advertising in the final weeks of the campaign, when the "media blitz" is supposed to have the most effect. However, when the polls showed early in the campaign that the "No on 394" side was trailing badly, its response was to flood the airwaves with radio and television ads for an incredible nine weeks.[64]

The anti-Initiative ads attacked "394" for its alleged high cost to taxpayers. The announcer's voice told listeners that the Initiative would require bond referendum elections every six weeks to approve spending for WPPSS's nuclear construction. The elections alone would cost "millions" and produce construction delays costing "hundreds of millions," and the final result would be the cancellation of needed power plants at a cost of "billions." The advertisers' purpose appears to have been to suggest to voters that they could stop further WPPSS cost overruns and delays by voting against the Initiative. This was the opposite of the truth, and the result of the ad campaign was to further reduce the "No on 394" committee's already tarnished credibility with the news media.[65]

"The opponents of Initiative 394 have run a campaign of disinformation . . . a sleazy campaign," chided *Seattle Post-Intelligencer* columnist Shelby Scates:

The anti's are . . . [making] you think we have an expensive excess of democracy in the Northwest. Maybe that's the case in Beverly Hills, whence these hired guns will crawl when they've collected their fee for the hit. Not here. What's expensive is WPPSS. It's not pronounced "Whoops!" without feeling. What else is expensive is the $100,000 shelled out, mainly by WPPSS contractors, to the firm of Winner/Wagner.[66]

Earlier in the campaign Winner/Wagner had tried another maneuver from its bag of campaign tricks: a mass mailing designed to produce the appearance of popular support for the "No on 394" committee. The initial step is to send a mailing to several hundred thousand voters early in the campaign, before most people know anything about the Initiative. Within a couple of weeks, ten thousand or so will return the prepaid postcards. Winner/Wagner then prepares a full-page anti-Initiative newspaper ad proclaiming that the "Citizens Committee of 10,000" urges voters to reject the Initiative. If there is enough space, all the names are printed. The ads are run in the state's major newspapers, simultaneously with another mailing to several hundred thousand more voters. Two weeks later, the same newspaper ad appears, this time backed by the "Citizens Committee of 20,000." And so it goes, every two weeks up to the election, with constantly growing numbers of supporters. These appeals do not ask for money or volunteers, since Winner/Wagner's anti-Initiative campaigns are amply funded.

Zemke, a bachelor, received a mailer addressed to "The Zemke Family" from the "No on 394" committee and recognized the tactic from the previous year's Winner/Wagner anti-Initiative campaign in Oregon. To counteract it, Zemke added the title "Yes on 394, the Committee of 186,000" to the name of the "Don't Bankrupt Washington" group. The new title was printed on news releases and used by workers answering phones in the campaign office. The opposition protested that petition signers were not really active supporters of the Initiative, but Zemke argued that their own

"Committee of 10,000" was a sham. After a week or two, the "No on 394" committee dropped the tactic, realizing that it could never get 186,000 citizens to sign and return its cards.[67]

Zemke had outsmarted the opposition once again. But these victories were minor compared with the battle for radio and television advertising, all too often the downfall of Initiative proponents facing a well-funded Winner/Wagner anti-Initiative effort. Television and radio ads can cost tens of thousands of dollars to produce and tens of thousands more to broadcast often enough to reach voters. In the last week of September, the "Don't Bankrupt Washington" Committee seemed incapable of mounting such a media campaign: accounting records filed with the state Public Disclosure Commission indicated that the group had spent all but $12,000 of the $53,000 it had raised. The opposition, by contrast, had by this time raised three-quarters of a million dollars and spent half of it.[68] Initiative 394 was getting clobbered in the political arena that counts the most: broadcast advertising.

Fighting Back: Money for Media

Zemke at this point abandoned the underfunded media campaign techniques of past Initiatives in favor of such professional tools as expert polls, out-of-state fundraising, and professionally created television and radio advertising.[69] First he commissioned a nationally known New York polling firm to design a poll to assess public perception of the issue and determine which pro-Initiative arguments were strongest in the minds of the voters. In addition to testing various arguments, the poll showed the public to be solidly in favor of the Initiative. This was an important factor in convincing major donors that unlike the Western Bloc campaign, this one could win.[70]

In late September Zemke and Seattle campaign consultant Blair Butterworth went to New York to work with the famous advertising entrepreneur Tony Schwartz to produce radio and television ads. Schwartz had become famous in 1964 as a result of a single, highly effective ad for Lyndon Johnson's presidential campaign. Shown just once, during a movie being broadcast nationwide on prime-time television, it depicted a little girl picking petals off a flower, followed by a nuclear explosion. Although Johnson's opponent, Barry Goldwater, was not mentioned in the ad, polls showed that his support plummeted by 15 percentage points within days.[71]

Since Schwartz personally supported the Initiative, he charged the "Don't Bankrupt Washington" Committee one-third of his normal fee: only $15,000, plus production costs.[72] Zemke estimated that $100,000 would be needed to pay for broadcasting the ads. While in New York, he and Butterworth met with potential supporters, like Alida Rockefeller Dayton, who made the largest single contribution to the campaign: $45,000 worth of broadcast time slots on Washington State stations. In Washington, D.C., they met with leaders of national environmental groups to plead their cause. While only a few groups gave money, the leaders of others helped Zemke by introducing him to the philanthropists who were their own biggest contributors. The east coast fundraising tour netted $65,500 for the pro-Initiative forces.[73]

Meanwhile, however, the opposition had received a $50,000 contribution from the architects of Three Mile Island, Babcock and Wilcox of Lynchburg, Virginia, and hefty sums from Wall Street brokerage firms that made money selling WPPSS's tax-free revenue bonds to investors. Merrill, Lynch was bullish against the Initiative to the tune of $20,000; Goldman, Sachs and Salomon Brothers each kicked in $15,000; Paine, Webber and Kidder, Peabody each gave $10,000.[74]

The "Vote No" forces broke the state record for Initiative campaign fundraising by 22 October, when the "No on 394" committee reported to the Public Disclosure Commission that it had passed the $1 million mark. Among the late contributors were out-of-state utility companies with nuclear power plants, like Consolidated Edison of New York, Baltimore Gas and Electric of Maryland, and Southern California Edison ($5,000 each); oil companies like Union Oil of California ($10,000), Mobil, Chevron, and Exxon Nuclear ($5,000 each); and last, but by no means least, aluminum companies, which are massive users of electricity (Reynolds, Kaiser, Alcoa, Intalco, and Anaconda each gave at least $30,000).[75]

Yet for all their access to big money, Initiative opponents could not stop the bad news coming from WPPSS. Less than a month before the election, "Whoops," by then the nation's largest issuer of tax-exempt bonds, ran out of money to continue construction of two of its five nuclear plants.[76] WPPSS bonds were rapidly turning into worthless paper.

Once back in Washington State, Zemke put into effect his plans to raise the bulk of his funds from local supporters. In the last week in September the "Don't Bankrupt Washington" Committee started an aggressive phone bank operation to complement its previous direct mail fundraising effort. Respondents were asked to help in any way they could: contribute money, volunteer their time, or sell tickets for a raffle. Raffles alone brought in $50,000. Between 25 September and 22 October, the "Yes on 394" side raised a total of $110,000.[77]

A Simple Message

On 18 October the "Yes on 394" media counterattack opened with radio ads, which were augmented a week later by television ads. The pro-394 committee spent $40,000 for a two-week radio ad campaign, and $50,000 for one week of television broadcasts. The principal radio ad was simple and direct, using the universally recognized pronunciation "Whoops" for the acronym WPPSS. In 30 seconds the ad recounted the sorry history of the agency, identified the ad's sponsors, and urged a "yes" vote:

You know when WPPSS announced they were going to build new power plants, they said they would cost 4 billion dollars, then whoops—they went up to 8 billion—whoops to 14 billion—whoops to 20 billion and now whoops 24 billion dollars. The WPPSS contractors say you should vote no on Initiative 394. We're the Don't Bankrupt Washington Committee, we paid for this ad, and we say let's just vote yes on Initiative 394 to let the voters decide if a new power plant should be built. Sorry about that WPPSS.[78]

In the television version, the same soundtrack was used, with the added visual elements of a photograph of the cooling towers of a nuclear power plant and a changing printout of prices corresponding to the announcer's litany of WPPSS's changing cost estimates.[79] Another ad answered the opposition's "costly elections" argument by briefly explaining Initiative 394, then concluding with the rhetorical question, "Which costs more—voting or building a nuclear plant? Vote 'yes' on 394."[80]

More than a year after the campaign, media consultant Schwartz called Initiative 394 one of his most successful campaigns, out of hundreds he has worked on. When asked what suggestions he had for other poorly funded Initiative campaign organizations, he cited fundraising and keeping costs down by refraining from "filmmaking":

They have to learn the importance of getting their act together and raising money from their supporters. . . . In Washington State, they've learned this lesson. In most cases, you find that the people in favor of an Initiative spend the money the wrong way, or don't recognize that they could raise the money needed for proper use of media. . . .

The most important part of the ad is the spoken message. The visual is just material to support and not interfere with the listener hearing the message. This type of ad [the WPPSS ad quoted in full above] is very inexpensive. There's the cost of the announcer, then no more than seven or eight hundred dollars of production costs. The purpose of the ad is communication, not filmmaking. You can make a statement . . . and it can work like gangbusters, and you don't need a million dollars worth of equipment to do it.[81]

The Final Push

In any tight political race, there is the temptation for campaign managers to launch a final advertising broadside just before election day by placing ads containing claims they well know are half-truths, distortions, or even blatant falsehoods, in the hope that there will not be time for the other side to make its rebuttal. Zemke, aware of this possibility, checked financial disclosure records filed with the secretary of state a week before the election to analyze the "No on 394" committee's latest expenditures. Sure enough, it had paid for full-page ads in Sunday newspapers around the state. On the Saturday before the election, Zemke made a point of getting an early edition of a Sunday Seattle paper. The "No on 394" committee had proven unable to resist the temptation. "Initiative 394 will shut down power plants we've already paid for!" screamed its ad.[82]

It was too late for pro-394 forces to produce and place rebuttal ads, even if money had been available to pay for them. Quickly, Zemke called the editorial departments of all the state's major newspapers, asking them either to confirm the truth of the opposition's ads or to pull them. He reminded them that they had, a few years before, refused to print a political ad until its sponsor documented its claims. (In that instance a candidate opposing former Washington governor Dixie Lee Ray had attributed to her several quotations that were so outrageous that editors could not believe she had uttered them; they wound up printing the ad once the opposing candidate proved their accuracy.)[83]

Although none of the editors agreed to stop the "No on 394" ad, they did give front-page coverage to the dispute. Zemke also informed several radio and television commentators of the controversy, resulting in many broadcast news items and a few editorials warning voters to beware of the opposition's latest ad. One television station manager went so far as to hold up a copy during a televised editorial in which he told viewers, "This ad contains lies!"[84]

As the ad dispute raged in the state's media, the "Don't Bankrupt Washington" Committee's effort to get out the vote was in full swing. Starting 10 days before the election, "Yes on 394" phone workers reminded supporters to vote, in addition to asking for a contribution and for volunteer help. Other volunteers distributed leaflets at bus stops and shopping areas and held large "Yes on 394" signs at major freeway exits in urban areas of the state.[85]

When the polls closed, Zemke and the other I-394 campaign organizers, satisfied that they had run the best campaign their limited financial resources allowed, sat back to await the results. With the combined forces of Wall Street, WPPSS, and the nuclear industry arrayed against them, a loss would be no great shock. Their opponents had spent over seven times as much money on their campaign, running up a record-breaking total of $1.25 million. Even so, the pro-394 campaign had been a fundraising success, bringing in more money than any previous grassroots Initiative campaign group. They had spent $204,000 and run up an additional campaign debt of $20,000.[86] If they lost, it would be difficult to raise the money to pay it off. But they never had to worry about that, because when the returns were counted, 58 percent of the votes were in the "Yes" column. The voters had shown that their anger over WPPSS mismanagement could not be deflected by an expensive ad campaign.

It was a victory for environmentalists, who now had a way to restrain a bureaucracy whose enthusiasm for nuclear power had outrun both environmental and economic considerations. And it was a victory for democracy by voter Initiative because the electorate had shown that big money does not always win.

Whoops Fallout

Heavy turnout by Initiative supporters swept the liberal Democrat Randy Revelle to an upset victory in the race for the office of King County (Seattle) executive, which is regarded as the state's second most important elective office. Revelle's opponent, the conservative Republican Ron Dunlap, had been leading comfortably in pre-election polls by a 60–40 margin, but he lost the election by two percentage points. The *Seattle Times* political editor Dave Schaefer reported that in those neighborhoods of Seattle where the "Yes on 394" vote was highest, turnout was 5 to 10 percent greater than in other areas, and this factor "appears to be crucial" in Revelle's victory. Dunlap himself agreed on this point: asked why he lost, Dunlap replied, "I think it was the strength of [Initiative] 394. It brought out a lot of people who are not too favorable to Republicans."[87]

Zemke, pursuing his post-election advantage as champion of the voters' will, stated that the Initiative "puts WPPSS on notice that future bungling, and attempts to circumvent the Initiative, will not be tolerated."[88] Although his words had a tone of righteous bravado, they addressed the reality that Initiative 394's opponents were not likely to give up, despite their defeat at the polls. Within weeks after the election, the three banks that had acted as bond trustees for WPPSS filed suit in federal court, seeking to overturn the Initiative on the grounds that it was an unconstitutional impairment of contracts made between WPPSS and bondholders prior to the election. The Ninth Circuit Court of Appeals validated part of this claim in a January 1983 decision voiding the Initiative's bond referendum requirement for three of WPPSS's five partially constructed nuclear plants.

It is difficult to isolate Initiative 394's effects on WPPSS from the financial pressures that in 1981–1983 brought WPPSS's nuclear projects to a standstill, but it is safe to say that the Initiative hastened this result. Wall Street bond brokers refused to sell WPPSS bonds for the duration of the I-394 court case—that is, from July 1982 to May 1983, when all appeals were exhausted by the "Don't Bankrupt Washington" Committee. This was the period in which WPPSS made the decision to scrap two of its nuclear plants and indefinitely postpone completion of another two. As of 1988, only one WPPSS plant has been completed.

The more citizens throughout the nation joined the effort to wrest control of their energy future from the nuclear industry, the more risky any future investment in that industry became. By threatening nuclear power and forcing government and industry to pay more attention to safety problems, the Initiatives of the 1970s and early 1980s delayed the spread of nuclear power. When the threat of the Initiatives had passed, the cost of nuclear power had risen so high that starting new plants from scratch was no longer a viable option. By the mid-1980s several utility companies were forced to abandon half-built plants costing billions of dollars. Ed Koupal would have been proud to know that his Western Bloc campaign had, in the end, been a major contributor to the demise of nuclear power's glowing prospects. In 1974 the industry had planned a thousand nuclear plants to be operating by the year 2000. A decade later, fewer than 100 were operating and more than 800 had been canceled—without any of the blackouts, brownouts, job losses, and economic stagnation predicted by the nuclear industry.

Epilogue

In the aftermath of the 1986 Russian nuclear power plant disaster at Chernobyl, anti-nuclear groups in several states renewed their efforts to pass ballot Initiatives—this time seeking to shut down existing plants. The first such Initiative was on the November 1986 Oregon ballot. The measure, sponsored by the environmentalist group Forelaws on Board, would have shut down the Trojan nuclear plant near Portland. Polls showed voter support for a shutdown early in the campaign, but that was before nuclear utility companies (primarily Portland General Electric) fought back furiously with a $2 million "Vote No" campaign—a spending record for Oregon Initiatives. Voters rejected the Initiative by a nearly two to one margin. A similar fate met the Maine Yankee shutdown Initiative placed on the ballot by the Maine Nuclear Referendum Committee in 1987.

But the fight was not over. Sacramentans for Safe Energy, an anti-nuclear group in California's capital city, sponsored a June 1988 countywide Initiative to shut down the trouble-plagued Rancho Seco nuclear plant, which had been closed for repairs throughout 1986 and 1987. The Initiative got a 49.7 percent favorable vote—the best showing yet (as of November 1988) for an Initiative to shut down an operating nuclear plant. Another shutdown Initiative, on the November 1988 statewide ballot in Massachusetts, was defeated by a two-to-one margin following yet another record-breaking utility-sponsored "Vote No" campaign managed by Winner/Wagner & Mandabach (as the firm was named in the mid-1980s). Massachusetts utility companies spent over $8 million, outspending proponents by a twenty-to-one ratio.

Consumer and environmental groups won only 1 of the 14 state Initiative campaigns on utility regulation issues held nationwide in the years between 1972 and 1976. From 1977 to 1987, however, as a result of more thoughtfully drafted Initiatives, better planning, and more experienced leadership, they won 14 of 29, despite the spending advantage of the utility companies.

BIG BUSINESS STRIKES BACK: THE BATTLE FOR THE "BOTTLE BILL"

In 1966 a San Francisco television documentary explored the problem of finding local sites for urban garbage disposal. Its theme song suggested that the public "Throw it down the kitchen sink/if it won't burn/No deposit/No return." It was already becoming clear that this ironic advice was no good.

Dr. Robert H. Keller, Jr., 35 years old in 1970, was a college professor who believed that hands-on experience with real life problems is just as important to education as classroom lectures. In that year he led a small group of students in an extracurricular project that seemed simple but, as the students learned, was not: the eradication of litter in a park near the Bellingham, Washington, campus of Fairhaven College, the liberal arts branch of Western Washington University. Neither volunteer litter pickups, nor signs telling people not to litter, nor ordinances imposing fines for littering proved effective. Discussing alternative solutions, one of Keller's students recalled that four years earlier a Spokane teenager had proposed a statewide ballot Initiative to require a deposit on "no deposit, no return" bottles.[89]

Though the Initiative had not qualified for the ballot, Keller's group decided that the idea went to the heart of the litter problem. It would prevent litter by giving people a financial incentive. They obtained a copy of the unsuccessful petition, which had been filed with state officials in January 1966 by W. N. Dahmen on behalf of his son, Randall Douglas Dahmen, who was too young to vote.[90]

They also found that the provincial parliament of British Columbia, just a few miles to the north of Bellingham, was debating a similar proposal, as was the Oregon legislature in Salem, to the south.[91]

Keller's students decided to base their proposal on the Oregon version, but rather than lobbying the legislature, they took their case directly to the people of Washington State with an Initiative petition to put it on the November 1970 ballot. By the time they drafted the proposal in legal form, it was mid-April, and Keller knew that it was probably too late to start a petition drive that would produce the necessary signatures by the deadline in the first week of July. But the students were too impatient to wait until the following year, so Keller filed the petition on their behalf on 23 April.[92]

By luck, the petition kick-off coincided with a wave of nationwide publicity about the ecology movement. Keller got phone calls and letters from people all over the state offering to help. Established ecology groups like the Sierra Club and the Washington Environmental Council offered their support. Practically overnight, the tiny group blossomed into a statewide network of two to three hundred petition circulators, who proved so enthusiastic that they went far beyond the goal and collected 188,102 signatures in eight weeks[93]—at that time the greatest petition total in the state's history.

In July a bank in Mt. Vernon, Washington, offered two cents for each empty beverage container brought in, and in one day citizens turned in 550,000 cans and bottles. This confirmed to Keller and his supporters that the "Bottle Bill," designated Initiative 256, would actually work: the Initiative required a five-cent refund on each beer and soft drink container. They expected little opposition from soft drink, can, and bottle manufacturers, since these interests were sponsoring ad campaigns touting the economic and ecological benefits of recycling and returnable bottles. In preparing a "Vote Yes" argument to be printed in the state government's election information booklet, which was to be sent to each voter before the election, Keller's group quoted liberally from these ads. "Wouldn't you rather borrow our bottle than buy it?" asked the Coca-Cola Company, rhetorically. "Pepsi Costs Less in Returnable Bottles," billboards proclaimed.[94]

Behind their public relations fronts, however, the long-term goal of the nation's big beer and soft drink companies, canners, and bottlers was to phase out the cheaper returnables in favor of the more profitable "no deposit, no return," or throwaway, container. The big companies had successfully lobbied legislatures since the 1940s to prevent passage of deposit laws, which had been sought by smaller, local bottlers (who used returnables) threatened by competition from big out-of-state manufacturers of throwaways.[95] Now the same legislation had been revived with the formidable new force of the ecology movement behind it. The "Pepsi Generation" had indeed "come alive" (in the phraseology of the late 1960s Pepsi ad campaign) but the beverage industry was none too pleased. With help from their corporate headquarters, the industry plotted a brilliant strategy to defeat the Initiative.

The strategy used the "carrot and stick" approach: if voters passed the Initiative, promised the industry, unemployment would result; or, they could support the industry's "Litter Control Act" Initiative. The latter proposal, unveiled 20 August 1970,[96] allowed the beverage industry to oppose the Bottle Bill while claiming to support the ecology movement. The industry Initiative proposed more anti-litter "education" (such as "Keep American Beautiful" ad campaigns), more outdoor public garbage cans, and the employment of more people to pick up litter. Ignoring the fact that these remedies had failed to stop litter in the past, the industry advertised its Initiative as a "comprehensive" approach to cleaning up *all* litter, rather than only bottles and cans.[97]

With this development, backers of the Bottle Bill could not harness the public's overwhelming dislike of litter, but instead were forced into the more difficult task of explaining why their Initiative was better than the industry's. Proponents of the Bottle Bill also discovered that the beverage industry had outflanked them on another front: when the young ecologists sought endorsements from labor unions, arguing that a container deposit law would create more jobs than would throwaways, they found that the industry had gotten to the unions first and convinced the retail clerks that they would be forced into an unwanted role as garbage collectors, that beverage sales would plummet, that producers and distributors of drinks in throwaway containers would be forced to shut down, and that unemployment would worsen.[98]

The retail clerks proved willing volunteers in the industry-backed petition drive to qualify the "Litter Control Act" for the 1972 ballot, even as the 1970 Bottle Bill campaign was under way. Meanwhile, Bottle Bill supporters fanned out through residential neighborhoods with mimeographed leaflets (they did not have enough money for printing) supporting their own Initiative.[99]

On 7 October, less than a month before the election, Washington State Gov. Dan Evans came to Fairhaven College for a speech and afterward took Keller aside and told him, "You may as well fold up your tables and go home. The Bottle Bill can't lose." Evans explained that pollsters working for the state's Republican Party had found that voters supported the Initiative by a margin of 76 percent in favor, 16 percent opposed, and 8 percent undecided. Evans supported the Initiative, as did Attorney General Slade Gorton.[100]

The industry was not to be beaten so easily, however. The corporations hired a Seattle public relations firm to unleash a "Vote No" media blitz of unprecedented intensity. In mid-October it saturated the airwaves with doomsday warnings that the Bottle Bill could "set the state in an economic tailspin that could destroy us" and cautioned voters that the state should not become "victim of a classroom project, an experiment in politics." The "Vote Yes" forces could not afford to broadcast a single ad and were unaware that the Federal Communication Commission's Fairness Doctrine gave them the right to ask for free response advertising.[101]

Keller's volunteers, who included rural farmers as well as urban young people, suffered a narrow, heartbreaking loss on election day: they got 48.7 percent of the vote. The beverage industry had spent over $300,000 on their "Vote No" campaign, compared with $4,500 on the "Vote Yes" side—a disparity of 67 to 1. Though the defeat was bitter, Keller insisted that the campaign "had a fantastic educational effect" on participants. "I still get letters from students who worked on it," he said, 15 years later. "We all started out with no practical experience in politics. Not only did we learn about the realities of politics and advertising; we also learned the broader environmental effects of litter, such as energy waste."[102]

Keller's campaign opened the way for other grassroots Initiative campaigns of the 1970s in Washington State. "Before that campaign, most people thought you needed money to put an Initiative on the ballot. We showed that all you need is popular support."[103] Washington State citizens circulated and signed enough petitions to put six Initiatives on the state ballot in 1972.

That same year the nation's first Bottle Bill, passed by the Oregon legislature, took effect. Vermont's Bottle Bill, also passed by the legislature, took effect in 1973. The results were dramatic: within two years Oregon's roadside beverage container litter, measured by volume, had decreased 88 percent, and the total volume of all roadside litter in Oregon had decreased 47 percent.[104]

With these statistics proving that Bottle Bills are worth fighting for, environmentalists returned to the Initiative petition when their efforts to convince legislatures failed. Dade County (Miami) in Florida was the next Bottle Bill Initiative battleground. Beverage companies in 23 states poured in $180,000 to finance a "Vote No" ad campaign, and the 1974 Initiative lost by a 57 percent margin. The industry used the campaign to refine its anti–Bottle Bill technique. For the first time it branded the bill a "forced deposits" law, making it sound distinctly totalitarian, and it disguised the "Vote No" campaign with a misleading, benevolent-sounding name: the "Dade Consumer Information Committee."[105]

These tactics, along with the strategy developed in Washington State, became standard beverage industry procedure in 15 statewide Bottle Bill Initiative campaigns over the next seven years. In 1976 Bottle Bill advocates fought the beverage industry to a draw, winning enactment of Initiatives in Maine and Michigan by large margins, narrowly losing in Massachusetts, and getting buried in Colorado.

After that, however, they were outgunned every time by industry's money and professional campaign managers.

Environmentalists easily defeated industry-sponsored ballot measures to repeal Bottle Bills (in Maine in 1979 and in Massachusetts, where a bill had been passed by the legislature, in 1982), but were unable to pass Bottle Bill Initiatives in any new states. In 1982 the Washington, D.C.–based citizen group Environmental Action coordinated Bottle Bill Initiative campaigns conducted by local groups in Colorado, Washington, Arizona, and California. Coloradans, who were on their second try, lost by a huge three to one margin; Washington State environmentalists, on their third try, lost almost as badly. Arizonans, too, were not even close to winning.

By this time the industry's tactics had been refined even further. Grocery store chains, allied with the beverage industry in opposition to Bottle Bills, printed "Vote No" messages on grocery bags, had clerks put "Vote No" leaflets into them, set up "Vote No" advertising displays in stores, and attached "Vote No" cards and stickers to six-packs and even individual bottles during the month prior to the election. This grocery store propaganda was cheap and effective, allowing the beverage industry to reduce the cost of its campaigns—though it still spent several times as much as Bottle Bill proponents.

The industry's campaign managers pulled out all the stops that year in California, realizing that if this trend-setting state adopted the Bottle Bill, the rest of the nation would not be far behind. The industry chose the political consultants Robert Nelson and Eileen Padberg as the team most likely to succeed. Padberg had proven herself two years earlier by managing the tobacco industry's successful ad campaign against a California Initiative that would have required the government and some businesses to establish smoking and nonsmoking sections to protect the health of nonsmokers.

A late August statewide poll showed that among the 64 percent of the voters who were aware of the Bottle Bill, supporters outnumbered opponents by a two to one margin.[106] Nelson and Padberg started their media barrage early. Radio ads began in early August; television ads started before Labor Day.

The industry-funded ads (whose sponsorship was concealed behind the name "Californians for Sensible Laws") attacked the Bottle Bill as a "hidden tax" (in fact it imposed a refundable five-cent deposit on each container). They claimed that it would cause rodent and roach infestations, and the use of dangerous chemical pesticides to control them, in grocery stores. They even claimed that it "could destroy California's voluntary recycling industry," the argument being that recycling bottles and cans for the sake of a deposit was a "forced" rather than a voluntary action.[107] To back up this claim, television ads showed sorrowful children in uniforms resembling those of Boy Scouts and Campfire Girls asking why people were trying to shut down the recycling efforts of "us scouts." When officials of the Boy Scouts and Campfire Girls complained, Padberg replied icily: "The use of the word 'scout' is totally generic. We checked it with our lawyers and they cleared it."[108]

To counter these claims, the pro–Bottle Bill group, Californians Against Waste, brought in former Oregon governor Tom McCall to film an ad and hold a series of press conferences in California. McCall, who had pushed the nation's first successful Bottle Bill through the Oregon legislature 11 years earlier, was eager to participate even though he was dying of cancer and confined to a wheelchair. "I'm going to fight to the last for the things I believe in," he explained to audiences.[109]

To counter McCall's impact, Nelson and Padberg designed ads portraying seemingly random interviews with Oregon citizens, all of whom denounced the Oregon Bottle Bill. In fact, public opinion polls in Oregon had shown public support for the law ranging from 90 to 95 percent, and not only were the "typical" Oregonians interviewed paid to act their parts, but most of them were employees of a beer distributor! Richard B. Spohn, former Nader's Raider and now head of the California Department of Consumer Affairs, called the ad "consumer fraud," adding, "In a season of sleazy political ads, they have found rock bottom."[110]

Nevertheless, the "Vote No" campaign had the desired effect: Californians defeated the Bottle Bill by a 56 to 44 margin. Over a 13-year period, the beverage industry and environmentalists clashed in 17 major Bottle Bill Initiative battles. The industry prevailed in 13 of them and reported to state campaign finance disclosure agencies nearly $18 million in campaign spending; environmentalists prevailed in 4 and reported $2.7 million in campaign costs.[111] Industry spending to defeat these Initiatives was small, however, compared with its lobbying expenditures against Bottle Bills in legislatures: though more difficult to verify, nationwide lobbying costs may have run as high as $20 million *each year.*[112]

Even in the states where Bottle Bills lost, the Initiative challenges forced the industry to start up its own aggressive recycling efforts (though these were only about half as effective as Bottle Bills in encouraging recycling) and to phase out the dangerous pull-tabs on drink cans.

From 1982 through 1986, the Bottle Bill's status remained the same: nine states had deposit laws, of which seven had been enacted by legislatures and two by voter Initiative. The beverage industry's "containment" strategy appeared to be working. But it faced another challenge in 1986, when Jonathan Puth, a veteran of the 1982 Colorado Bottle Bill Initiative campaign, led a successful petition drive to put the issue on the 1987 ballot in Washington, D.C. In the same year California's legislature reacted to the threat of a second Initiative campaign by passing a compromise bill that required a one-cent deposit for bottles and cans and required grocery stores to set up collection points in over two thousand store parking lots throughout the state. Most of these recycling centers were in operation by the end of 1987. Meanwhile, the beverage industry in the East spent over $2 million (nearly double the previous D.C. campaign spending record) to defeat the D.C. Initiative. Proponents won a respectable (in view of their 14 to 1 spending disadvantage) 45 percent of the vote.[113] And the D.C. Bottle Bill sponsors did win some concessions from opponents. The industry established eight recycling collection points throughout the city, and members of the city council debated alternative recycling bills that, said sponsors, would outperform any Bottle Bill in encouraging recycling. The beverage industry followed a similar strategy to defeat Bottle Bill Initiatives on the November 1988 ballot in Montana and in Mercer County (Trenton), New Jersey.

Overall, voters throughout the nation proved as susceptible to beverage industry claims as their elected legislators. Why? The beverage industry is dead-set against Bottle Bills, while the electorate is only mildly supportive of them. For Initiatives to succeed, the majority of the people must really *want* them to succeed. In the future, as urban garbage disposal costs continue to mount, the electorate's desire for stronger recycling measures may well push Bottle Bill Initiatives, or other recycling legislation, over the threshold of victory.

5

Two Case Studies

The careers of activists as far apart as Berkeley, California, and Oak Park, Illinois, illustrate the scope and power of the ballot Initiative. Consider the cases of Martin Schiffenbauer, a California tenant activist, and the Quinn brothers, Illinois campaigners for political reform.

THE INITIATIVE WARS OF BERKELEY

Berkeley, California, was racked in the 1960s by a series of protest demonstrations originating on the University of California campus. The series started with the Free Speech Movement in 1964, continued with anti–Vietnam War protests in the next several years, and culminated in the violent "People's Park" riots of 1969. In the 1970s the campus quieted down, but the protest movements did not die out: the protesters just exchanged confrontation politics for Initiative petitions. Every election from 1970 through 1984 had at least one Initiative on the ballot.

Each of these campaigns was the work of dozens of dedicated people, but one activist stands out as having started the earliest, lasted the longest, and accomplished the most: Martin Schiffenbauer, a native of Brooklyn who played a crucial role in most of the Berkeley Initiative campaigns of 1970–1984. His accomplishments would be the envy of an elected legislator—yet he has never run for public office.[1]

Born in 1938, Schiffenbauer was brought to Berkeley by his doctoral work in experimental psychology. He settled there permanently in 1969, the year of People's Park. Berkeley's city government, having gone into debt hiring police officers from other jurisdictions to control the demonstrators, imposed a tax on utility bills to pay it off. It was this that sparked Berkeley's own Ballot Initiative Revolution.

People's Park demonstrators and sympathizers hated the tax so much that some of them refused to pay it. In 1970 Schiffenbauer proposed a better solution: a ballot Initiative to repeal the tax. He became one of the founders of RIOT (Refusers of Illegal and Oppressive Taxes), which organized a successful petition drive to put the repeal measure on the April 1971 city election ballot. Schiffenbauer also joined other volunteers who were circulating petitions for an Initiative entitled "Community Control of Police." The main goal of this Initiative was to reduce police brutality by making the police more accountable to their local communities. The proposal divided the city into three electoral districts, from which local police commissions were to be chosen by voters. This measure, too, qualified for the ballot, but lost at the polls, while the tax repeal gained voter approval.

The Rent Control Struggle

In late 1971 Schiffenbauer helped draft Berkeley's first rent control ordinance and circulated petitions to put it on the June 1972 presidential primary ballot. Despite an expensive "Vote No" campaign funded by landlords, Berkeley voters passed the measure by a 52 percent margin, probably because George McGovern's presidential candidacy brought out liberal and radical voters.

This victory was short-lived. The Alameda County Superior Court struck down the Initiative in 1973 on the grounds that it did not provide sufficient "due process" for landlords seeking rent increases. The California Supreme Court upheld this ruling in its *Birkenfeld* decision, which set out guidelines for acceptable rent control ordinances and became the basis of all of the state's local rent control ordinances. The 1972 Berkeley Initiative thus had a powerful, albeit indirect, effect.

The initial 1972 rent control victory had, moreover, impressed Berkeley's left-wing community with the power of the Initiative process. Later that year, groups sponsoring seven separate Initiatives conducted petition drives that qualified their measures for the April 1973 city ballot. They joined together in the "April Coalition" to promote a favorable vote on the seven:

• A "Neighborhood Preservation" ordinance, which set up a hearing and permit procedure for demolition or construction of any building. (Approved by a 59 percent margin.)

• A marijuana decontrol Initiative, which would have prohibited police from making arrests on charges of marijuana possession without the approval of the Berkeley City Council. (The measure passed, but it could not override state and federal marijuana laws. Sponsors, including Schiffenbauer, knew in advance that the Initiative might not stand up in court, but campaigned for it as a strategy to attract liberal and radical voters to the polls.)

• Four Initiatives dealing with police regulation. Two gained voter approval: a Police Review Commission measure similar to the "community control" Initiative defeated in 1971, and a "mutual aid pact" measure regulating procedures for temporary use of police from other jurisdictions.

• An Initiative sponsored by RIOT to mandate municipal ownership of the city's electricity distribution system, which was—and still is, as of 1988—owned by the nation's largest investor-owned utility, PG&E. (The Berkeley City Council passed the Initiative, making a public vote unnecessary, but PG&E hired petition circulators to force a Referendum. The utility poured money into "Vote No" advertising, and the measure lost.)

Later in 1973 Los Angeles–based People's Lobby's statewide petition drive (see Chapter 3) inspired a local lawyer, David Mundstock, to draft a similar Initiative promoting political ethics and campaign law reform. Schiffenbauer, together with other still-active members of the April Coalition, petitioned to put the measure on the June 1974 ballot. This was the start of a regular collaboration between Schiffenbauer and Mundstock in drafting Berkeley Initiatives.

The city council thought the political ethics Initiative too stringent and placed its own alternative version on the ballot. Voters approved both versions, but the city council version got more votes, so it took effect. A key provision of the council version was a $250 limit on contributions to ballot measure campaign committees. With that provision in place, sponsors hoped that monied interests like PG&E could no longer defeat an Initiative by donating vast sums to the "Vote No" side.

By late 1976 Schiffenbauer was working with the Berkeley Tenants Union on a new rent control Initiative, which qualified for the April 1977 ballot. The campaign contribution limit was in effect, but Berkeley's landlords flouted it. Their campaign committee, Citizens Against Rent Control, collected contributions exceeding the limit and went to court to challenge its validity on the grounds that the law violated their right to freedom of speech.

The lower court agreed, allowing landlords to amass a "Vote No" war-chest many times larger than the amount raised by the pro-Initiative Berkeley Tenants Union. The Initiative was defeated by a two to one margin of voters, not only because of the lopsided campaign spending, according to Schiffenbauer, but because of low turnout, which tends to favor conservatives.

In June 1978 Californians statewide voted overwhelming approval of the property-tax-cutting Proposition 13. This gave Schiffenbauer an idea for a rent control Initiative with a new twist. Since one of "Prop. 13's" major inequities was its failure to pass on property tax savings to renters, Schiffenbauer proposed a rent control law requiring landlords to pass on to tenants 80 percent of their Prop. 13 savings for one year. The city council responded by putting on the ballot a weaker alternative, "Measure J," to compete for votes with the Schiffenbauer Initiative, designated "Measure I." Schiffenbauer coined a slogan to clarify the difference for Berkeley voters: "I = Initiative, J = Jive." In November 1978 Berkeleyites voted 60 percent in favor of "I," but only 30 percent for "J."

In the June 1980 election, the city council put a permanent rent control ordinance on the ballot, and landlord interests were again allowed to contribute unlimited amounts to a "Vote No" campaign while the validity of the contribution limit was on appeal to higher courts. (The U.S. Supreme Court finally doomed the contribution limit in *Citizens Against Rent Control* v. *City of Berkeley* 454 U.S. 290–299 [1981].) Despite the unequal spending, Berkeley voters approved rent control by a 57 percent margin. However, rent control forces suffered a setback the following year when landlord-backed candidates swept the city council elections and proceeded to appoint a pro-landlord majority to the rent control enforcement board. Schiffenbauer had a brief tenure on this board—his only stint in public office—but resigned in 1981. He consulted with members of the Berkeley Tenants Union, who agreed to sponsor an Initiative that would strengthen the 1980 rent control ordinance. It appeared on the ballot in June 1982 as "Measure G," alongside a landlord-backed Initiative to weaken rent control, "Measure H."

This time Schiffenbauer's slogan was: "G is Good, H is a Hoax." The voters agreed and approved "G."

Residential rent control was not the only issue in this election. Small business owners were being forced out by huge rent increases, and one of those facing eviction after 30 years of doing business was Charles ("Ozzie") Osborne, operator of the city's last soda fountain. Osborne had been an ace fighter pilot in World War II, and later made his fountain a Berkeley institution. Ozzie's neighbors and customers sympathized, but Schiffenbauer provided the solution: a commercial rent control Initiative. In the June 1982 election, the voters approved the nation's first commercial rent control law.

What a Difference an Election Date Makes

By this time Schiffenbauer had noticed how the low turnout in municipal elections consistently favored conservative candidates and causes. Reasoning that municipal elections held simultaneously with national elections would have a higher turnout, and probably more liberal outcomes, he petitioned for another Initiative for the June 1982 ballot. Voters gave their approval to an ordinance shifting municipal elections from the spring of odd-numbered years to national election dates in the fall. As a result of the change, voter turnout in municipal elections in Berkeley zoomed from 33,000 in April 1981 to 39,000 in November 1982, and to 52,000 in 1984. (The Initiative also saves Berkeley taxpayers $40,000 in election costs every two years.) The additional left-leaning voters swept eight candidates of the left/liberal Berkeley Citizens Action slate into the nine-member council, as well as the city auditor's office and all the school board seats.

From Rent Control to Electroshock Therapy

In November 1982 rent control was again an issue—the Berkeley Tenants Union was sponsoring an Initiative to require popular election, rather than appointment, of members of the rent control enforcement board. The measure, put on the ballot with Schiffenbauer's aid, passed by a wide margin. A bigger issue on Berkeley's general election ballot that year, however, in terms of its innovative nature and the national attention it attracted, was the Initiative to ban electroshock therapy for mental patients. Berkeley's sizable contingent of holistic medical practitioners, as well as former electroshock patients, had enlisted Schiffenbauer to help draft the ordinance and plan the campaign. This ordinance, although approved by voters, was struck down by the courts because state law preempts local law in matters of medical regulation.

Schiffenbauer has become something of a guru to Initiative sponsors in Berkeley: almost everyone starting an Initiative campaign for left, liberal, or environmentalist causes comes to him for advice. Perseverance has been Schiffenbauer's hallmark. After the April 1971 rejection of the Community Control of Police Initiative, he was part of a group that reworked the proposal and got it passed by voters in 1973. After the failure in November 1972 of a statewide Initiative to legalize marijuana, Schiffenbauer and others led the campaign for a local pro-marijuana Initiative. Two years later the legislature passed a law reducing the charge for marijuana possession from felony to misdemeanor status. When the city council of Berkeley passed a weak recycling measure, he and the Berkeley Friends of Recycling organized a successful 1984 Initiative campaign for a much more ambitious one. In addition, Schiffenbauer has assisted sponsors of liberal-backed statewide Initiatives by collecting signatures for them while he circulates his own local petitions. Table 5-1 displays the efforts and achievements of the Berkeley Initiative Revolution, sparked in large part by Marty Schiffenbauer. In 1984, Schiffenbauer, a freelance writer and editor, reported that he lived on a mere $400 a month (including the cost of his rent-controlled apartment)—thus providing living proof that the success of local Initiative campaigns is not necessarily dependent on money.

Table 5-1
Chronology of Berkeley, California, Initiatives, 1971–1984

Election Date	Description of Measure	Result
April 1971	Repeal of utility tax used for outside police forces	Passed
April 1971	Community control of police	Failed
June 1972	Rent control	Passed[a]
April 1973	Neighborhood preservation	Passed
April 1973	Marijuana decontrol	Passed[a]
April 1973	Police Review Commission	Passed
April 1973	Police mutual aid pact	Passed
April 1973	Police weapons control	Failed
April 1973	Police residency requirement	Failed
April 1973	Municipal ownership of electricity distribution system	Failed
June 1974	Political ethics, campaign contribution limits	Passed[b]
Nov. 1974	Municipal ownership of electricity distribution system	Failed
April 1975	Equalizing of appointments by city council members	Passed
June 1976	Removal of traffic barriers (conservative-backed)	Failed
June 1976	Two Initiatives to stop proposed industrial park	Passed
April 1977	Removal of traffic barriers (conservative-backed)	Failed
April 1977	Rent control	Failed
Nov. 1978	Rent control for one year ("Measure I")	Passed
April 1979	Removal of city funds from Banks with South Africa Investments	Passed
April 1979	Lowest priority given to marijuana enforcement	Passed
June 1980	Rent control (placed on ballot by city council)	Passed
June 1982	Strengthening rent control ("Measure G")	Passed
June 1982	Weakening of rent control ("Measure H," backed by landlords)	Failed
June 1982	Commercial rent control	Passed
June 1982	Change of municipal election dates from April to November	Passed
Nov. 1982	Popular election of Rent Control Board	Passed
Nov. 1982	Banning of electroshock therapy	Passed[a]
June 1984	Ending of U.S. aid to Israeli settlements (advisory)	Failed
Nov. 1984	Improvement of recycling program	Passed

[a]Initiative overturned by court action or other legal problems.
[b]City council's version passed, but it included most provisions of the Initiative version.

THE ILLINOIS COALITION
FOR POLITICAL HONESTY

It was a typical day at the state capitol in Springfield, Illinois, when a state legislator rose from the floor of the state house of representatives to introduce a visiting constituent who was watching from the gallery. Normally, such introductions are greeted with a round of courteous applause from the assembly. But on this day in May 1976, the politicians stood and booed the visitor for a full three minutes. "Is this any way to greet an Irishman?" asked the legislator who had introduced his constituent. "He's not worthy of being called an Irishman," replied acting Speaker of the House Michael J. Madigan of Chicago,[2] an associate of the late mayor and political boss Richard Daley.

The visitor so rudely received by the Illinois house of representatives was neither criminal nor spy nor traitor but something far worse in the eyes of the politicians—a reformer. He was Patrick Quinn of the Chicago suburb of Oak Park, and his offense was a "Political Honesty" petition with 635,158 signatures on it. This was more than enough to place on the state ballot three Initiatives, all of which attacked the extraordinary advantages enjoyed by the legislators. The first proposed to end their long-standing practice of collecting their full year's salary on the first day of a legislative session (thereby getting full pay even if they were absent every day for the rest of the year). The second was a measure prohibiting individual legislators from voting on bills in which they had a personal financial interest. The third proposed to ban "double-dipping"—collecting two government salaries simultaneously.[3]

The petition was unprecedented in Illinois history. It was the first to fulfill the signature requirement for a *binding* Initiative to change the state constitution. The procedure used was authorized in the state's new 1970 constitution: since the turn of the century, citizens of Illinois had had the right to place *nonbinding* Initiatives on the state ballot, but this process had not been used for four decades.[4] The number of signatures on the Quinn petition was also unprecedented, as was the fact that the petition was the product of a new, all-volunteer grassroots organization founded by Quinn, his brother Thomas, and a few friends just a year earlier.

Tom Quinn graduated from Stanford University in California in June 1974, the same month that California voters passed the Political Reform Initiative, Proposition 9 (see Chapter 3). Back home in Illinois, Tom got his older brother Pat, then on the staff of Gov. Daniel Walker, interested in the idea of sponsoring a similar political ethics Initiative in Illinois. In mid-1975 Pat quit his job, and the brothers called together reform-minded friends for a meeting around the Quinn family dinner table in Hinsdale, Illinois. There they hatched the dream of a statewide citizens group to promote a statewide Initiative. By Labor Day their Initiative petition was ready for circulation, and they sent it out to people on the combined Christmas card mailing lists of everyone in the group. By January 1976 they had 100,000 signatures. This attracted news coverage, and the movement snowballed.[5]

By the end of April, with over 600,000 signatures, Pat Quinn notified the state Board of Elections that his group intended to turn in the petition. Since no statewide petitions had been turned in for decades, and since this was a new kind of petition, the board members were not at first sure what rules should be applied. They settled on using the same regulations that had been applied to petitions earlier in the century. One regulation on which the board was adamant was that all petitions submitted must be attached to each other in a single book. The Quinns' "Coalition for Political Honesty" painstakingly punched holes in each of 30,000 petition sheets, strung them together with airplane wire, assembled a 30-foot-long cardboard box around the petition, mounted the entire thing on wheels, and paraded it through the streets of Springfield before turning it in to state officials. Pat Quinn dubbed it "the world's largest book," and the news media loved it.[6] At the time, the three Quinn brothers (Pat, Tom, and Ron) were in their twenties.

The seasoned politicians were not about to let these young upstarts defeat them. They filed a lawsuit to keep the Initiative off the ballot, claiming that it was unconstitutional. The state constitution said that Initiatives "shall be limited to structural and procedural subjects contained in Article IV," which sets out the structure and basic procedures of the legislature. The Political Honesty Initiative dealt with the procedures but not the structure of the legislature and therefore, said the politicians, was outside the scope of the Initiative process. Despite the Coalition's spirited legal defense of its Initiative, the Illinois Supreme Court adopted this reasoning as its own in *Coalition* v. *State Board of Elections* (65 Ill. 2d 453, 1976), and kept the Initiatives off the ballot.

The Coalition salvaged a partial victory even in the face of this crushing defeat: within a month after the petitions were turned in, the publicity forced the legislators to end their practice of getting a whole year's pay on their first day of service, and henceforth they received their salary in regular installments like normal people.[7] Though the Coalition Initiative would not be on the November 1976 ballot, the group asked candidates for state legislative seats to support a "Political Honesty Platform" composed of the double-dipping and conflict-of-interest provisions of the Initiative, plus a constitutional amendment to give Illinois citizens the right to enact laws on any subject by Initiative. They got 112 candidates to endorse these changes, but that was not enough to secure their passage in the 1977–1978 legislature.[8]

During that time, Tom Quinn went back to Stanford Law School, and Pat Quinn began law school at Northwestern University in Chicago, juggling part-time jobs with study and volunteer leadership of the Coalition. The legislators, just after the 1978 election, took what they saw as a golden opportunity to raise their salaries with minimal threat of voter retribution. In a single day, 29 November 1978, the state senate amended an otherwise innocuous bill to include a pay raise from $20,000 to $28,000, passed the bill, and sent it to the house of representatives, which in turn passed it and sent it to the governor, who was vacationing in South Carolina.[9]

Without a moment's hesitation the governor directed that his veto be affixed to the bill, in his absence, by machine, a response designed to give the legislature a chance to override the veto and put the bill into effect before the public could protest. The operation was so cynical that an immediate outcry arose. Pat Quinn and the Coalition for Political Honesty urged citizens to indicate their displeasure by sending a teabag to Gov. James Thompson.[10] Some 40,000 people did just that, invoking the anniversary of the Boston Tea Party, 15 December.[11] As a result, Thompson called the legislature back into session early in January, seeking a compromise by which some of the salary increase would be rolled back. The legislature, however, would agree to give up only $3,000, and that for only one year.[12]

Cutting the Politicians Down to Size

In other states the Coalition could have forced a Referendum on the salary raise with a Referendum petition, but Illinois had no such provision in its constitution. However, the constitution's provision for "structural and procedural" reform of the legislature, even as narrowly interpreted by the state supreme court in 1976, offered another means of striking back. The legislature could simply be restructured to have fewer members. This remedy had in fact already been proposed in 1970 during the state's constitutional convention and had been promoted by an abortive 1973–1974 petition drive led by former convention delegates and the state's League of Women Voters.[13]

Both previous attempts to cut the size of the legislature had involved a second issue; elimination of the state's confusing, anti-competitive "cumulative voting" system of electing state house members. This odd system, unique to Illinois, had been effect since 1870. Voters in each district had many choices: they could cast one vote for each of three house candidates, or they could cast all three votes for one candidate, or they could cast two for one candidate and one for another, or they could cast $1\frac{1}{2}$ votes (yes, $1\frac{1}{2}$ votes!) for one candidate and $1\frac{1}{2}$ for another.[14] Few voters understood the system. Furthermore, in most districts there were only four serious candidates on the ballot (two Democrats and two Republicans), of which the top three vote-getters would be elected. It was nearly impossible to defeat an incumbent, since name recognition alone would normally produce enough votes to prevent an incumbent from coming in fourth.[15]

The citizen outrage sparked by the legislative pay raise gave the Coalition enough momentum for a new campaign. The brothers Quinn and their Coalition seized the 1973–1974 Initiative idea, printed up new petitions, and kicked off a new statewide petition drive in mid-January 1979. Their Initiative proposed to abolish "cumulative voting," replacing it with a simpler system of single-member districts where each person would get one vote. At the same time, the state house of representatives would be cut from 177 to 118 members. The Coalition christened their measure the "Legislative Cutback Amendment" and adopted the slogan, "It's time to cut the politicians down to size."[16]

The proposal would promote accountability, since citizens could much more easily keep track of a single representative than of three. The district boundaries would have to be redrawn to create 118 single-member districts in place of the 59 three-member ones, but redistricting was due to take place in any event after the 1980 census.

To the legislature, the threat of the 1976 "Political Honesty" Initiative was minor compared with this. If passed by voters, the "Cutback" would eliminate the jobs of 59 legislators, as well as changing the odd "cumulative voting" system they held dear because they *won* under it. To undercut the Coalition's petition drive, therefore, on 11 August 1979 they passed a law to restrict petition circulation. The law stated that the signers and circulator of each petition sheet must reside in the same election jurisdiction. This requirement was complicated by the fact that in some cases an "election jurisdiction" was a county, but other jurisdictions had different boundaries. The new law prevented petition circulators from going to a neighboring city or county to solicit signatures, made it impractical to solicit signatures at places where people gather from miles around, such as shopping centers or state fairs, and made it next-to-impossible for petition drive coordinators to make a count of valid signatures, since a single signer from another town, city, or county could invalidate a whole petition sheet.[17]

The Coalition attempted to comply with the law and turned in a total of 477,112 signatures on 2 May 1980, but the Board of Elections used the "one signer in the wrong jurisdiction" rule to throw out more than three-quarters of this number and proclaim that the Initiative had not qualified for the ballot. The Coalition challenged the law in court, charging that it unnecessarily restricted the citizens' right to petition under the First Amendment of the U.S. Constitution, as well as the right of voter Initiative under the Illinois constitution. The state supreme court ruled in favor of the Coalition on 2 September 1980 and placed the Initiative on the November ballot.[18] The victory was sweetened by the court's award of $80,000 in legal fees to the Coalition's attorneys.[19]

A group of legislators and lobbyists quickly formed a "Committee for Representative Government" to oppose the Initiative, its name deceptively implying that the measure would somehow threaten representative government. Leaders of the committee included former Illinois governors Richard Ogilvie and Samuel Shapiro, State Rep. Giddy Dyer (from the Quinns' hometown of Hinsdale), and an array of well-heeled lobbying organizations: the Illinois Association of Realtors, the Education Association, the state Medical Society, bankers' groups, the Trial Lawyers Association, the United Auto Workers, the National Organization for Women/Equal Rights Amendment Committee (NOW), and Phyllis Schlafly's Stop ERA. Pat Quinn commented wryly: "I see we've been able to do something that no one else has been able to do. . . . We brought together Phyllis Schlafly and the National Organization for Women." The state's Farm Bureau opposed the Initiative, as did the Farmers' Union, the American Federation of State, County, and Municipal Employees, the Illinois Bar Association, the state Municipal League, the Illinois Nurses Association, Independent Insurance Agents, the Chicago machine Democratic organization, Chicago's anti-machine organization (Independent Voters of Illinois), Republican legislative leaders, and Governor Thompson.[20] These opponents argued that the "Legislative Cutback" Initiative would reduce the representation of women and minorities in the house, fail to reduce costs, and increase the influence of special interests. (Had this last charge seemed plausible, most of the groups opposing the Initiative would undoubtedly have switched sides.)

The Coalition for Political Honesty spent about $25,000 promoting the Initiative with radio ads, but most of the campaigning on both sides was done in grassroots style with debates before live audiences and on television, distribution of leaflets, and the lobbying of editorial boards of newspapers and television stations to get endorsements. In the year and a half before the 1980 election, the Coalition raised about $100,000 by repeated mailings to its 20,000-strong supporters list. Almost all the money raised was in amounts of 5, 10, or 20 dollars.[21]

On election day 1980, the Initiative won 68.8 percent voter support statewide. It won biggest in Peoria and the surrounding counties, where over 80 percent favored it, probably because of the strong support of Peoria's main newspaper, the *Journal-Star*. In the city of Chicago, 55 percent voted "yes"; in suburban Cook County 70 percent did so. Outside this major population area, the vote averaged 73 percent in favor. Even in Sangamon County, where the state capital is located, 55 percent said "yes."[22]

Although the change is difficult to quantify, the voting power of monied interests and party machines was definitely reduced. Well-organized groups of voters motivated by a single issue or candidate could no longer cast blocks of three votes per candidate to overwhelm the votes of citizens unaware of the peculiarities of cumulative voting. The "Legislative Cutback Amendment" finally ushered in the era of "one person, one vote" in Illinois after a century of the highly manipulable cumulative system. One result was that the number of women and blacks in the state house of representatives *increased*, contrary to the claims of those who had opposed the "cutback."[23]

The Coalition Shows Its Staying Power

The Coalition had just about exhausted the possibilities of allowable Initiatives under the narrow 1976 court ruling. In order to place future Initiatives on the state ballot, a new constitutional amendment was needed to end the restrictions on Initiatives and give the state's voters a "full-fledged Initiative" power, in the words of the Quinns.

Knowing that the legislature would be of no assistance in passing one—from the Illinois politicians' point of view, it could only lead to more attempts to ban "double-dipping" and tighten conflict-of-interest laws, which they had so far successfully avoided—the Coalition in 1981 turned again to a constitutional Initiative petition. The Coalition argued that since expanding the scope of the Initiative process would alter the "structure and procedure" of lawmaking, such a change fitted the state supreme court's 1976 interpretation of an allowable subject for balloting. On 2 May 1982 the Coalition filed 275,000 signatures, just enough to secure ballot placement. Opponents, including a "big business–big labor" alliance that brought together the Illinois Manufacturers Association, the state chamber of commerce, and the state AFL-CIO, filed suit to prevent ballot placement and won a ruling on 2 August 1982 that killed the Coalition's Initiative.[24]

The court had knocked the Coalition out of one arena, but the never-say-die Quinn brothers led their group to fight on in another. Under a long-neglected set of state laws, voters could place nonbinding advisory Initiatives on local ballots—but only by petition of a prohibitive 25 percent of the number of voters who had cast ballots in the most recent election. Pat Quinn, now a lawyer, contended that the signature requirement was unconstitutional and won a court ruling lowering it to 10 percent. The Coalition resolved to use local Initiatives to create a mandate for a proposed state law to create a "Citizens Utility Board (CUB)," a voluntarily funded staff of experts paid to advocate the interests of utility consumers before state regulatory agencies. The Coalition persuaded the Cook County (Chicago) government to place the question on the ballot in November 1982, and 81 percent voted "yes." It then petitioned to put it on the ballot in 111 downstate communities in an April 1983 election, and 83 percent of the voters supported it.[25] Though the Initiatives had no binding legal effect, this outpouring of public support was instrumental in winning the legislature's approval of CUB that same year. Illinois became the second state in the nation, after Wisconsin, to establish one.[26]

But this was not the only Quinn project of 1982–1983. In 1981 a tax-fixing scandal had been exposed in the Cook County Tax Appeals Board, the body responsible for setting property taxes in this area of six million residents. Crooked tax lawyers and employees of the board had bilked honest taxpayers of $50 million by giving illegal tax breaks to dishonest ones. "It was a swamp of corruption that had been going on for years and years," recounted Pat Quinn, who ran for tax appeals commissioner in the Democratic primary election in March 1982, against the incumbent, who was backed by the notorious Chicago Democratic machine. The hyperactive Quinn won the primary by a healthy margin, even though he was also leading the Coalition's "full-fledged

Initiative" petition at the time, and he won the general election in November by a landslide. Upon his election, he handed over the mantle of executive director of the Coalition to his brother Tom.[27]

Under Tom Quinn's leadership, the Coalition not only carried out the successful CUB campaign, but used the same procedure to place on local ballots in spring 1984 an advisory Initiative asking the state legislature to cut the state's utility tax in half. The Illinois government had reaped a windfall from this tax, which added 5 percent to each gas, electric, and telephone bill. As the rates for these services skyrocketed in the 1970s and early 1980s, the tax went up proportionately. Meanwhile, the legislature had opened up tax loopholes for large businesses.[28]

On 20 March 1984 voters in 75 Illinois communities (which included about 10 percent of the state's population) cast ballots on the utility tax reduction measure, and 85 percent approved. Although such a vote could not have the impact of the "Legislative Cutback Amendment," it still sent a message to the state legislature about what the people wanted. The legislature did not react immediately, but on 22 May 1985 the state house of representatives passed a bill to stop the tax from increasing along with inflation—not a total victory for the Coalition by any means, but still an accomplishment.[29]

By this time the Coalition's advisory Initiatives had become a rite of spring in Illinois. On 2 April 1985 the issue was reform of the Cook County judicial selection system, which the Coalition placed on the ballot in 14 suburban Cook County jurisdictions. The issue had become pressing in the wake of the Graylord scandal, in which 25 people, including five sitting judges, were indicted for case-fixing. The Coalition proposed that the old method of selecting judges be abolished in favor of a merit system of gubernatorial appointment of judicial candidates nominated by panels of citizens. Voters in all 14 jurisdictions supported the plan.[30]

After 10 years of struggle, Pat Quinn, now a married man with two young children, Chicago's appointed revenue director, and member of the governing board of the Coalition for Political Honesty, assessed the Coalition's record: "Between 1900 and 1975, there were only about 100 state and local [citizen-initiated] referendums on ballots throughout the state. Over the next 10 years, the Coalition sponsored about 500." In April 1986 the Coalition sponsored local ballot measures calling for legislation to create a state Consumer Insurance Board to represent consumer interests in insurance regulatory matters. And in November 1986 it sponsored referendums in over 50 towns calling for stricter political ethics laws.

"All these local referendums help people get used to the idea of voting on statewide issues," Quinn says. "This is bound to help build support for eventual enactment of the 'full-fledged Initiative amendment,' by which voters will be able to pass laws on any subject, by petition and popular vote."[31]

6

Tax Revolt:
Conservatives Take the
Initiative

The news of Ed Koupal's death on 29 March 1976 must have been the occasion for secret rejoicing in the California state capitol. Never again would this disrespectful crank harass the professional politicians with his annoyingly effective brand of direct democracy. Few realized that a right-wing reincarnation of Ed Koupal was already organizing a statewide Initiative petition drive. The similarities between Ed Koupal and this rising star, Howard Jarvis, were striking. Jarvis was an unknown in California politics whose obscenity-ridden condemnation of politicians would help make him a folk hero. His began his political career in his later years and, like Koupal, refused to give up his statewide petition efforts despite repeated failures. On 2 December 1977, when he and his supporters submitted to election officials a record 1.2 million signatures on his tax cut Initiative petitions, his name became a household word from one end of the state to the other, and the politicians were forced to take him seriously.

Howard Arnold Jarvis had a lifetime of volunteer political action behind him. His first important political venture was as an advance man on a whistle-stop train tour in the western states with President Herbert Hoover, who was making his doomed re-election bid in 1932. Hoover, having presided over three years of the worst economic depression the nation had ever seen, had become the focus of citizens' frustrations. At each train stop, it was Jarvis' job to make an introductory speech for the president, then physically defend Hoover from the rotten fruits and vegetables thrown by angry listeners. Jarvis wielded a pillow for this purpose, making use of his experience as baseball player on a coal company team in Utah. "I'll bet I saved him from getting hit with 500 tomatoes," Jarvis recalled. "It stood me in good stead for Proposition 13."[1]

Jarvis was born 22 September 1903 in the small mining town of Mercur, Utah, to a Mormon mother and a strict, North Carolina–born father. He studied law at the University of Utah in the early 1920s, supporting himself through summer work as a laborer in the silver and copper mines and mills and, briefly, a professional boxer and trainer. After obtaining his law degree, he went into the newspaper publishing business by buying his hometown paper in Magna, Utah. He expanded the operation into a successful chain of newspapers that sold throughout rural Utah.[2]

In the early 1930s Jarvis was appointed to the state tax commission by Gov. George H. Dern. Jarvis later looked back on this job as the start of the long road to Proposition 13.[3] In 1935 he moved to Southern California and over the following years owned businesses that produced, among other things, electric irons, garbage disposals, gas space heaters, and aircraft parts. Off the job Jarvis was an insider in Southern California Republican Party politics. He became precinct chairman of Los Angeles County's 14,000 precincts and helped manage Dwight Eisenhower's California campaigns in 1952 and 1956 and Richard Nixon's early campaigns, including the 1960 presidential bid.[4]

In 1962 Jarvis took what he thought was to be a final fling in politics, campaigning to win the California Republican nomination for the U.S. Senate. After coming in last in a three-way race, Jarvis retired from both business and politics.[5] That same year, however, he attended a living room meeting of about twenty people who were concerned about rising property taxes, and they asked him to help start a citizen lobby group devoted to tax reduction. He accepted and was soon completely committed to the cause.[6]

By 1965 Jarvis had merged his small ad hoc group with others in Southern California and incorporated the coalition as the United Organizations of Taxpayers (UOT).[7] For the next 10 years, Jarvis stated the case of irate taxpayers before city councils, county boards of supervisors, school boards, and state legislative committees.

In 1968 Jarvis' group attempted to put its first statewide Initiative on the ballot. It failed disastrously, gathering only about a fifth of the half-million petition signatures required. The group then decided to support Los Angeles County Property Assessor Philip Watson's property tax reduction Initiative.[8] Watson, unlike Jarvis, had the money to hire petition circulators and got enough signatures to qualify his Initiative for the 1968 election ballot,[9] but the voters rejected it by a two to one margin. The issue had been temporarily defused by the legislature, which, with the support of Gov. Ronald Reagan, passed a property tax exemption that provided temporary relief from steadily rising property taxes and headed off this embryonic tax revolt.[10]

Property taxes were directly linked to inflation in property values, being based on a percentage of assessed value. Until Proposition 13, that value was based on the purchase price of comparable nearby properties. Consider, for example, a block of homes built decades ago. If a single house was sold, the taxes on the entire block would go up.[11] The highly populated areas of both Southern California and the San Francisco Bay Area were filled with neighborhoods in which the houses had been built in the 1920s, 1930s, and 1940s for five or six thousand dollars each. By 1970 they were worth 10 times that amount—and were taxed proportionately. Many of their elderly owners, now on fixed incomes, could no longer afford the taxes and were forced to abandon their homes. This injustice spurred Jarvis and his followers on to ever-greater efforts.[12]

California's extraordinary inflation in property values in the 1960s and early 1970s was the result of three factors: inflation, population growth, and natural geographical limits on the expansion of detached, single-family houses in the biggest urban areas of California. The San Fernando Valley was full; the Los Angeles basin was hemmed in by the Pacific Ocean on one side and mountains on the other; most of the farmlands surrounding San Francisco Bay had been buried beneath suburban streets. Yet the population of these areas kept growing, forcing property values up by increased demand and constricted supply.

California residential property values in the early 1970s typically doubled, and in some cases tripled, in less than five years, and so did the property taxes.[13] The new property tax bills shocked homeowners, not only because they had to be paid in one lump sum each year, but, more important, because reassessment took place at three- to five-year intervals, which meant that they were hit with huge and abrupt hikes.[14]

In 1971 Jarvis and UOT made their second attempt to put a property tax reduction Initiative on the California ballot. This time they collected 650,000 signatures statewide—well over the half-million required. Unfortunately for proponents, however, more than 200,000 of these signatures were disqualified by county election officials on the basis of technicalities, thus keeping the measure off the ballot.[15] Los

Angeles County Assessor Watson then launched another property tax cut petition drive on his own in 1972. Again his measure qualified for the ballot, and again this spurred the legislature and Governor Reagan to head off the Initiative with their own temporary property tax relief plan. Watson's Initiative was overwhelmingly defeated.

At the same time that inflation was driving up property taxes, it was driving up state income taxes as well. Unlike property taxes, which are collected by local governments, income tax is collected by the state. In late 1972 the economist Milton Friedman helped Governor Ronald Reagan draft an Initiative to slow the growth of state spending, which would, they argued, stop the upward spiral of the state income tax.[16] The following year, Reagan's supporters, hoping to boost his chances of gaining the presidency in 1976, raised the money to hire petition circulators. They succeeded in getting the required number of signatures, and Governor Reagan called a special election for voters to consider "his" Initiative in November 1973.

Prospects for voter approval of the Initiative looked good, but two weeks before the election, Governor Reagan appeared on a television talk show and was asked whether the average voter really understood the Initiative. "He shouldn't try. I don't either," responded Reagan, a gaffe that cost him dearly. Opponents urged voters to reject an Initiative so complex that its own creator could not understand it, and the measure lost by a 54 percent margin.[17]

At the end of 1973, massive oil price increases added even more fuel to the inflationary fire, driving up wages, prices, and, of course, taxes. In 1976 Jarvis and the UOT launched two statewide petition drives; the first fell short by 10,000 signatures, the second by only 1,400. Assessor Watson and the Sacramento tax cut activist Paul Gann ran a competing petition drive, and they also failed.[18] The lesson was obvious to Jarvis and Gann: if they had been working together, their Initiatives would have qualified for the ballot. In 1977 they joined forces for what would be Jarvis' fifth statewide petition attempt, beginning their drive on 6 July, and aiming at the legal deadline of 2 December 1977.

Jarvis became a regular guest on George Putnam's noontime radio talk show on station KIEV in Los Angeles and on Ray Briem's midnight-to-dawn show on KABC radio in the same city. The audience ratings of these shows soared whenever Jarvis was on.[19]

Meanwhile, Jarvis' wife, Estelle, had organized a group of women volunteers whom she would deposit at grocery stores each morning and round up each evening with another 1,000 signatures. Gann toured the vast area of Northern California's 50 counties, recruiting volunteers and signers in each one. The drive expanded far beyond these stalwarts; hundreds of people who had never been politically active before became involved. The momentum Jarvis had built up with his previous efforts was paying off. By the deadline, 1.2 million signatures had come in. And the drive had been one of the cheapest in California history. All the petition circulators were volunteers, so the total cost, including printing, postage, office space, telephones, and advertising, was only $28,500.[20]

The measure, known at first as the "Jarvis-Gann Initiative," proposed a state constitutional amendment limiting property taxes to 1 percent of assessed value, based on 1975–1976 assessments, and allowing tax bills to increase by only 2 percent annually. Property would be reassessed at its sale price, and only when sold. This meant that the sale of a single house on a block would no longer push up the taxes on all the neighbors' homes. Under Jarvis-Gann, the average property tax bill would be cut by 57 percent, for a total (statewide) cut in local governments' revenues of $6 billion[21]—approximately one-sixth of the combined state and local government revenue.

In February 1978 before advertising campaigns began for and against the Jarvis-Gann Initiative (labeled "Proposition 13" on the upcoming June ballot), the San Francisco–based

Field Institute's statewide poll found 20 percent in favor, 10 percent against, and the rest undecided. Opposition activists, drawn mainly from the ranks of state and local government officials and public employee unions, were confident that they could defeat the Initiative because of the cautious tendency of undecided voters to vote "no" when there is a well-financed "Vote No" ad campaign. They hired the Los Angeles–based campaign management team of Charles Winner and Ethan Wagner,[22] who had just two years before managed a successful "Vote No" campaign against an Initiative to restrict nuclear power, and raised over two million dollars, enough to reach every Californian several times with the "Vote No" message.

Jarvis and Gann matched the opposition practically dollar for dollar, employing the services of Bill Butcher and Arnold Forde to direct both advertising and fundraising by mass mail solicitations to citizens.[23] The legislature, hoping to once again head off sentiment for tax cuts, passed a more modest relief measure, placing it on the ballot as "Proposition 8." If passed by voters (in fact it lost by a 53 to 47 percent margin), it would have cut homeowner property taxes by 30 percent, enlarged the tax credit for renters, and raised property taxes on business to make up for a portion of the tax cuts.[24]

The "No on 13" campaign theme was that the Initiative would have a disastrous effect on local government services, such as schools, police and fire protection, and sewers. It was also projected that "13" would result in the loss of nearly half a million jobs.[25] This was disputed by Jarvis, who argued that the state had built up a massive revenue surplus and could contribute toward local government services. The amount of the surplus was a matter of controversy: Jarvis claimed that it was $6 to $7 billion, and most state officials claimed that it was between $1 and 2 billion, but Democratic State Treasurer Jesse Unruh, who opposed "13," made his own estimate of $6 billion, thus helping to confirm Jarvis' contention.[26]

Jarvis' combative and abrasive style guaranteed media coverage. When Assembly Speaker Leo McCarthy accused Jarvis in a debate of sponsoring Proposition 13 to benefit the Los Angeles Apartment Owners Association (which employed Jarvis as a part-time director), Jarvis countered with the charge that the "*real* dirty money" was the money made from public employee unions, whose donations made up nearly half of McCarthy's own election war-chest. McCarthy replied that he held the money for all Democratic candidates, and Jarvis shot back: "You mean you launder it, like Watergate?"[27]

Although the Los Angeles Apartment Owners Association was the largest single contributor to the "Yes on 13" campaign ($16,000), almost all the $2.1 million raised by the campaign came in amounts of less than $100 from thousands of small contributors. On the "No on 13" side, by contrast, there was $100,000 from the California Teachers Association, $30,000 from the Los Angeles County Employee Association, $25,000 each from Bank of America, Atlantic Richfield, Southern California Edison, and the California State Employees Association, and $15,000 each from the Southern Pacific Railroad and Standard Oil of California.[28]

Late in the campaign, polls showed that the undecided voters were not joining the "Vote No" ranks as anticipated but were lining up two to one in favor of the Initiative. Gov. Jerry Brown muted his harsh attacks on "13" in the final weeks of the campaign and began planning how to deal with the measure should it pass.[29] On 6 June 1978, 64.8 percent of California's voters approved Proposition 13. Not only that, but "13" turned out half a million more voters than had participated in the previous statewide primary election, and more ballots were cast for and against the proposition than were cast in any of the candidate contests on the same ballot.[30]

The victory for "13" swept across most demographic divisions. Majorities of both Republicans and Democrats voted for it, as did majorities of voters in every income and education level. Those opposed to the Initiative included renters (53 percent), government employees (70 percent), and blacks (80 percent).[31] Proposition 13 carried 55 of California's 58 counties. The three dissenters were the long-time liberal bastion of San Francisco, Yolo County (which includes the university town of Davis and some Sacramento suburbs), and Kern County, where a sizable anti-13 vote in Bakersfield edged the county into the "No" column.[32]

THE AFTERMATH OF PROPOSITION 13

The first weeks after the Initiative passed were, for the legislature and Governor Brown, some of the most frantic, and productive, of their careers. Brown and his Department of Finance rewrote the entire state budget in three weeks, working feverishly to meet a constitutionally mandated 1 July deadline. They cut the state budget from $17.4 billion to $14.7 billion and allocated $4 billion to beleaguered local governments.[33] (The surplus on hand turned out to be $7.3 billion.)[34] They saved the remainder of the surplus for local government support for the following year. The legislature jumped on the Tax Revolt bandwagon, adopting bills to cut state income taxes by $1 billion, partially indexing the state income tax (to aid people pushed into higher income tax brackets even though their real income remained the same), increasing income tax credits, including a renters' credit.[35]

In November 1978 Jarvis' co-sponsor Paul Gann, acting independently, kicked off a petition drive for a state constitutional amendment Initiative that he christened "Spirit of 13." Its intent was similar to Reagan's 1973 Proposition 1 in that it proposed to limit total state spending by setting a cap on the state budget that would be adjusted annually for population growth and inflation. There was no organized opposition, and voters in November 1979 adopted Gann's "Spirit of 13" by a three to one margin.[36] However, the measure had no impact until 1987, when state revenue finally rose above the limit (Governor Deukmejian returned the billion-dollar excess to taxpayers in the form of rebates).

Jarvis was not content to rest on his laurels after passage of "13." In 1979 he launched a petition drive for a statewide Initiative to cut state income taxes in half.[37] This time, rather than organizing hundreds of squads of volunteer petition circulators, Jarvis hired Butcher and Forde's consulting firm to conduct the entire petition drive by mail, sending out petitions first to the addresses on Jarvis' lists of Proposition 13 supporters and asking them for donations as well as signatures. These donations were used to finance additional mailings to other potential supporters, such as the complete list of California's registered Republicans.[38]

Jarvis saw his income tax Initiative as analogous to Proposition 13, since inflation was driving up income taxes as it had driven up property taxes. In another way, however, the situation differed: the billion-dollar income tax cut enacted by the legislature in 1978 in the wake of Proposition 13, as well as "13" itself, had relieved the pressure on taxpayers that had been the main factor in the Initiative's success. And this time there was no state surplus to soften the impact of a huge revenue loss.

The income tax cut Initiative was labeled "Proposition 9" on the June 1980 ballot and became known as "Jarvis II," or, to its detractors, "Jaws II," in reference to the huge bite the Initiative could take out of government services. Essentially the same cast of backers and opponents took the same positions that they had taken in the 1978 campaign, and again both sides were fairly evenly matched in campaign spending. But this time a 61 percent majority of the voters decided that they had had enough tax cuts.

Jarvis, stung by this defeat, scaled down his expectations and drafted another Initiative, which qualified for the June 1982 ballot through the direct mail expertise of Butcher and Forde. The measure proposed to fully index the state income tax. This minor reform faced only token opposition and passed by a nearly two to one margin.

In 1983 Jarvis unveiled "Jarvis IV": a petition for a state constitutional amendment Initiative aimed at reversing a series of state supreme court decisions that had interpreted the ambiguous language in Proposition 13 to allow local governments to circumvent its requirement that voters approve any new or increased taxes by a two-thirds majority. "Jarvis IV" included $1.3 billion worth of rebates to property owners who had been taxed according to the court's interpretation of "13" rather than Jarvis's.[39]

Thanks once more to Butcher-Forde's computerized direct mail petition circulation and fundraising operation, "Jarvis IV" qualified for placement on the November 1984 ballot. Jarvis tried to make the 1984 campaign a replay of "13," to the extent of christening his new measure the "Save Proposition 13" Initiative. Local government officials and public employee unions opposed the Initiative fiercely, repeating the warning of the Wall Street bond-rating firm Standard and Poor that ratings on local government bonds would be lowered if the Initiative passed.[40]

The 1984 "Vote No" campaign featured vicious attacks on Jarvis' personal integrity, especially in the television advertisements. Opponents also attacked the Proposition itself by arguing that the taxpayers who would get a rebate under the 1984 Initiative were the ones who had already benefited most from Proposition 13. This was because under "13," property can be reassessed only at the time of sale. Anyone who bought property after "13" passed—including the latest buyers, who had the highest assessments—would get no rebate under "Jarvis IV." A new owner might pay double the tax of a next-door neighbor living in an identical house. The tax gap between just-sold and not-sold-since-"13" property continued to widen throughout the 1980s.

Most of the criticisms of 1984 had been leveled against Proposition 13 in 1978: the attacks on Jarvis as a noisy crank, the uneven benefits, the threats of cuts in government services. This time Californians backed off, rejecting "Jarvis IV" by a 55 percent margin. Proposition 13 had been a crisis measure, and it had served its purpose.

Despite this rebuff from the voters, which California political analysts interpreted as proof that the Tax Revolt was dead, Jarvis pressed on in his effort to save Proposition 13 from unfavorable court decisions. He redrafted the 1984 Initiative, scaling it back so that his 1986 version, "Jarvis V," merely reinstated his 1978 intention of making all local tax increases subject to majority approval by the local governing council, and two-thirds voter approval.[41] By mid-1986 the measure had qualified for the November ballot, but a court decision restricted the effect of the Initiative before it even passed. Any limit adopted would not apply to charter cities, where the vast majority of the state's population reside.

Jarvis, in his mid-eighties, succumbed to a blood disease on 12 August 1986.[42] His Initiative attracted only token opposition, and very little attention, in the absence of the controversial-to-the-last, raspy-voiced gadfly. Voters approved the Initiative by a 58 percent margin, sending a message to the politicians that they stood by Jarvis' handiwork, even eight years after the initial Revolt.

What had he wrought? According to Jarvis, the tax limitation Initiatives enacted by voters in California between 1978 and 1982 had, as of mid-1985, saved taxpayers $125 billion.[43] California's state and local government spending continued to grow, but in some areas the tax limits meant that local government could not raise enough revenue to meet the needs of the expanding population. The state's comparative ranking in per-pupil educational spending dropped from 17th in 1977/78 to 35th in 1982/83, partially rebounding (because of economic growth) to 27th in 1984/85.[44] The number of public employees continued to grow, but construction and maintenance of public works—"infrastructure" items such as roads, sewers, public buildings—were delayed to such an extent that a 1985 governor's report estimated that an extra $51 billion would be needed for this purpose over the next decade.[45] Still, the disruption was minor compared with the dire prophecies of Proposition 13 foes.

A decade after its passage, Proposition 13 can be judged a rational and successful mechanism employed by Californians to put the brakes on tax increases when their elected representatives had failed to do so. The Initiative process that made Proposition 13 possible has also been vindicated by the California voters' sparing use of their unlimited ballot-box lawmaking power. Of five major tax cut Initiatives offered them on ballots over a span of 17 years (in 1968, 1972, 1978, 1980, and 1984), they approved only one, and that one worked.

THE NATIONWIDE TAX REVOLT

The root cause of California's tax revolt—inflation—was a nationwide phenomenon. Californians were not the only ones to resort to the Initiative process to get tax reductions. In 1968 tax cut advocates had secured ballot placement for Initiatives in Oregon, Nebraska, and Montana, all of which were rejected by large margins, just as in California. Significantly, however, at this historical low point of Initiative use nationwide (only 10 state Initiatives qualified for ballots that year), 40 percent were tax reduction measures. This was a higher proportion than in any election after Proposition 13, and in retrospect it appears that the "Nationwide Tax Revolt" that burst into the national news in 1978 had its first stirrings a decade earlier.

In 1969 a potential tax revolt began brewing in Washington State as a result of a court decision forcing county assessors to assess property at the "50 percent of true and fair value" required by the state constitution, rather than the 20 to 25 percent they had been using. The decision meant that property taxes would more than double in a single year. The legislature responded quickly to the crisis, passing a bill in 1970 to lower the tax rate[46] and thus head off the huge tax hikes that would have otherwise resulted from the court decision.

Washington State provides a useful example of the way in which the legislature and citizen groups can work on the same issue. In 1970 Lester P. Jenkins began a petition drive for a 20-mill property tax limit. Jenkins' group collected 229,785 signatures by the 30 December 1970 deadline— nearly twice the number then required to qualify the measure for the 1972 ballot.[47] The 1971 legislature, taking its cue from Jenkins' Initiative, passed a bill to make the 20-mill limit part of the state constitution. Both the legislature's amendment[48] and the Initiative were put to the voters in November 1972, both won by a landslide, and both are still law (the two measures do not conflict, since the Jenkins Initiative was a statute, not a constitutional amendment). The legislature had responded to the satisfaction of the electorate.

Elsewhere in the early 1970s, outside California there was little tax cut Initiative activity, but inflation continued to worsen. Liberal groups in Michigan fought back in 1974 with a successful Initiative to end the state's sales tax on food and drugs, which inflation had turned into a government revenue bonanza.[49] The tax had hit the poor hardest, since the poor spend the greatest proportion of their money on food. But everyone suffered from food price inflation, and a 55 percent majority took this opportunity to ax the tax.

By 1976 the Initiative roster showed that conservatives nationwide were again starting to sponsor tax cut Initiatives. There were eight tax cut/tax limit Initiatives on ballots in five states, not counting two liberal-backed anti-food-tax proposals. Of the eight, two passed: an Initiative cutting the sales tax from 4 percent to 3 percent in North Dakota, and a property tax relief measure in neighboring Montana. The following year, on the eve of California's Tax Revolt, voters in Washington State passed an Initiative eliminating the food tax there, and came within a hair (0.05 percent) of passing another measure to repeal a fuel tax hike just passed by the legislature.

What Proposition 13 did for the rest of the nation was add the catalyst of hope to latent and lagging tax cut drives everywhere. Nobody liked tax hikes, but, like death, they seemed inevitable. But Proposition 13 showed that people could control taxes. The effect was immediate. In 1974–1976, only 10 tax cut/tax limit Initiatives were on state ballots. In 1978–1980, there were 23.

Most of the measures patterned after Proposition 13 failed. Over half of the tax Initiatives that *passed* in 1978–1980 set moderate limits on future growth of state spending (Michigan, California, Washington, Missouri). Tax Revolt fever may have swept the nation, but in most cases it did not result in drastic tax cuts. Only in Idaho (where homeowners' share of the property tax burden had nearly doubled in 1969–1978) and supertaxed Massachusetts (known as "Taxachusetts" in the late 1970s because of its rapid tax increases) did voters follow California's lead by adopting Initiatives to dramatically slash taxes.

THE TAX REVOLT IN MASSACHUSETTS

From 1968 to 1979 Massachusetts' combined state and local tax burden jumped from 103 percent of the national average to 124 percent.[50] Gov. Michael Dukakis, elected on a platform of "no new taxes" in 1974, ended up raising taxes substantially to cover a deficit (left over from the previous gubernatorial administration) and declining tax revenues (the result of a failing economy).[51] By 1978 the state's property taxes were the second highest in the nation,[52] and Dukakis was defeated in his bid for re-election.

The legislature's answer to the tax problem was to shift the burden. It approved a 1976 constitutional amendment to create a graduated income tax (by which people with higher incomes would be taxed at a higher rate) to replace the state's flat-rate income tax.[53] The measure required voter approval before it could take effect, and it was placed on the November 1976 ballot. A conservative group, Citizens for Limited Taxation (CLT), founded in 1973, organized opposition to the measure, and voters defeated it by a nearly three to one margin.[54]

Three years later CLT, under the leadership of its president, Edward F. King (no relation to the later governor Ed King), and executive secretary Donald Feder, conducted a successful petition drive for a constitutional amendment limiting state taxes. Unlike other states, Massachusetts gives the legislature power to amend a constitutional Initiative before it goes to the ballot, or even to block it from the ballot entirely. In this case the politicians so gutted the Initiative that CLT no longer supported it.[55]

In the summer of 1978, CLT drafted a statutory Initiative (i.e., one related to a law, not a constitutional amendment) and submitted it to Attorney General Francis X. Bellotti. In a controversial judgment, Bellotti declared the Initiative unconstitutional and stopped the petition drive from going forward. Undaunted, CLT redrafted its petition to comply with Bellotti's objections and filed it again the following summer; "Proposition 2½" was born.[56]

The Initiative took its name not from its ballot position (as in California), but from its provisions: it would limit property taxes to 2.5 percent of assessed value, and limit the annual growth of property tax revenue in each local jurisdiction to 2.5 percent.[57]

The Massachusetts High Technology Council, the state's computer industry trade association, had filed its own tax limit Initiative proposal, but dropped it and joined forces with CLT in its petition drive for "2½."[58] The necessary signatures were collected by early December 1979, and the following year the legislature considered the measure. On 6 May 1980, it turned down "2½" by a lopsided vote of 145 to 5.[59] But under Massachusetts' complicated Initiative procedure, legislators could neither amend a statutory Initiative nor block it from the ballot. Proposition 2½ qualified for the November 1980 ballot.

Leadership in the 1980 campaign fell to Barbara Anderson, a CLT volunteer who had become executive director. Her major argument in support of the Initiative was that Massachusetts property taxes were 70 percent higher than the national average.[60] Leading the opposition was the Massachusetts Teachers Association, which claimed that 40 percent of the employees of local governments—including teachers—would have to be laid off if voters approved "2½." This warning was based on proponents' own estimate that "2½" would cut property taxes by 40 percent.[61] "Vote No" forces promulgated the idea that voters would be hurting themselves if they passed "2½": campaign posters showing a pistol with its barrel mounted backwards were captioned, "How 2½ Works."

During the fall of 1980, Proposition 2½ was the subject of more heated debate in Massachusetts than the presidential race between Carter and Reagan. The electorate understood that "2½" was serious, unlike many presidential campaign promises. A poll in the first week of October showed the Initiative leading 43 to 40 among those voters who considered themselves likely to vote,[62] but support declined when "Vote No" advertisements hit the airwaves. Supporters rebounded in the final weeks, thanks to the financial support of the High Technology Council, which provided the funds necessary to broadcast the "Vote Yes" arguments.[63]

On election day 59.6 percent of the voters supported Proposition 2½. Unlike California's "13," Proposition 2½ specified that the property tax cut would be phased in gradually. Any locality having property taxes over the 2½ percent limit had to reduce its taxes by 15 percent (of the original rate) each year until it reached the limit.

Other elements that softened the impact of "2½" were the rapid rise of home values in Massachusetts in the 1980s (which raised assessments and thus the tax revenues based on them) and "2½s" provision that local governments might override the 2½ percent limit on annual tax increases if two-thirds of the local voters (later changed to a simple majority) approved. The local jurisdictions also could, and did, impose user fees for certain services. Since passage of "2½," Massachusetts' private sector has boomed. By mid-1983 the state's unemployment rate was the lowest in the nation, nearly 40 percent below the national average.[64] Economists like Milton Friedman and Arthur Laffer, who had supported "2½" as an example of their "supply side" economics at work, claimed that the state's experience was proof positive that tax cuts stimulate the economy. Certainly other forces were involved in the state's economic recovery, but "2½" may well deserve some of the credit.

One of the criticisms leveled against "2½," as against Proposition 13 before it, was that "big business" would benefit most. Proponents, however, pointed out that 73.6 percent of property taxes in the state came from residential property.[65] Proposition 2½ also included provisions to benefit non-property-owners by granting renters a state income tax deduction equal to half their rent paid, and by cutting the motor vehicle sales tax from $66 per $1,000 to $25 per $1,000, which benefited all car buyers. The popularity of "2½" was so strong that when Governor Dukakis attempted to weaken it in early 1983, a storm of citizen opposition forced him to drop the bill.[66] By 1988 Massachusetts had so successfully adjusted to life with "2½" that Dukakis was able to display his state as a showcase of good government during his presidential campaign.

In Idaho, the critics who said that the benefits of the state's 1978 property tax cut Initiative would go mainly to business turned out to be right, primarily because the legislature changed the Initiative after it passed, resulting in an accelerating shift of the property tax burden from business to homeowners. To deal with this problem, Kenneth Robison of Boise enlisted the state's liberal and labor groups to form the Citizens Crisis Coalition, which sponsored an Initiative to shift $19 million of the annual property tax burden from homeowners back to business, without any further loss of revenue.[67] Idaho voters, upset that their property taxes had kept rising despite the 1978 Initiative, passed the new and more equitable measure by a 57 percent margin in November 1982.

Although the Tax Revolt had dramatic tax-cutting effects only in California, Idaho, and Massachusetts, it also had an important impact on other parts of the nation. Even the dozens of Initiatives nationwide that were rejected by voters served to focus public attention on rising taxes and prompted efforts by elected legislators to ease the tax burden. According to Tax Revolt expert Alvin Rabushka, a senior fellow at Stanford University's Hoover Institution, 47 states adopted some type of tax relief in 1978 and 1979.[68]

Most important, the success of Tax Revolt ballot Initiatives in just a few states shattered the apathetic fatalism of a nation that had come to regard taxes as beyond the control of citizens. The voters' responses to the Tax Revolt encouraged liberals as well as conservatives to promote tax solutions at the ballot box. In North Dakota, voters passed an Initiative to double the state tax on oil production (1980);[69] in Missouri, they passed a measure sponsored by the state Education Association that raised the sales tax by 1 percent and allocated half the new revenue to schools, returning the rest to taxpayers in property tax relief (1982).[70]

Once the pressure of inflation was off, and the Reagan administration's tax cut bill of 1981 took effect, voter interest in cutting state and local taxes declined. By 1984 only a single, minor tax cut was approved by Initiative vote at the state level anywhere in the nation. This was Washington State's measure to cut the sales tax on a new purchase in proportion to the value of a trade-in, as with a car or boat. It affected *only* items purchased with a trade-in.[71]

EPILOGUE

Although the Tax Revolt may have peaked in 1978–1980, the 1986 election cycle showed that it still had support. Ten tax Initiatives qualified for ballots in five states, and three were successful: the Jarvis measure to shore up Proposition 13 in California; a Massachusetts Initiative to limit the growth of total state spending (sponsored by the same group that initiated Proposition 2½), and a Montana Initiative to hold property taxes to 1986 levels. In 1988, however, voters rejected tax cut Initiatives in Colorado, South Dakota, and Utah. Meanwhile, in California, voters approved exemptions in the state spending limit for increased education funding (Proposition 98) and a 25-cent per pack sales tax increase on cigarettes to pay for health care (Proposition 99).

The nationwide record of citizen voting on 20 years' worth of state ballot Initiatives shows a cautious, rational, judicious approach to tax reform. Voters enacted only one-third of the 100 tax-related measures initiated by their fellow citizens in 1968–1986.

One can argue that the Tax Revolt has proven once again the wisdom of Thomas Jefferson's faith in the electorate. He disagreed with other upper-class patriots of his day, who argued that a violent "Tax Revolt" of their own era, Shays's Rebellion in Massachusetts, showed the masses of people unfit to govern themselves. Jefferson wrote to James Madison on 20 January 1787, in reference to Shays' Rebellion, that "even this evil is productive of good. It prevents the degeneracy of government and nourishes a general attention to the public affairs. I hold that a little rebellion now and then is a good thing, and as necessary in the political world as storms in the physical."

Shays' Rebellion left four rebels dead, shot by Massachusetts state militia.[72] Perhaps there was no other way for citizens to fight back against an unresponsive government in those days. But in the twentieth century, in countless cities and 23 states, the Initiative process has provided a way for voters to exercise their sovereignty legally, peacefully, and effectively. Those who oppose direct citizen control of taxes and government spending forget the most important factor in this debate: it's *our* money.

7

Ballots Against Bombs

The idea of preventing war by popular vote on a ballot Initiative seemed a novel tactic to the activists of the 1980s Nuclear Weapons Freeze Campaign, but the Progressive leaders of seven decades earlier came up with it first. In 1915, when it began to look as though the United States would become involved in World War I, William Jennings Bryan, Robert M. La Follette, Jane Addams, and other prominent reformers called for a national war referendum. Addams called it "our best hope" for peace.[1]

Senator La Follette introduced a bill to allow a national advisory Initiative (that is, it would not be binding upon the federal government) that would require a national popular vote before any break in diplomatic relations with a European country, such breaks being a prelude to war.[2] A national referendum before any declaration of war by Congress was also proposed. Though Congress held hearings on the bills in February 1917, none of them came up for a vote in time to give Americans a choice on the declaration of war two months later.[3]

The idea emerged again as a plank in both the Democratic Party's national platform and La Follette's third-party platform in 1924, and 17 separate bills were introduced in Congress on the subject over the next 10 years,[4] but none were seriously considered. With the threat of war gone, the peace movement that had been so vocal in the early years of World War I had evaporated.

In the mid-1930s, with war again looming in Europe, Indianapolis' Democratic congressman Louis Ludlow became the new champion of the war referendum cause. He first introduced his proposed constitutional amendment mandating a national referendum on declarations of war, and restricting war profiteering, on 14 January 1935. In 1937 a poll by George Gallup's American Institute of Public Opinion showed that 73 percent of the public supported the bill.[5]

When congressional leaders blocked the bill from coming to a vote on the House floor, Ludlow successfully initiated a "discharge petition" to get the bill out of the House Judiciary Committee.[6] The Ludlow Amendment would have left Congress and the president free to declare war without a referendum "in case of attack by armed forces, actual or immediately threatened, upon the U.S. or its territorial possessions, or by any non-American nation against any country in the Western Hemisphere." Except in these cases, however, "the people shall have the sole power by a national referendum to declare war or to engage in warfare overseas."[7]

Supporters included Congressmen Everett Dirksen of Illinois, Jerry Voorhis of California (who was defeated a decade later by the young Richard Nixon), and Hamilton Fish.[8] President Franklin D. Roosevelt enlisted his cabinet members in the fight against the bill. One of them, Postmaster General James A. Farley, spent a day telephoning Democratic members of the House. Another Roosevelt ally, Speaker of the House William B. Bankhead of Alabama, hinted darkly about "alien influences" behind the Ludlow bill.[9]

The roll call vote was 209 to 188—Ludlow lost. Robert M. La Follette, still in the U.S. Senate, attempted to attach the war referendum proposal to another bill two years later, but this failed (on 27 October 1939) by a 73 to 17 vote.[10] By that time Nazi Germany had already crushed Poland, and Congress was unwilling to restrict the president's, or its own, war-making powers. When Congress *did* declare war after the Japanese attack on Pearl Harbor, it was under circumstances that would not have required a referendum even if the Ludlow Amendment had been in effect.

When Ludlow retired in 1948, he admitted that it was "too late for war referendums."[11] However, as the undeclared war in Vietnam dragged on into the 1970s, several congressmen reintroduced the Ludlow Amendment of the 1930s as a way to end American involvement. On 1 April 1971, Congressmen John Rarick of Louisiana, Robert L. Leggett of California, and Parren Mitchell of Maryland introduced a bill with the same wording as Ludlow's, under the title "People Power Over War Amendment."[12] The bill never gained serious consideration. There were, however, a few local votes on the Vietnam War. San Francisco's 1967 measure was the first to be initiated by voter petition.

THE MOUSE THAT ROARED: THINKING GLOBALLY, VOTING LOCALLY

On an April weekend in 1967, 55,000 people filled San Francisco's Kezar Stadium for what was the biggest-yet west coast protest rally against the Vietnam War. That same weekend, several dozen of these protesters initiated a new anti-war tactic by starting a petition drive to place on the citywide ballot a proposition that would allow voters to express their position on the war.[13]

The sponsors of the petition were the Pacific Democrats, a local affiliate of the California Democratic Council (CDC). The leaders (Mrs. Marylouise Lovett, a former president of the California Federation of Young Democrats, and Edward Farley, a CDC activist) set up their petition drive headquarters at 55 Colton Street, the same $100-a-month loft just vacated by the organizers of the Spring Mobilization rally at Kezar.[14]

Within two months Farley and Lovett's group had collected over 22,000 signatures and submitted them to Basil Healy, the city registrar of voters. Healy refused to certify the Initiative for ballot placement, claiming that only matters of *city* policy could be placed on the city ballot. Farley and Lovett took their case to court, and although their attorney, Benjamin Dreyfuss, lost the case in San Francisco Superior Court, he won it on appeal in the state supreme court. In the landmark *Farley* v. *Healy* decision, California's highest court ruled that voters had the right to place any subject they pleased on the ballot.[15]

The Initiative was labeled "Proposition P" for the November 1967 ballot, and it read: "Declaration of Policy: Shall it be the policy of the people of the City and County of San Francisco that there be an immediate cease fire and withdrawal of U.S. troops from Vietnam so that the Vietnamese people can settle their own problems?"[16]

San Francisco's mayoral candidates took stands on the issue (Joseph Alioto and Harold Dobbs opposing, Jack Morrison in favor), but the debate quickly spread beyond the city's boundaries. From Sacramento came a press release from Governor Reagan, an avowed supporter of the war: "I don't think cities should have a foreign policy. Any responsible citizen should give serious consideration as to whether it [the Initiative] does indeed lend comfort and aid to the enemy."[17]

Sally Hellyer, a member of San Francisco's Art Commission and originator of another group backing the anti-war Initiative, "Independent Sponsors of Proposition P," solicited endorsements from celebrities around the world. Among those who responded favorably were Beatles John Lennon and Paul McCartney, the French existential philosopher Jean-Paul Sartre, the French author Simone de Beauvoir, and the television celebrities Robert Vaughan, Leonard Nimoy, and Ben Gazzara.[18]

On 27 October the Hearst-owned daily newspaper the *San Francisco Examiner* sent telegrams to every member of the U.S. Senate in Washington asking how they would vote on Proposition P. Of the 36 who responded by election day, 33 were opposed; the outspoken Vietnam War critic Senator William Fulbright straddled the fence; and only Senators Gruening of Alaska and Young of Ohio supported the Initiative.[19]

San Francisco's two major newspapers, the *Chronicle* and the *Examiner,* both took editorial positions against "P," though a group of 100 dissenting *Chronicle* staffers, including columnists Herb Caen and Arthur Hoppe, took out a "Yes on P" ad in their own paper. A group of well-known local businessmen, including millionaires Benjamin Swig and Mortimer Fleischacker, took a stand against the measure as "The San Francisco Committee for Peace with Freedom and Honor in Vietnam," while a local veterans' group leader stated naively, "We believe our President [Lyndon Johnson] knows what he's doing."[20]

Voters rejected Proposition P by a nearly two to one margin, 132,402 against to 76,632 in favor. Anti-war forces attributed the defeat to the strict wording of the Initiative, which many thought called for too precipitous an exit from Vietnam. "I don't think any of the Senate critics [of the war] would have voted for the measure to unilaterally withdraw our troops. . . . I think the San Francisco vote would have been in favor of de-escalation and negotiation," commented the dovish South Dakota senator George McGovern.[21]

Proponents reworded their petition, put it back on the ballot, and won voter approval with little fanfare the following year. In the end, the few, scattered local votes on the Vietnam War played only a minor role in the larger anti-war movement. But they demonstrated the feasibility of placing world issues on local ballots by citizen petition.

THE NEW MOVEMENT TO STOP WAR BEFORE IT STARTS

In 1978 San Franciscan Michael C. Miller submitted 19,397 signatures to the city registrar of voters to place on the November ballot an advisory policy Initiative calling on the federal government to reduce military spending.[22] His action went virtually unnoticed outside the city, but his Initiative passed with 61 percent in favor.[23]

By itself, the measure could have virtually no influence on federal military expenditures. But peace activists in Madison, Wisconsin, soon put a similar Initiative on their city's ballot, and it passed with 65 percent in favor in April 1979. In Berkeley, California, activists petitioned to put such an Initiative on the ballot in the June 1980 primary election, and voters passed it by a 61 percent margin. In November of that year, similar measures gained ballot placement in Oakland, California; Detroit, Michigan; and the Massachusetts towns of Brookline, Newton, Cambridge, Somerville, Medford, and Waltham; all but the Waltham Initiative passed. Boston followed in November 1981 with a smashing 72 percent victory.[24] The organizers of these campaigns convened in late 1981 and formed the Jobs With Peace National Network to propagate more ballot Initiatives.[25]

By 1986 Jobs With Peace activists had sponsored 28 more local ballot measures around the nation, winning approval of nearly all of them.[26] Many of the measures approved included provisions mandating the local governments to make an annual calculation of how much money local taxpayers pay for military purposes, and how much they get back in military contracts, the point being to show that military expenditures are a net drain on the local economy.[27] These campaigns served to focus citizens' attention on the connection between a bloated military budget and faltering local economies, particularly in urban and industrial areas. Combined with other military-related ballot Initiatives of the early 1980s, the result was increased pressure on Congress to reduce military spending.

In October 1979 anti–nuclear weapons activists Phil McManus, Dan Haifley, and Ian Thierman[28] started a petition drive for a Santa Cruz county-wide Initiative to ban the manufacture and testing of nuclear weapons within the county. Since the Lockheed Missiles and Space Company assembled crucial parts of its nuclear-tipped Polaris, Poseidon, and Trident missiles at a plant within the county, the Initiative (designated "Proposition A" on the ballot) represented a direct assault on the nuclear weapons industry.[29]

Lockheed was a major economic power in the county. An $11 million annual payroll, 370 employees, 140 more or less dependent subcontractors and vendors, and an inexhaustible corporate treasury financed by American taxpayers made it a formidable opponent. A Lockheed spokesperson said, "We'll spend whatever it takes" to defeat the Initiative. Forty days before the 3 June 1980 election, the company had already spent $52,000 to influence the roughly 100,000 voters of Santa Cruz county. In addition, Lockheed threatened to shut down the plant forever if the voters passed the Initiative, despite the fact that the proposed law gave Lockheed five years to convert the plant to uses other than atomic weapons manufacture.[30]

Lockheed sent every voter in the county several "Vote No" mailers, and every voter received calls from a Lockheed-funded telephone panel purporting to be pollsters asking "questions" designed to influence them to vote against the Initiative. Voters who expressed sympathy for the company's position during the first call received half-hour-long follow-up calls and were paid three dollars "for their time," a move that was apparently legal although disturbingly similar to vote buying.[31]

Two weeks before the election, Lockheed's campaign spending reached $152,000. It was seven times greater than proponents' spending, making this the most expensive political campaign in the county's history. Initiative backers carefully parceled out their limited funds to pay for tens of thousands of "Vote Yes" tabloid newspapers and brochures to be handed out by volunteers, and a single, sobering television ad that began with footage of a Trident missile bursting from the ocean's depths as a grim voice intoned, "We have enough nuclear weapons to destroy the Soviets 30 times over." Then footage of an atomic bomb exploding: "We don't need more nuclear weapons." The film showed buildings falling and trees going up in flames from the bomb's heat, as the announcer urged viewers to heed the message printed across the screen: "Vote Yes on A."[32]

On election day nearly 70 percent of the county's voters turned out to vote. The Initiative went down to defeat, 63 percent to 37 percent. Proponents won a majority in the city of Santa Cruz, where a University of California campus is located, but lost disastrously in outlying areas. Still, Santa Cruz city, population 41,483, had become the nation's first jurisdiction in which a majority of voters cast ballots against nuclear weapons production. And, as Phil McManus noted, the Initiative "did succeed in putting the arms race on trial." A slogan on a button summed up the campaign: "Yes on A— The Courage To Start."[33] Lockheed was never again invulnerable in Santa Cruz County. In 1985 the company applied to the county board of supervisors for a grading permit so that it could expand its nuclear-missile-component facility. The defeated proponents of the 1980 Initiative rallied against the permit application, lobbied their elected supervisors, and won an important victory. On 8 January 1985 the supervisors rejected Lockheed's permit application by a three to two margin, thereby blocking the A-bomb-maker's expansion.[34]

Meanwhile, the Nuclear-Free Zone Campaign had become the principal inheritor of the Santa Cruzans' "Courage To

Start." Its first spokesperson was Eugene McDowell, a resident of the tiny (population 1,200) Washington, D.C., suburb of Garrett Park, Maryland. When McDowell found out that citizens in several foreign countries, including England, had passed local laws declaring their cities or regions "nuclear-free zones," he decided to lead the way in his own community.[35]

In May 1982 Garrett Park citizens banned the production, transportation, storage, processing, disposal, or use of nuclear weapons within their community by a vote of 245 to 46, thereby establishing the nation's first nuclear-free zone. In November 1982 the citizens of Ashland, Oregon, passed a nuclear-free zone Initiative. On 4 July 1982 Nuclear-Free America, a national clearinghouse, was formed in Baltimore to encourage formation of more nuclear-free zones,[36] and during the following year dozens of communities nationwide passed nuclear-free zone bills in city or town councils, town meetings, or referendums.[37]

The most common characteristic of these nuclear-free zones was that they harbored no nuclear-weapons-related activity even before passage of their Initiatives—that is, the ordinances merely reinforced an existing situation. But in Cambridge, Massachusetts, the site of Harvard University, nuclear-free zone activists made another frontal attack on the weapons industry. They sponsored a ballot Initiative that would ban nuclear weapons *research* in addition to the production, storage, and so on of the actual bombs and missiles.

Once again anti-nuclear activists—this time led by Richard Schreuer of the Boston chapter of Mobilization for Survival—had provoked the nuclear weapons industry to fight. The stakes were high: Cambridge's Charles Stark Draper Laboratory employed 1,800 people, mostly in nuclear weapons research, supported by $120 million a year in defense contracts.[38] The Draper Lab and other defense contractors, including Lockheed, General Electric, AT&T, Sperry, and Honeywell, spent over half a million dollars on a "Vote No" campaign—equivalent to \$18.97 per vote cast on the issue, one of the most expensive political campaigns in the nation's history.[39]

The opposition seized on the fact that "research" would be banned by the Initiative, and claimed that all research related to nuclear weapons—even disarmament research—would be banned, despite the Initiative's wording to the contrary. The relentless television, telephone, and mail advertising tried to make "academic freedom," rather than nuclear weapons, the central campaign issue. The Nobel prizewinner George Wald, a Harvard biology professor, said of the "Vote No" campaign: "I have never encountered dirtier politics, dirtier in the sense of spilling disinformation."[40]

On 8 November 1983 Cambridge voters defeated the Initiative 17,331 to 11,677—60 percent to 40 percent. Still, Nuclear Free America's newsletter, *The New Abolitionist,* described the campaign as "a tremendous success. The . . . issue engaged more public debate than any other in the city's history . . . [and] forced the community to assess its own role in the nuclear arms race and to take a stand, one way or the other."[41]

Nuclear-free zone backers waged their next big Initiative campaigns in Ann Arbor, Michigan, and Santa Monica, California, in 1984. Nuclear weapons research was at issue in both cases, and the Ann Arbor campaign was in many ways a replay of the Cambridge struggle. The Ann Arbor Initiative lost by a 64 to 36 margin.[42]

In Santa Monica, however, the weapons contractors employed a new tactic: surprise. The Rand Corporation (a military research thinktank) lulled Initiative proponents into a false sense of security by issuing statements claiming that it did not oppose the Initiative because Rand's Santa Monica office did not handle nuclear work. When proponents checked campaign spending disclosure reports (required by law to be filed with city officials in late October 1984, two weeks prior to the election), there was no report filed by the opposition.[43]

Rand strategists waited until the day after the disclosure deadline to officially form their "Vote No" committee and swing into action. A week before the election, full-page "Vote No" newspaper ads appeared. Simultaneously, "Vote No" literature was sent to every voter. Santa Monicans rejected the Initiative by a 62 to 38 margin.[44]

Despite these defeats coordinator of Nuclear Free America, Albert Donnay, pointed to a steady stream of successes elsewhere. By November 1988 a total of 160 U.S. towns, cities, and counties, with a combined population of over 16 million, were officially declared nuclear-free zones.[45] In some the designation did not mean much legally, but others, such as Marin County, California, and Takoma Park, Maryland, passed ordinances so strict that city officials were prohibited from using city funds to purchase anything from companies with nuclear weapons contracts. As a result, even General Motors cars and General Electric lightbulbs are off limits for city purchasers in Takoma Park. According to former mayor Sam Abbott, the city has saved money by going to alternative suppliers.[46]

THE NUCLEAR WEAPONS FREEZE: A NATIONAL CHAIN REACTION

In March 1981 over 300 activists from around the nation gathered to form the Nuclear Weapons Freeze Campaign. The possibility of organizing a national referendum on the issue was not even discussed. The five-year strategic plan adopted by the participants called for lobbying elected officials at the state, local, and national levels. But over the next 15 months, independent Freeze groups across the nation underwent a spontaneous chain reaction, deciding one by one to take their message directly to the people by putting the Freeze on the ballot. By the time the polls closed on 2 November 1982, an unprecedented one-third of the nation's electorate scattered throughout 25 states had cast their ballots for or against a bilateral U.S.-Soviet "freeze" on the testing, production, and deployment of nuclear weapons. It was the closest equivalent to a national referendum in U.S. history.

Though the Freeze movement blossomed with extraordinary rapidity, the political roots of its key leaders went back to the tumultuous days of Vietnam War protest in the late 1960s. Randall Kehler, who was director of the loose-knit national Freeze coalition in the early 1980s, graduated from Harvard University in 1966 with a bachelor's degree in government. He went on to Stanford University (in Palo Alto, California) for graduate study on secondary education policy. He recalls his feelings during that early period of the war: "I wasn't raised to be a pacifist or anti-militarist. I was ready to go into the military, until I was morally offended by the war." He dropped his studies at Stanford and hired on as a full-time staffer at the San Francisco office of the War Resisters League. Upon receiving his draft card in 1967, he sent it back to the Selective Service and refused to be inducted. Arrested two years later, he was sent to prison and served 22 months. Fourteen years after his release, he said, "In similar circumstances I'd do it again."[47]

About the same time that Kehler refused to cooperate with the draft, others made their anti-war protest by volunteering in the presidential campaign of Minnesota Sen. Eugene McCarthy. Two of the most important leaders of that campaign were Jo Seidita and Harold Willens. Jo Seidita was a homemaker and mother of four from the San Fernando Valley in California who had organized a statewide petition drive to put McCarthy on California's 1968 presidential primary ballot. Harold Willens was involved in the McCarthy campaign as a major fundraiser. He was a Southern California textile machinery manufacturer who used his many contacts with fellow millionaires to make personal appeals for contributions (which he called "investments in the nation's future"). Willens had been a Marine intelligence officer and Japanese language translator during World War II, and in this capacity he was one of the first Americans to visit Hiroshima and Nagasaki after the atomic bombings.[48] He favored McCarthy not only as the candidate most likely to end the Vietnam War but also the one most likely to respond to Willens' concerns about the nuclear arms buildup.[49]

While the Vietnam War protests served as training grounds for Kehler, Seidita, Willens, and thousands of other activists, the war had a much broader effect on protesters and nonprotesters alike by creating a distrust of government that made them more receptive to the concept of "do-it-yourself" lawmaking by ballot Initiative. Yet the end of the war meant the collapse of the mass public mobilization that many activists had hoped to link to other issues. In September 1979 Randall Kehler, now a high school teacher, joined with friends who shared his concern about the nuclear weapons buildup to found the Traprock Peace Center in Deerfield, Massachusetts. Kehler became full-time director of the center. In December of that year, two members of the Washington, D.C.—based peace group Sojourners told Kehler about their success in persuading Oregon Sen. Mark Hatfield to sponsor a proposed amendment to the SALT II (Strategic Arms Limitation Talks) Treaty that would halt deployment of new nuclear weapons by both the United States and the Soviet Union.[50]

Neither the amendment nor the treaty passed Congress, but Kehler realized that the amendment was the kind of simple, straightforward arms control proposal that most Americans could both comprehend and support, unlike the complicated SALT II Treaty. Both sides have enough nuclear weapons already, so why not just stop building more of them? Such a move would stop the costly arms race, reduce the threat of nuclear war posed by each new advance in weapons technology, and set the stage for reducing the worldwide stockpile of nearly 50,000 nuclear bombs.

Kehler and his Traprock group decided that the best way to build public support for the "moratorium" idea was to put it on the ballot.[51] They began collecting signatures in the spring of 1980, hoping to gain ballot placement in the four state senatorial districts that made up Western Massachusetts. They succeeded in three of them, which covered about four counties.[52]

During the campaign, skilled volunteers put together pamphlets and produced television and radio ads promoting the Initiative, now labeled "Question 7" on the November ballot. Daniel Ellsberg, the former Pentagon war planner who had leaked the Pentagon Papers in 1971, made a speaking tour of Western Massachusetts at the behest of Initiative sponsors. "Western Massachusetts has a chance to lead the United States to nuclear disarmament," Ellsberg told audiences at local colleges. Initiative backers were on hand at each speech, circulating sign-up sheets, and recruiting hundreds of volunteers. The owner of an advertising company donated space on seven huge billboards that urged, "Vote for a Mutual Nuclear Weapons Moratorium."[53]

In December 1979 Randall Forsberg, a 36-year-old doctoral candidate in political science at the Massachusetts Institute of Technology,[54] issued a "Call to End the Nuclear Arms Race" that was essentially the same as the Initiative. She dropped out of her academic program to become founder and director of the Institute for Defense and Disarmament Studies in Brookline, Massachusetts, in January 1980.[55]

While Randall Kehler publicized the moratorium idea at the grassroots level in Western Massachusetts with his ballot measure campaign, Randall Forsberg circulated it among arms control experts and peace activists in the Boston area. Many were skeptical about the chances of these efforts. A conservative mood was sweeping the state in the form of public support for the tax-cutting Proposition $2\frac{1}{2}$ and sweeping the nation as well, in response to the presidential candidacy of Ronald Reagan. Under these circumstances, how could a nuclear weapons moratorium proposal win in a traditionally conservative, Republican area like Western Massachusetts?[56]

Yet on election day, when the results were in, both Randalls were vindicated. Voters backed the moratorium in 59 of the 62 cities and towns where it was on the ballot—including 30 of the 33 towns where majorities voted for Reagan for president![57] Overall, the result was 60 percent in favor of Question 7. "This proved that Reagan's mandate had more to do with getting rid of Carter than expanding the arms race," said Kehler. The national news media ignored this important counterpoint to the Reagan landslide. The only national news source outside the peace movement journals to carry the story was the *Nation*.[58]

Kehler and Forsberg then joined forces, changed the name of the proposal to "Nuclear Weapons Freeze," and established a clearinghouse to respond to the requests for information that were coming in daily from activists across the nation.

The Chain Reaction Begins

Nicholas Seidita, psychologist, high school vocational education counselor, and husband of Jo Seidita, was inspired by the *Nation* article. He wanted to put the "Freeze" on the statewide ballot in California for the November 1982 election. The couple presented their idea first to the social concerns committee of their local church, the Sepulveda Unitarian, and came away with an endorsement. By March 1981 they had endorsements from 30 groups, most of them religious, including the statewide convention of the Unitarian Church.[59]

Harold Willens, the millionaire businessman and veteran of the McCarthy and McGovern presidential campaigns, joined the Seiditas at a September 1981 statewide planning meeting. With each succeeding presidential campaign in the 1970s, Willens had edged closer to influencing nuclear arms policy.[60] When Willens backed Carter in 1976 and Carter won, Willens thought that the Georgian would take the lead in stopping the arms race.

"He and I sat and talked about this issue . . . and that was the first time that I had an open door to the White House. Then came what I call his 'betrayal.'"[61] Looking back on this disillusioning experience, Willens said that he "learned . . . one of the bottom-line lessons of American history—namely, that Washington [i.e., the nation's elected leaders] never innovates, Washington only validates what it senses the citizenry wants."[62]

Willens contributed $25,000 of his own money to finance the California Initiative effort, and set about raising more money.[63] He concentrated his appeals on New York and Los Angeles, the two cities that he learned in his years of anti-war fundraising, have the highest "giving capability" in the nation. Willens' view is that these two cities have more generous millionaires than anywhere else; residents of New York and Los Angeles have a "broader perspective" than the rich elsewhere, and there are more Jewish charitable donors. "That probably comes from the tradition, the centuries of subjugation and ostracism and therefore being concerned with justice, equality, a higher human concern, higher than just another Bentley or Rolls-Royce or mink," he believes. Jewish himself, Willens was born in the Ukraine, the son of a tailor. As a child he saw Jewish homes burned by Russians, and his own family threatened with death by drunken soldiers on an anti-Semitic rampage.[64]

Midway in the petition drive to put the "Freeze" on the California ballot, Willens placed a full-page ad in the *New York Times* asking readers to give to the California campaign. The ad cost $26,000, but brought back $45,000 in contributions.[65] And, "more importantly," said Willens, "Monday morning I got calls from media people—you can't imagine how many people called, including some top people from *Time* magazine. Within two weeks they ran their first cover story on the [Freeze] issue."[66]

The Californians' monopoly on Freeze Initiative petitions did not last long. On 2 February 1982, David Wysocki and Debbie Hejl kicked off a statewide drive in Michigan.[67] On

26 March Malik Edwards and Kathleen Lundy announced another in Washington, D.C.[68] On 2 April Oregon Congressmen James Weaver and Les Au Coin announced one in their state. And on the same day the Wisconsin legislature voted to put a Freeze question on the state's 14 September primary ballot, making Wisconsin the first to schedule a statewide vote on the issue.[69]

Vietnam veteran and Bronze Star winner John McNamer, an electrician and small-time cattle rancher from Charlo, Montana, independently began a petition against the MX missile in August 1981. Freeze activists in contact with the national clearinghouse urged him to start over with a new petition drive to put both the MX *and* the Freeze issues on the ballot, which he did, starting in February 1982.[70] Another drive started in North Dakota. By 20 April it seemed too late for any additional states to get on the Freeze Initiative bandwagon, but Nancy Carroll of Phoenix, a Catholic nun, ignored predictions that it could not be done and started a petition drive. Within six weeks the Arizona campaign had 70,000 signatures, enough to qualify for the statewide ballot.[71]

By early July Freeze supporters nationwide had gathered over 2,365,000 signatures—probably the largest number for any petition in U.S. history. Resolutions supporting the Freeze were also passed by voters in a total of 444 New England town meetings, by city and county councils in 196 cities and 41 counties, and by both houses of 10 state legislatures.[72]

Why It Happened

The suddenness of the groundswell took veteran political operatives by surprise. In the first week of July 1982, a *New York Times* reporter questioned Matt Reese, a veteran campaign consultant, based in Washington, D.C., who had worked for Democratic candidates since the 1960 Kennedy campaign, about the significance of the Freeze movement. "It's a strong issue whose birth was secret. I didn't see it coming. I'm not smart enough to know how to use it yet," said Reese.[73]

What made Americans so eager to embrace the Freeze in 1982? As long as the SALT I and SALT II arms control negotiations were in progress, Americans could shut their eyes to the arms race and hope for the best from the negotiators. But President Reagan made it clear in his first few months in office that he was not interested in negotiating with what he termed an "evil empire." Top Reagan officials such as Vice President George Bush and Defense Secretary Caspar Weinberger had suggested that a nuclear war could be fought and won by the United States.[74]

The Freeze movement benefited from the belated discovery by the news media of the arms race and the Freeze campaign itself. Just as the news media made "ecology" a household word by focusing on environmental pollution in 1969 and 1970, even though pollution had been around for decades, so did the media's faddish attention to the nuclear arms race in 1981–1982 help build the Freeze movement.

The Opposition's Dilemma

The Freeze appealed to majorities of Republicans as well as Democrats and Independents, young and old, men and women.[75] The Reagan administration was able to forestall approval of the Freeze in Congress, but convincing the public was another matter. Rather than risk an embarrassing defeat, the White House kept such a low profile on the Freeze issue that proponents wondered whether Reagan was planning a last-minute "October Surprise" to turn public opinion around.[76]

The president made no secret of his opposition to the Freeze, saying in March 1982 that "a nuclear freeze at this time would legitimize a condition of great advantage for the Soviets."[77] But he offered no help at the grassroots level to right-wing groups fighting the Freeze. The most active was the American Security Council, a lobbying group with an annual budget of $4 million. A subsidiary organization, the

Coalition for Peace Through Strength, was formed by the council to fight against ratification of the SALT II Treaty in 1978 and took up the anti-Freeze banner after winning that battle.[78] By September 1982 the coalition counted a majority of the U.S. House of Representatives among its members, and nearly half the U.S. Senate.[79]

The right-wing television evangelist Jerry Falwell also took up the anti-Freeze cause, warning in a June 1982 fundraising letter that "the 'freez-niks' are hysterically singing Russia's favorite song: *a unilateral U.S. nuclear freeze*—and the Russians are loving it! . . . Because of these liberal activists, the survival of your family and mine is threatened."[80] The movement was in fact calling for a bilateral, not a unilateral, nuclear weapons freeze. Furthermore, the Department of Defense described the United States and the Soviet Union at this time as "roughly equal in strategic nuclear power,"[81] and Defense Secretary Weinberger, asked in a Senate committee meeting whether he would be willing to trade the U.S. nuclear arsenal for the Soviets', replied, "I would not for a moment exchange anything, because we have an immense edge in technology."[82]

Falwell's rhetorical excess did little or no damage to the Freeze campaign. More serious was the red-baiting article by *Reader's Digest* senior editor John Barron, printed in the magazine's October 1982 issue. In "The KGB's Magical War for 'Peace,'" Barron purported to "authenticate in detail" how the "nuclear-freeze movement . . . has been penetrated, manipulated and distorted to an amazing degree by people who have but one aim—to promote communist tyranny by weakening the United States." When it came to evidence of KGB influence on the Freeze movement in the U.S., however, the best Barron could do was report that two Russians had attended a public national Freeze convention.[83]

A month before election day 1982, despite the thinness of this evidence, President Reagan called the Freeze "a movement that has swept across our country that I think is inspired by not the sincere and honest people who want peace but by some who want the weakening of America, and so are manipulating many honest and sincere people."[84] Randall Kehler, now national coordinator of the Freeze campaign, responded with a restrained but angry statement:

> The President's unfortunate remarks show his lack of understanding of the nationwide freeze campaign. . . . His pejorative comments are an insult to the 2½ million Americans who signed petitions . . . hundreds of religious leaders, including 140 Roman Catholic bishops, over 750 state and local governments, scores of U.S. Senators and Representatives, dozens of our nation's finest scientists, and many of our most important national citizens organizations."[85]

Reagan, perhaps sensing that he had gone too far, sat out the rest of the campaign.

Nine states and over 30 cities or counties, including major ones like Dade County (Miami), Cook County (Chicago), and Denver, scheduled November 1982 votes on Freeze ballot measures. Wisconsin, which had a Freeze referendum on the state's 14 September primary ballot, approved it by a massive three to one margin; there had been no opposition. In other warm-up votes, on 5 October, the Freeze won by 54 percent in Longmont, Colorado, 53 percent in Anchorage, Alaska, and 58 percent in Juneau (it lost in Fairbanks, with only 46 percent in favor)—again without organized opposition.[86]

In the crucial state of California and next-door Arizona, opponents did organize and took advantage of assistance offered by the American Security Council. This included an anti-Freeze television documentary produced by the ASC, entitled "Countdown for America," and television ads starring the actor Charlton Heston, who had been debating the pro-Freeze actor Paul Newman throughout California. In California Freeze opponents were able to run the ads free of charge, under the FCC's Fairness Doctrine, to respond to Freeze backers' paid ads.[87] Thanks in part to the work of

Harold Willens, supporters of the California Freeze Initiative raised over $3 million—more than proponents raised for Freeze ballot measure campaigns in all the other states, cities, and counties combined.[88]

In Arizona, by contrast, proponents had virtually no money, but opponents placed full-page ads in major newspapers. Many retired military officers, including former general George Jones, organized the distribution of "Vote No" yard signs and pamphlets.[89] And the state's three highest elected officials, U.S. Sens. Barry Goldwater and Dennis DeConcini and Democratic Gov. Bruce Babbitt, came out against the Freeze. The combined effect of these efforts and Arizona's traditional conservatism defeated the Freeze by a decisive 59 to 41 margin on election day.[90]

Throughout the rest of the nation, however, there was good news for Freeze backers. Chicago voted 75 percent "yes," Massachusetts 74 percent "yes," Washington, D.C., 70 percent, and so on, with an overall national total of 11,606,832 for and 7,884,507 against the Freeze. The Freeze won in 9 out of 10 states, and 34 out of 37 cities and counties. California, where Freeze activists had been so confident that they would do better than proponents elsewhere, did rather poorly by comparison, with 52.5 percent voting "yes." The nationwide total, however, still came to 60 percent in favor, and voters had cast ballots in all or parts of 25 states scattered throughout the North American continent.[91] The people had spoken. But would their elected representatives in Washington listen?

The Struggle to Enact the Mandate

"Randall Forsberg should get a Nobel Prize for social engineering," commented Curtis Gans, a Washington, D.C. based political analyst and former organizer of protests against the Vietnam War. "The Freeze movement is a vehicle that makes it possible for Americans to oppose the development of nuclear arms and still be patriotic."[92] But it would take more than state and local ballot Initiatives to translate the voice of the people into federal government policy.

Since the Freeze votes were all on the state and local level, they had no legally binding effect on the federal government. Freeze backers hoped that Congress would follow the voters' mandate, but realized that they had a lot of lobbying to do on Capitol Hill. The House of Representatives debated the Freeze at greater length than any other issue for the previous decade, and finally passed a Freeze resolution on 4 May 1983 by a vote of 287 to 149. But the resolution had been so watered down by the opposition's amendments that it could only be called a partial victory. Freeze backers recognized the magnitude of their task when, three weeks later, the House voted by a similar margin to go ahead with production of the MX missile. Congress favored a Freeze as long as it did not get in the way of the arms race.[93]

Unfortunately for the Freeze campaign, by the election year of 1984 the news media had tired of reporting Freeze activities. The lackluster Democrat Walter Mondale was the peace movement's presidential candidate, and President Reagan brushed aside the nuclear arms race to win re-election on the basis of his personal popularity and an improved economy. Still, the Freeze could claim to have contributed to a change in Reagan. He began arms control negotiations with the Soviet Union that culminated in his 1987 signing of the Intermediate Nuclear Forces (INF) treaty to eliminate medium-range nuclear missiles.

According to Kehler, the Freeze movement could have been more successful had more states been included in the nationwide referendum campaign of 1982: "Our loss of momentum has been somewhat of a self-fulfilling prophecy by the media. Any movement which grew as fast as we did would eventually have to haul in its sails somewhat."[94] The 1982 national referendum banished the former conventional wisdom that said people are powerless to do anything about the biggest political issue of our time, the issue of human survival.

Four years later, in 1986, peace activists in many jurisdictions throughout the nation returned to the ballot Initiative strategy, though not on as grand a scale as in 1982, and not in as coordinated a fashion; the proposals varied widely. Voters approved the Freeze by 58 percent in an Alaska statewide vote; "Jobs With Peace" Initiatives won in Baltimore and Delaware County, Pennsylvania; voters in seven of nine local jurisdictions, including Berkeley and Marin County, California, approved nuclear-free zones (though Oregonians defeated the first *statewide* NFZ Initiative); and in rural districts of Massachusetts, the birthplace of the Freeze movement, 72 percent of the 84,000 voters who cast ballots on the issue approved an innovative proposal calling for a nuclear test ban and a 1 percent reduction of U.S. and Soviet nuclear arsenals, followed by gradual reductions toward a goal of near abolition of nuclear weapons by the year 2000.

Although the peace movement's ballot Initiatives of the 1980s fell short of their ultimate goal of reversing the arms race, the campaigns were quite successful in gaining the movement publicity, credibility, volunteers, and nationwide public support—a good, solid foundation for a citizens' movement that has, like the environmental movement that preceded it, settled in for a long-term struggle.

8

National Initiative

Voters in Switzerland and Italy made international news in the 1970s and 1980s by using their national Initiative procedures to decide national policy. Australia's Democratic Party and West Germany's Green Party campaigned to get national Initiative voting rights in their countries as well. The following summary of national Initiative activity around the world indicates the unprecedented extent of agitation for—and use of—direct democracy in recent years.

Switzerland

The Swiss have exercised the right to amend their federal constitution by national Initiative since 1891, and the right of national Referendum (to approve or reject laws passed by the national parliament) since 1875. Switzerland went through an upsurge of Initiative use in the 1970s and 1980s similar to that in the United States. Whereas prior to 1970 an average of only one measure per year qualified for the national ballot by petition, in the years between 1970 and 1987 no fewer than 65 such measures did so. In addition, 13 constitutional amendments were placed on the ballot by the parliament as alternatives to voter Initiatives. Over 20 additional Initiatives are expected to be on the national election ballots in 1988–1991.

The Swiss have voted on many of the same issues that have concerned Americans in recent years: air pollution control (1977), nuclear power (1979, 1984), alternative energy development (1984), and equal rights for women (1981). The last amendment, passed by a 60 percent majority, was proposed by the Swiss parliament as an alternative to an Initiative sponsored by women's groups. The most recent national Initiative passed by the Swiss, as this book went to press, was a 1987 environmentalist-sponsored measure to preserve a high mountain meadow area that would otherwise have been damaged by planned military exercises.

To put a constitutional amendment on the ballot, 100,000 signatures are required (about 2.6 percent of the electorate). Half that number of signatures are required to force a national Referendum on a bill passed by the parliament.

The latest Swiss national Initiative to stir controversy, as this book goes to press, is a Socialist-sponsored constitutional amendment to abolish the Swiss Army. It has qualified for the ballot and must be considered by the parliament before going to the voters, on 26 November 1989. On the local level, too, the Swiss are avid Initiative sponsors. In the city of Zurich alone, 79 Initiative petitions qualified for the ballot in 1970–1986.[1]

Italy

In Italy voters cannot enact new legislation by Initiative, but they can petition for national votes to repeal existing laws (or parts of laws). This procedure, allowed under Italy's 1947 constitution (itself approved by national referendum vote in 1946), was first employed by Catholics in an attempt to repeal Italy's 1970 law legalizing divorce. The nation's voters, though overwhelmingly Catholic, voted to uphold the divorce law by a 59 percent margin in 1974.

By 1988 Italians had voted on 15 voter-initiated national Referendums. Five of these, all on the ballot in November 1987, successfully overturned existing laws. Two dealt with judicial procedures. The other three concerned the regulation and subsidization of nuclear power, and their rejection by voters represented a remarkable victory for the small, environmentalist Green and Radical parties, which had petitioned these measures to the ballot. To put a national Referendum on the ballot, sponsors must collect at least 500,000 petition signatures.

Australia

Sen. Michael Macklin of Australia's liberal-progressive Democratic Party is leading his party's efforts to secure the right of national Initiative. Delegates to a national constitutional convention in the mid-1980s debated the proposal, but voted it down. The Democrats have continued to press for a national Initiative process. The debate grew hotter in 1987 and 1988 with the publication of a book advocating national Initiative, *Initiative and Referendum: The People's Law,* by a University of Queensland law professor, Geoffrey de Q. Walker.[2]

West Germany

West Germany's Green Party in December 1985 adopted the "Manifest für Direkte Demokratie" ("Manifesto for Direct Democracy"), calling for a national Initiative lawmaking process. In 1986, in the wake of the nuclear disaster at Chernobyl, a group known as "Initiative Volksentscheid Gegen Atomanlagen" ("Action Referendum Against Nuclear Power Plants"), led by Green Party federal representative Gerald Häfner, began pressing for a national referendum on nuclear power. By the end of 1987, the group had collected over

600,000 signatures on a petition calling for both a referendum on nuclear power and a national Initiative process. Häfner and his allies have discovered that the framers of West Germany's postwar constitution had intended to include a national Initiative power, but failed to agree on the details in time to meet a deadline they had set for completing the document.[3]

Netherlands

Two groups in the Netherlands are pressing for National Initiative rights: the "Bond voor Direkte Demokratie" ("Alliance for Direct Democracy"), and "Referendum Ja."

CREATING A NATIONAL INITIATIVE PROCESS IN THE UNITED STATES

Interest in a national Initiative process began at the turn of the century when, as we have seen, Progressive reformers in the United States introduced the Swiss Initiative and Referendum system at the state and local level (Switzerland had had a national Initiative process since 1891). As early as 1902 the Washington, D.C.—based reformer George H. Shibley wrote a pamphlet entitled *City, State and National Initiative Can Be Attained Without Constitutional Amendment,* published by the American Federation of Labor.

The demise of the Progressive movement in the years just after World War I ended discussion of a national Initiative process for nearly 50 years. Ed and Joyce Koupal of California's People's Lobby thought they were the first to come up with the idea in the early 1970s. Koupal's Western Bloc anti–nuclear power organizers, in turn, transmitted the idea to Jody H. Seaverson, then an aide to South Dakota's Democratic senator James Abourezk. In 1975 Seaverson suggested to Abourezk that he introduce a national Initiative proposal "for our Bicentennial bit."

Seaverson, noting the beginnings of a conservative trend in public opinion, wrote:

There is a force in motion in the country which says that government is getting too big for its britches. . . . So far, though, only the right-wingers are making any steam from it. . . . Why don't we see if any of these winds blow in another direction? . . . The general principle in play here is that self-government is better than "good" government. Any time we can figure out ways for people to make their own decisions rather than have "bureaucrats" and "politicians" make [decisions] for them, democracy is served. The first idea I have in mind is . . . a constitutional amendment giving the people national Initiative and Referendum powers.[4]

Abourezk spoke with Ed Koupal by phone about the national Initiative idea, and was sympathetic but unwilling to add another lonely cause to his list of maverick crusades in the Senate. The Seaverson memo was filed and forgotten until early 1977, when former Western Bloc organizers Roger Telschow and John Forster arrived in the nation's capital to start a national lobbying effort for a constitutional amendment to create a national Initiative process. They met with a member of Abourezk's staff, Kevin Murray, to see if the senator might be interested in sponsoring the proposal now that two enthusiastic Initiative promoters were available to help drum up public support.[5] (Murray had gone to college in California and was familiar with the upsurge in Initiative use there.)

Abourezk listened to Telschow and Forster's story of the western Bloc effort. Their enthusiasm was contagious. On 11 July 1977 Abourezk introduced Senate Joint Resolution 67, the Voter Initiative Constitutional Amendment.[6]

The Abourezk proposal benefited from good timing: it was introduced in mid-summer, a traditionally slow news period in the nation's capital. Telschow and Forster's "Initiative America" lobbying group was off and running with a burst of national publicity thanks to the conservative columnist George Will. In late July, the nationally syndicated commentator condemned Abourezk's bill. Telschow immediately drafted five letters to the editor of the *Washington Post,* responding to Will's column, and persuaded friends to sign and send them. It would take at least five letters, Telschow guessed, to get even one printed. He was wrong. On 3 August 1977, the *Post* printed all five.[7]

Meanwhile, Abourezk had persuaded Sen. Birch Bayh, chairman of the Senate Subcommittee on the Constitution, to hold hearings in December on the national Initiative proposal. Political scientists, state government officials, and activists like Joyce Koupal and Ralph Nader converged on Capitol Hill to testify. More publicity, most of it favorable, was the result.[8]

Next, the veteran pollster George Gallup added his support in the form of a nationwide opinion poll on the national Initiative plan. Citizens backed the idea by a three to one margin: 57 percent approved, 21 percent were opposed, and 22 percent were undecided. And this support came nearly equally from Democrats, Republicans, and Independents.[9] Gallup's poll was released to the news media in May 1978[10] and further publicized in his August 1978 *Reader's Digest* article, "Six Political Reforms Most Americans Want."

In California, Los Angeles County Supervisor Baxter Ward persuaded the Board of Supervisors to put a similar question on the 6 June 1978 primary election ballot. Voters there approved it by a margin of 66 to 34 percent.[11] This was the same election that saw Californians statewide approve the trend-setting Proposition 13 tax cut. Proposition 13 familiarized millions of Americans with the concept of enacting laws by petition and popular vote, but it also polarized the debate over the proposal to establish such a lawmaking process on the national level. After Proposition 13, the staunchly liberal Abourezk found that liberals in Congress were fearful that a national Initiative process would result in the passage of a national Proposition 13, and many refused to support the Abourezk bill for that reason. (Some Republicans anticipated the same result.)[12] Ironically, even without a national Initiative process, a national variation on "13" was approved by Congress three years later in the form of President Reagan's 1981 tax cut bill and the Gramm-Rudman balanced budget law.

Although Abourezk did not run for re-election in November 1978, Initiative America's Telschow counted 55 co-sponsors of the Abourezk bill who would take their seats in the House and Senate in January 1979.[13] On 5 February 1979 Senators Hatfield (R–Oregon), DeConcini (D–Arizona), Simpson (R–Wyoming), Gravel (D–Alaska), and Pressler (R–South Dakota) held a press conference with Initiative America announcing the reintroduction of the national Initiative proposal (this time numbered S.J. Res. 33). Hatfield was the veteran on the new Initiative America team, having been an original co-sponsor with Abourezk. Representing the House contingent were the Democratic Budget Committee chairman, James R. Jones, and the Republican presidential hopeful Jack Kemp.[14]

By this time Forster and Telschow had exhausted their financial reserves. Initiative America's fundraising mailings had failed to break even, and by early 1979 they were spending most of their time running a small printing business—Initiative Press—to pay their living expenses. They decided to let Congress carry the ball in 1979. All year long they waited, but nothing happened. The 55 co-sponsors had paid lip service to the concept of the national Initiative, but only Jack Kemp went so far as to mention it in some speeches and in a 1980 book on his political views.[15] Telschow and Foster's last hope was that one of the 1980 presidential candidates would pick up the proposal as a campaign issue. Both Jerry Brown and Ronald Reagan had indicated through staff members that they supported the proposal, but neither mentioned it in his campaign.[16]

The final blow came on 18 February 1981, when the *Washington Post* reported that Senator Hatfield was sponsoring a bill to overturn the first Initiative ever passed by the voters of Washington, D.C. (a measure to establish a government-sponsored lottery there). Telschow fired off a telegram:

> Initiative America urges you to immediately withdraw sponsorship of your bill to overturn D.C. Lottery Initiative. Your bill is inconsistent with your support of national Initiative amendment. . . . The foundation of voter Initiative is self-determination. How can an Initiative sponsor propose to negate these voting rights? Please acknowledge.[17]

Hatfield did not respond. Burnt-out, broke, and disgusted, Telschow and Forster disbanded Initiative America.[18] At the grassroots level, however, support for the Initiative process—as measured by the number of people throughout the nation signing petitions to put Initiatives on state and local ballots—continued to grow. At least 16 million people signed such petitions in 1982, and more Initiatives qualified for state ballots that year than in any election of the preceding 50 years.[19]

The discussion on a national Initiative process that Telschow and Forster had started in 1977 continued sporadically throughout the 1980s. John Naisbitt mentioned the idea in his 1983 bestseller, *Megatrends,* and the Rutgers University political scientist Benjamin Barber made a detailed national Initiative proposal of his own in his 1984 book, *Strong Democracy.*[20]

CREATING A NATIONAL INITIATIVE PROCESS

Congress, by majority vote of both houses, could create a nonbinding national Initiative process or mandate national referendums on any subject at any time. The results of such popular votes, however, would not have the force of law: under the U.S. Constitution, only Congress can *make* laws. Only an amendment to the Constitution passed either by a constitutional convention or by a two-thirds vote of both houses, and in either case ratified by at least 38 states, can give voters real national Initiative lawmaking power.

The various national Initiative proposals, plus the recent campaigns using state and local Initiative procedures to address national issues such as nuclear power, taxes, and nuclear weapons policy, plus polls conducted by the Gallup organization and by Patrick Cadell, have shown strong support for a national Initiative process for more than a decade. In addition, the expansion in the federal government's authority at the expense of the states' over most of the last century has increased the necessity for citizens' Initiative lawmaking powers beyond the state and local level. Since Congress is subject to the same weaknesses as state legislatures, the national government needs the Initiative process to ensure responsiveness to citizens no less than the cities and states. And certainly in this age of mass communication and worldwide economic interdependency, more and more policy issues can only be satisfactorily resolved at the national level.

The principal reservation raised in discussions of the national Initiative process concerns the potential power of monied interests to sway voters with slick, expensive advertising campaigns. Although this is a pervasive problem in American political campaigns (not just Initiative campaigns!) it seems to grow worse in proportion to the size of the jurisdiction. In a state as populous as California, only television and radio can reach a majority of voters with a political message.

Until 1987, the Federal Communications Commission's "Fairness Doctrine" ensured access to the broadcast airwaves by grassroots Initiative campaigns, but the FCC substantially weakened the doctrine in a 1987 ruling. Without guaranteed access to the broadcast media for cash-poor Initiative campaigns, the promise of national Initiative to make the federal government responsive to the electorate may well turn out to be hollow.

Although several states in the early 1970s tried to solve the problems of monied interests' influence by limiting Initiative campaign spending and contributions, these laws were invalidated by U.S. Supreme Court decisions on the grounds that they restricted First Amendment rights of free speech and freedom of association. The Court argued that there was no conclusive evidence that such unlimited spending power subverted the Initiative process (see *First National Bank of Boston* v. *Bellotti*, 435 U.S. 765 [1978], and *Citizens Against Rent Control* v. *City of Berkeley*, 454 U.S. 290 [1981]). An amendment to the U.S. Constitution may therefore be the only way to ensure that voters hear both sides in national Initiative campaigns.

Since a constitutional amendment is already required to give citizens federal lawmaking power, the same amendment could also deal with the fairness issue. Rather than limiting national Initiative campaign spending, however, a better approach would be to prohibit *paid* Initiative advertising on all electronic media and at the same time require all such media to set aside a specified percentage of their broadcast (or cable) time for use by opponents and proponents of Initiatives *free of charge*, as a public service in return for use of the public airwaves or the grant (by state or local government) of a cable franchise. In the interest of both fairness and better voter education, such a requirement should also extend to any print medium that runs public notices paid for by the government. A reasonable broadcast time or print space requirement would be one-tenth of 1 percent, per national Initiative on the ballot, per national election. The opposing sides would each get 0.05 percent, or about 7 minutes per day for 60 days (on television or radio); in a 100-page daily newspaper, it would work out to six-tenths of a page for 60 days. An alternative would be an amendment requiring media to give equal time (or print space) free of charge to the opposing side whenever a station or publication accepts paid advertising on that issue. Such a requirement could be made to apply to state and local Initiatives as well as national ones.

California and several other states publish a voter information handbook before each election providing the text, an analysis, and arguments for and against each ballot measure. These handbooks, cheaply printed on newsprint, are mailed to every registered voter. Such handbooks, even if they are studied by only a minority of voters, have proven to be a valuable source of balanced information that can be used to evaluate the campaign advertisements in the mass media.

Besides fairness in media access and voter information, the second most essential condition for a national Initiative process is a petition requirement high enough to prevent ballot clutter, and low enough to enable grassroots groups to qualify an Initiative for the ballot. At the state level, a requirement of 5 percent of the number of ballots cast in the last gubernatorial election works well. Given that the larger the jurisdiction, the tougher the signature quota (even though the percentage may be the same), a national Initiative signature requirement should be set at about 3 to 4 percent of the number of ballots cast in the previous Presidential election (about 4 million signatures.)

Other essential features of a good national Initiative amendment include a procedure for Congress to amend an Initiative if necessary (by no less than a three-fourths majority in both houses), and a reasonable time limit on petitions, such as one year. Without a specified time limit, Congress would be free to set an impossible one, like two weeks.

9

Campaign Manual

Unfortunately, there is no national law or provision in the U.S. Constitution that says that every state or local government must have the Initiative process. Many states and localities still lack this essential mechanism of self-government. There are two principal ways to get it.

One is for a *state constitutional convention* or local charter revision commission to pass an Initiative amendment. In most cases, however, the only way to make the necessary change is for the elected *legislature* or *city council* to pass an Initiative amendment to the state constitution or city charter. The way to get them to do it is good old-fashioned lobbying. The basic steps of a successful lobbying campaign are these:

Lobbying for the Initiative Process

1. Identify potential allies and solicit their support in the form of written endorsements, money, staff/volunteer time, leadership, or whatever they can give.

2. Form a coalition that is as broad-based and bipartisan as possible. Include Republicans and Democrats, liberals and conservatives, young and old, white and nonwhite ethnic groups, men and women.

3. Find sympathetic legislators to introduce the Initiative bill. Get a prime sponsor who is enthusiastic enough about the bill to organize support for it among the other legislators, and who will keep pushing it year after year.

4. Make sure that the bill is carefully drafted along the lines of the model bill described below. Inevitably, opponents will try to kill the bill with weakening amendments, while claiming that they are adding "safeguards." Don't let them get away with it. Expose their opposition and publicize it as an attack on the people's right to self-government.

5. Make sure that the bill gets lots of publicity.

6. Have constituents bombard their legislators with letters and phone calls supporting the bill when it comes up for a vote in committee or on the floor of either house of a legislature. Make sure that supporters turn out in droves for any committee hearing.

7. Work to elect candidates who support your bill, and campaign against incumbents who do not.

8. Don't give up if your bill doesn't pass the first time—or the second time or the third, fourth, or fifth. Let the legislators know that you mean business, and keep after them.

9. Don't hurt the cause by illegal or discourteous behavior toward opponents, like heckling speakers in committee hearings. But don't be timid about giving strong criticism when it is appropriate.

For more detailed instructions on lobbying, get a copy of Marc Caplan's excellent manual, *Ralph Nader Presents: A Citizen's Guide To Lobbying.*[1]

An alternative way to *get* the Initiative process is to *use* the Initiative process. This is only possible, however, in cases where a jurisdiction *with* the Initiative process has power over one *without* it. For instance, if there is a *state-wide* Initiative process, voters may use it to propose and pass a new state law creating Initiative procedures at the *city and county* level. Or, if a state constitution (or city charter) allows Initiative constitutional *amendments* (or Initiative charter amendments), voters may propose and pass an amendment to create an Initiative procedure for *statutes* or *ordinances*. Hawaii's pro-Initiative group, the Initiative Committee, used this procedure in 1982 to pass an Oahu charter amendment that gave voters the power to pass Initiative ordinances. This may sound complicated, but the idea is simple: constitutions (and charters) set out the rules on how laws are passed. If the Constitution (or charter) does not include a procedure for passing *laws* by petition and popular vote, change it!

A Model Initiative and Referendum Amendment

The following is a model state constitutional amendment to create the Initiative and Referendum process at the state level. Such an amendment should be clear and brief, yet must include essential items such as petition requirements so that the legislature cannot easily change them in the future. The amendment should include the following items:

1. A provision giving voters the power to propose and enact laws and resolutions that have *the same force and effect* as enactments of the legislature

2. A provision giving voters the power to propose and enact state constitutional amendments

3. A provision giving voters the power to block (by petition) and reject (by popular vote) new laws passed by the legislature (i.e., the Referendum procedure)

4. Definitions of Initiative and Referendum

5. A lower signature requirement for Initiative statutes or resolutions, and a higher requirement for constitutional

amendments. This gives Initiative proponents an incentive to make their proposal a law instead of trying to put it into their state constitution. If signature requirements for proposed statutes and constitutional amendments are equal, proponents will sponsor constitutional proposals (because the Legislature can't change them). This can result over the long term in cluttered, unwieldy constitutions.

6. A specific signature requirement framed in terms of a percentage of the total number of ballots cast in the preceding gubernatorial election. It should be high enough to require that proponents show substantial voter support, but low enough to allow grassroots citizen groups to put an Initiative on the ballot: between 3 percent and 6 percent of the number of ballots cast in the preceding election.

7. A timetable setting petition deadlines at least three months before each election, so that interested parties have at least two months to organize and wage campaigns for and against an Initiative.

8. A time limit of one year for circulation of an Initiative petition. Without such a time limit written into the constitution (or local charter), the legislature (or city council) would be free to impose a shorter limit that could make it nearly impossible for proponents to get the required signatures.

9. A section setting out the procedure under which an Initiative approved by voters may be amended by the legislature. It is necessary to allow some procedure for changes, but the legislature should be prevented from taking such action unless absolutely necessary. One way is to allow the legislature to change an Initiative only by three-fourths vote of both houses. Another way, described in the model amendment below, is to require that any changes made by the legislature must also be approved by the voters.

10. A section stating what essential information must be printed on a petition—for instance, the actual text of the measure and/or an impartial summary drawn up by an official such as the attorney general

11. A section granting Initiative and Referendum powers to the voters in any municipalities that do not already have these rights

12. A "self-executing" clause to make sure that the Initiative process will take effect without any further action by the legislature. Without such a clause, the legislature can kill the Initiative process simply by refusing to pass a bill covering minor procedural details.

13. A requirement that the state government send a pamphlet to each household before any election with an Initiative on the ballot, including the text, a summary, and arguments for and against each measure

14. A section on the resolution of possible conflicts between two Initiatives passed in the same election

This following model fulfills all these requirements.

Article _____. Initiative and Referendum

Section 1. The legislative power of this state shall be vested in the Legislature, but the people reserve to themselves the power to propose laws and amendments to the constitution, and to adopt or reject the same, at the polls independent of the Legislature, and also reserve the power, at their own option, to so adopt or reject any act, or part of any act, passed by the Legislature.

Section 2. (a) The Initiative is the power of the electors to propose statutes, bond acts, resolutions, and amendments to the constitution and to adopt or reject them.

(b) An Initiative measure may be proposed by presenting to the Secretary of State a petition that sets forth the text of the proposed statute, resolution, or amendment to the constitution and is signed by electors equal in number to 4 percent in the case of a statute, bond act, or resolution, and 6 percent in the case of an amendment to the constitution, of the votes cast for all candidates for Governor at the preceding gubernatorial election. No time limit less than 365 days shall be imposed for the circulation of an Initiative petition.

(c) The Secretary of State shall then submit the measure at the next general election held at least 130 days after proponents present the petition signed by the requisite number of voters. The Secretary of State shall have 40 days to determine if the petition contains more or less than the requisite number of signatures.

Section 3. (a) The Referendum is the power of the electors to approve or reject statutes or parts of statutes except emergency statutes approved by three-fourths vote of the members in each house of the Legislature.

(b) A Referendum measure may be proposed by presenting to the Secretary of State, within 90 days after the adjournment of the legislative session at which the statute was passed, a petition signed by electors equal in number to 4 percent of the votes for all candidates for Governor at the preceding gubernatorial election, asking that the statute or part of it be submitted to the electors. The Secretary of State shall have 40 days to verify the signatures.

(c) The Secretary of State shall then submit the measure at the next statewide election held at least 100 days after the petition is presented to the Secretary of State.

Section 4. (a) An Initiative or Referendum measure approved by a majority of votes thereon takes effect five days after the date of the official declaration of the vote by the Secretary of State unless the measure provides otherwise. If a Referendum petition is filed against part of a statute, the remainder of the statute shall not be delayed from going into effect.

(b) If provisions of two or more measures approved at the same election conflict, those of the measure receiving the highest affirmative vote shall prevail.

(c) The legislature may amend or repeal Referendum statutes. It may amend or repeal an Initiative statute by another statute that becomes effective only when approved by the electors, by majority of votes thereon, unless the Initiative statute permits amendment or repeal without voter approval.

(d) Prior to circulation of an Initiative or Referendum petition for signatures, a copy shall be submitted to the Attorney General, who shall prepare a title and summary of the measure. Such title and summary, not to exceed 100 words total, shall be printed on each petition.

(e) The Legislature shall provide methods of publication of all Initiative or Referendum measures referred to the people with arguments for and against the measures so referred. The Secretary of State shall send one copy of such a publication to each individual place of residence in the state and shall make such additional distribution as he/she shall determine necessary to reasonably ensure that each voter will have an opportunity to study the measures prior to the election.

Section 5. Initiative and Referendum powers may be exercised by the electors of each municipality as provided by law. Petition requirements for municipal Initiative or Referendum measures shall not exceed 6 percent of the registered voters in any municipality with over 10,000 registered voters, nor 10 percent of the registered voters in all other municipalities.

Section 6. This article is self-executing, but legislation may be enacted especially to facilitate its operation.

The Next Step: Winning a Ballot Campaign

Because it takes a state constitutional (or charter) amendment to create the Initiative process in a state (or city) that does not have it, and because such an amendment must be ratified by voters, victory in the legislature is only half the battle. Most voters support the Initiative and Referendum process—if they know what it is. In a state that does not have it, most people may be unfamiliar with the concept.

Pro-Initiative forces must reach as many voters as quickly as possible with the simplest possible explanation of what Initiative is, urging a "yes" vote to get it. The methods of organizing such a campaign are the same as those for any ballot measure campaign (see "How to Run a Winning Initiative Campaign," below in this chapter). The themes of the campaign can be summarized in a few phrases, which should be repeated in every broadcast advertisement and elaborated upon in leaflets, newspaper ads, and other print advertising. For example: "Initiative and Referendum Means Citizen Power! Your Voting Rights—The Essence of Democracy—Let The People Decide—Vote Yes!"

Initiative and Referendum—Making It Work

Assuming that the voters approve the I&R amendment to their state constitution (or city charter), one task remains before it can be used: passing a bill setting out the details of petition and campaign procedures. Such bills specify the format of a petition, procedures for verifying the names on it, requirements for disclosure of campaign spending and contributions to committees backing and opposing each Initiative that gets on the ballot, and penalties for violators.

Legislators opposed to Initiative and Referendum may try to put restrictive provisions into these bills. Good bills must be carefully guided over such legislative hurdles. Unfortunately, even after a good bill is passed, citizens need to be constantly on guard against bills to restrict use of the Initiative process. One such sneak attack on the people's voting rights was launched in 1965 by Caspar Weinberger, then serving as a Republican member of the California State Assembly, representing San Francisco.

Weinberger's plan to kill the Initiative process failed.[2] But throughout the nation, year after year, legislators with the same intent introduce bills designed to obstruct Initiatives. The only antidotes are constant vigilance and strenuous protest the moment politicians begin discussing encroachments on the people's legislative powers.

HOW TO PUT AN INITIATIVE
ON THE BALLOT

There are four key steps in qualifying an Initiative for a state or local ballot: (1) researching the Initiative procedure; (2) drafting the proposed law; (3) creating an organization; and (4) organizing a petition drive.

Research

Initiative procedures vary widely from state to state, and between local jurisdictions *within* each state (See Appendix IV, Petitioning: A State-by-State Guide to Rights and Requirements).

Initiative campaign leaders must become experts on procedures in their jurisdiction to avoid running afoul of the many rules and regulations through which they must steer their proposal. Being forced to start over after petition circulators have already collected thousands of signatures can doom an entire campaign.

Seemingly tiny mistakes can be crucial. One completed petition was denied ballot placement because the copies that were circulated lacked the words "Be it enacted by the people" at the beginning of the fine-print text of the proposal. To avoid such mistakes, sponsors must take the following precautions.

Read the state constitution and election laws, including court and attorney general opinions affecting Initiative procedures. Even a footnote to a decades-old court decision can prove crucial. Perhaps the best example of this is the Ohio state supreme court decision of 3 June 1931, in *State ex. rel. Hubbell* v. *Bettman.* This allows Initiative proponents to put several Initiatives on the state ballot with a single petition. It was first put to effective use 45 years later by a 23-year-old petition drive organizer with no formal legal training (see Chapter 4). Lesson: it pays to read the fine print!

Check with the secretary of state (or other officers responsible for handling completed Initiative petitions) to determine the exact number of petition signatures required by law *and* the average proportion of signatures on past petitions that were ruled invalid. If 20 percent of the names on the average petition have been ruled unacceptable, sponsors should set their goal at 25 or 30 percent over the minimum number required; if the invalidation rate averages 30 percent, plan to get 40 percent over the requirement; and so on.

Compare notes with other groups that have conducted Initiative drives in the same jurisdiction so you can anticipate problems that are likely to occur, and get suggestions on the best local sites for collecting signatures and the most effective solicitation techniques. They may even provide the names of their best petition circulators, who may be willing to volunteer again—or train other volunteers.

Determine filing requirements, deadline dates, and the required format of petitions (some states even specify the type size to be used in different parts of the petition and the size of the paper to be used). Sponsors should allow plenty of time to meet each deadline. In Massachusetts, for example, before a statewide Initiative petition can be circulated, the measure must be filed with the state's attorney general in the first week of August the year *before* the Initiative is to be on the ballot.

Allow extra time for problems that may come up, including possible lawsuits seeking to block ballot placement of the Initiative. Some states, like Oregon, provide for a "challenge period" allowing legal challenges to the official title and summary *before* a petition drive starts. Opponents can cut over a month off a petition drive with such a lawsuit—a cheap but potentially effective way to block an Initiative if sponsors start the process too late.

Drafting

Careful drafting is crucial because not a single word or comma of an Initiative may be changed once the petition drive starts. A seemingly minor flaw in wording can give the opposition an issue with which to turn a majority of voters against the proposal on election day. Flaws can also destroy the effectiveness of your proposal should it pass. Therefore sponsors should do the following:

Research laws proposed by others working on the same issue. Laws already in effect in other states, laws under consideration in other states or in Congress. Sponsors should try to model the Initiative on laws that have worked elsewhere.

Consult with the experts on the issue. Authors, scientists, lawyers, regulatory bureaucrats, leaders of other organizations. Sponsors should get their comments on the proposal and how to improve it. A public opinion poll is useful at this point to determine what aspect of the issue is most popular with the public, so that sponsors can be sure to include it in their proposal, and, conversely, to find out where public opinion and the proposal may differ. Generally, it is much more difficult to get a "yes" vote on a controversial proposition than a "no" vote.

Draft the proposal to take advantage of the maximum extent of voter support, yet keep it strong enough to accomplish the goal. For instance, a law that would require voter approval for any new nuclear power plant—but not actually ban nuclear power—takes advantage of the overwhelming agreement among voters that they should be allowed to decide whether another nuclear plant is built. Such a law may be all that is necessary to push a utility company into abandoning its plans to build such a plant.

Get expert legal advice on wording of the proposal. Some states allow (or require) Initiative proponents to submit a draft to the legislature's bill drafting office. Another way to consult the experts is to have an elected legislator introduce the proposal and conduct hearings on it in the legislature before sponsors finalize the wording. Sponsors should have attorneys check every section of the Initiative for constitutionality (or conformity to the local charter) and to find any conflicts with existing law. Most Initiatives should include a "severability clause," which states that if any part of the Initiative is found to be invalid, the rest of it shall remain in effect.

Try to make the Initiative concise, straightforward, and comprehensible to the average voter. Since legal language is required, this is not always possible. But sponsors should keep in mind that one common opposition tactic is to reprint some particularly obscure section in anti-Initiative ads that urge citizens to "Vote No—it's too complicated!"

Anticipate the opposition's arguments about the Initiative's possible undesirable effects and consider including sections to mitigate these effects. This way, sponsors can head off some of the opposition before it starts. For instance, the Bottle Bill Initiatives in the 1970s and 1980s were opposed not only by beverage bottlers and canners but by grocery stores, which did not want to handle returnable cans and bottles. Had the Initiatives made grocery stores' obligations more convenient (or profitable), the stores might not have joined the opposition.

Check the printer's galleys or plates. Make sure that there are *no* mistakes—not so much as a missing comma—before petitions are printed.

Creating an Organization

An Initiative needs two kinds of supporters: the volunteer activists who collect petition signatures, and the influential groups and "opinion leaders" whose endorsements, singly or cumulatively, exert an influence on some segment of the electorate.

Solicit endorsements widely. The "opinion leaders" and organizations should be numerous, well-known, and respected, and they should represent a broad political spectrum. Any list of endorsers should include elected officials, clergy, celebrities, business people, labor leaders, men, women, Republicans, Democrats, Independents, blacks, whites, and Hispanics, and—this is important—experts on the subject of the Initiative, print and broadcast media editorialists, and "natural enemies" who support your Initiative. For example, a crucial "natural enemy" endorser for a Bottle Bill Initiative would be a beverage bottling or canning company. "Natural enemy" endorsements cast doubt on the opposition's claims.

Recruit volunteers from organizations whose members are likely to support the Initiative strongly. The groundwork for such a recruitment effort can be laid by soliciting endorsements from the organizations, with the understanding that an endorsement means that the group will allow recruitment of its members.

Send mailings to members of endorsing organizations. The people who show up at the group's meetings are likely to be already involved in too many activities to spare the time for an additional commitment. For smaller organizations, sponsors can phone everyone on the mailing list.

When recruiting, ask volunteers and organizations to make commitments to work a certain number of hours, collect a certain number of signatures, coordinate the petition drive in a specific geographical area, or raise a specified amount of money.

Get additional volunteers by instructing petition circulators to recruit any signer who expresses strong support for the Initiative.

Get endorsements early, and in writing. That way, sponsors can call on endorsers for assistance throughout the campaign and secure their endorsement before the opposition approaches them.

Organizing a Petition Drive

Use arithmetic to plan the petition drive. Calculate the number of signatures needed per day, per region, per volunteer, per group. Volunteers should be assigned quotas per day or per week. In addition to giving petition drive leaders control over the campaign (so that adjustments can be made along the way if quotas are not met), such planning makes each individual's task more manageable in his or her own mind. A goal of 50 signatures per person per day, or 10 per hour, seems easier to accomplish than a simple order to "produce 10,000 signatures" to a meeting of 50 volunteers.

Use the table method to collect signatures. Pioneered by the late Ed Koupal in California in the early 1970s, this method still beats all others when employed as described here.

A metal folding table is best, but one or two card tables, or even an ironing board, will do. All campaign literature, extra pens, petitions, tape, and so on should be neatly stored in a box under the table.

Petitions should be taped to the table, all around the three edges facing passersby, so that they can come up and sign. This way, several people can sign at once, under the watchful eye of a circulator. The tape is necessary to keep petitions neatly secured to the table—so that neither wind nor absent-minded signers can snatch them away.

To attract attention, circulators should attach colorful signs bearing simple messages to the sides of the table or nearby. A bold red "Sign Here" sign can be used for any cause, and it serves to bring the curious close enough to hear the pitch.

Volunteers should bring the following items.

Table Method Materials Checklist

- A stack of blank petitions
- A stack of explanatory pamphlets
- Cardboard box or duffel bag to store materials under the table
- Folding table or ironing board
- Coffee can for donations
- Posters to hang on sides of table
- Masking tape
- A dozen or more ballpoint pens (not felt-tip and ink pens; the signatures might smear if they got wet)
- Water or other drinks (never on table—they might spill)

Choose table locations carefully. Table location can make the difference between getting five signatures an hour and getting a hundred. Tables should be set up in areas with a steady, high volume of pedestrian traffic for an extended period of time—shopping malls are ideal. Arrange with mall management beforehand for permission to set up a table. In Washington State, Oregon, and California, state supreme court decisions have secured the right of citizens to circulate petitions in privately owned malls. (See "The Right to Petition," in Appendix IV).

Other good locations are county fairs and urban block parties or street fairs, busy downtown sidewalks, particularly near popular subway stops, large food or discount stores, university campuses, and the entrances to municipal buildings or county courthouses where people come to pay taxes, register to vote, get driver's licenses, pay traffic tickets, and so on.

Always work the exits. People are more often in a hurry when they are going into stores and municipal offices than when they are coming out of them. So don't bother them twice;

just solicit them as they are on their way out and are more relaxed from having completed their business.

If an election occurs during the petition drive, plan a major, one-day effort to get volunteers to collect signatures at polling places. The advantage of polling-place soliciting is that nearly all passersby are voters and therefore eligible to sign the petition.

In most states weather can be an important enough factor to doom a petition drive if it is bad and organizers have not planned for it. Plan some locations that can be worked regardless of weather.

Work in groups. Teams of two, three, or more people are recommended. A single volunteer working a table is much more apt to get tired or frustrated and give up, or never show up in the first place, than a duo or trio. Groups support each member's morale and gather signatures more efficiently—which is a morale booster in itself.

Table methodology as developed by Ed Koupal and other activists requires one volunteer to stand directly behind the table. Another volunteer approaches each person walking by and asks if she (or he) is a registered voter in the jurisdiction in which the Initiative will be on the ballot. If the answer is "yes," the volunteer directs her attention to the table and says, "Would you please sign our petition for [whatever positive phrase sums up the intent of the Initiative]."

If the potential signer hesitates or asks questions, the circulator should answer briefly and remind her that this petition is "only to get it on the ballot so everyone can vote on it." It is not necessary that signers make an immediate decision to support the Initiative.

Always be polite and cheerful. It is important to generate positive feelings among signers and passersby to attract more people to the table. If circulators are in a place where permission is required, such as a shopping mall, one complaining customer can get them thrown out.

As the signer moves toward the table, the volunteer behind the table makes eye contact, hands the voter a pen, and shows him or her exactly where to sign, "Sign here just the way you are registered to vote." This last is very important: if a woman who is registered under the name "Mrs. John C. Jones, 221 Baker Street," signs the petition as "Mary F. Jones, 221 Baker St.," the signature will probably be disqualified.

Both volunteers should remain standing—sitting is too passive. A sitting person is resting, not signing up voters.

Above all, there should be no arguing or debating at or near the petition table! This turns people off immediately, and they will avoid the table. At the same time, arguing drains the volunteer's energy. If a person tries to argue, do not respond in kind. Answer the question briefly, hand him or her a blank petition and a pamphlet, and turn to another customer. If necessary, walk away. Volunteers should not converse at length with signers or attempt to answer lengthy questions. While such a conversation is in progress, a hundred people may walk by unsolicited. The goal of the table operation is to get petition signatures, not educate voters. All efforts to educate voters will be futile if the Initiative does not qualify for the ballot.

Ask for a donation as each person finishes signing the petition. Many people interested enough to sign the petition will also be willing to give at least a dollar. Each table should have a coffee can for the donation—it is among the easiest fundraising methods around.

Have volunteers hand in their signatures to the petition drive coordinator each week, so that the coordinator can keep a running total and gauge the success of the campaign. The coordinator should *never* count signatures unless they are *in hand*—those reported by phone may be exaggerated, since people don't like to admit by phone that they didn't collect as many signatures as they said they would. Another advantage of bringing the signatures to a central collection point each week is that news media advisories can be put out regarding the progress of the campaign, and sponsors can prove that they are not fabricating the totals. Security (see below) is another advantage.

Handle, store, and submit completed petitions with care. A completed petition is worth more than its weight in gold—and it should be treated that way. Completed petitions should be stored in *several* secret, safe locations. Sponsors should *not* leave them in the organization's office overnight. Burglaries and break-ins do occur. As petitions are turned in to headquarters by volunteers, organizers should check a few of them from time to time to see if the names on them match up with official lists of registered voters. This way, sponsors can tell if circulators are making mistakes—like neglecting to ask signers whether they are registered voters. It will also allow sponsors to estimate what proportion of signatures are valid.

Finally, get a receipt from government officials attesting to how many petition sheets have been turned in. Arrive early enough to allow time for the officials to count the sheets. Photocopy the receipt(s) and store copies in safe places. Even in government offices, petitions can be lost to burglaries, fires, and unwitting discards. Sponsors should also keep photocopies of each petition sheet as insurance against such a disaster.

HOW TO RUN A WINNING INITIATIVE CAMPAIGN

Once the petitions are turned in, campaign leaders should meet to decide upon a detailed plan for winning. If possible, they should have a professional consultant, with ballot measure campaign experience, advise the drafters of the plan. If that is not possible, at least make sure that *someone* with experience in managing such campaigns and knowledge of the issue participates.

A campaign plan has three essential components: a definition of the campaign's message or theme, a strategy for recruiting and employing volunteers and contributors, and a mass media publicity strategy. The presence of a professional campaign consultant is optional.

The Campaign Message

The campaign theme should summarize the purpose of the Initiative in such a way that a majority of voters will favor it. The theme should encourage people to vote for something they already believe in. It is more than just a slogan; it is the unifying element of the campaign and the foundation of societal consensus on a public issue. It is also a flag by which the voters can distinguish this issue from all the other items on a crowded ballot. Sticking with a single theme, moreover, enhances the campaign's credibility. Voters feel more secure about supporting the Initiative if the downstate supporters, the upstate supporters, and the radio, television, and newspaper ads are all saying the same thing.

Credibility must also be safeguarded by "quality control" of all written and spoken information distributed by your campaign. Facts must be checked. Nobody should be allowed to print literature or speak on behalf of the campaign without clearing the text with the central headquarters first. Better yet, all printed literature should be prepared by the central office, since this saves time and money as well as preventing contradictory statements.

Volunteers

If the volunteers are few, put them to work phoning contributors and asking them to give more of their money and time. If there are more volunteers than are needed for a phone bank operation, send a few back to the shopping malls with a card table and a box of leaflets. There, they can distribute the leaflets and solicit small contributions.

Early campaign efforts should focus on expanding the base of contributors and volunteers. This can be done through mailings to members of organizations that have endorsed the Initiative, phone calls, and many other techniques, which can be found in books like Joan Flanagan's *The Grass Roots Fundraising Book*.[3]

As for volunteers, be sure to treat them with respect, not neglect. If they are not happy, they will quit—remember, they are not being paid. For tips on how to keep them satisfied, get a copy of *A Celebration of Volunteers* from the Northern Rockies Action Group.[4]

Preparing a Mass Media Campaign

In any statewide or big-city campaign, mass media must be used—radio, television, newspapers, and the mail. There are two ways to get your message across in these media: paid and "free." With the former, the campaign has complete control over the content and timing of advertising; with the latter, the campaign's control is limited. Planning for both should begin at least three or four months prior to election day.

Most ballot measure campaigns rely on "free" mass media (news coverage and editorials) during their petition drive. Throughout that period, campaign leaders should be holding news conferences, mailing out regular press releases, staging attention-grabbing "media events," and courting the editorial boards of newspapers and television and radio stations. Some of the free advertising during the final months of the campaign will be a continuation of this process. To get good news coverage at the end of your campaign, begin educating reporters and editors about the issue even before the petition drive begins, and keep sending them information.

In addition to news coverage, free media advertising can be gained by letters to the editor, interviews with celebrities invited to appear on behalf of the cause, and "free speech messages" (or responses to unfavorable editorials) on radio and television. Staged "media events" should be creative but must get your message across without alienating people. To get television coverage, it helps if the event includes children, animals, or other colorful moving objects. Television film crews want movement and color. Campaign spokespersons should be prepared to stand in front of television cameras and make a statement that sums up the event and the Initiative in 10 or 15 seconds.

In a campaign with well-funded opposition, sponsors should plan to invoke the FCC's Fairness Doctrine. The doctrine says that if broadcast media show one side of a controversial issue, they have to show the other as well, even if the other side does not have the money to pay for advertising. If the opposition is advertising heavily, proponents get a chance to respond.

To get the maximum benefit from the Fairness Doctrine, advance planning is essential. The best manual on the doctrine for ballot measure campaign leaders is *Talking Back,* a book that includes case histories and copies of letters actually used in such campaigns.[5] In paid media advertising, expert help is essential. Newspapers often have their own graphic designers who will design an ad for customers at no extra cost.

Any type of publicity or advertisement *must* include prominently the ballot proposition number (or letter) and instruction on how petition sponsors want people to vote— for instance, "Vote YES on 7," or "Vote NO on B." This goes for leaflets, television ads, press releases, everything. And the theme should be stated the *same way* in every ad, using the same style of lettering and the same logo. Repetition is the key to a successful ad campaign. Without it, some voters can become confused about which way to vote.

Newspapers, television, radio, and the mail are the four most important mass media. Billboards, bumper stickers, yard signs, window signs, and posters on telephone poles are secondary—their main value is in boosting the morale of volunteers. Seeing such signs confirms to them that they are working on a real campaign. Some professional political consultants use no signs at all, believing that most people do not read them, and that most of those who do ignore them.

Buying time. The "media buyer" is a key contact. In ad agencies and political consulting firms, the media buyer is the person who works with radio and television stations to schedule the broadcasting of ads. Rather than wade through the technicalities of "rating points," nonprofessional campaign organizers should find an experienced media buyer to shop around for the best television or radio slots on which to reach the voters at a price the campaign can afford.

Producing television and radio ads. Production of a single beer commercial can cost hundreds of thousands of dollars. Campaign television ads, however, can be produced for well under a thousand—possibly even for free. Radio ads can also be done for free: here is how the Nuclear Weapons Freeze Campaign in Western Massachusetts did it in 1980.

Campaign leaders prepared a 30-second script for a radio ad, to be read as a dialogue between a male voice and a female voice. They then notified a radio station that they would pay for broadcasting an ad if the station would help them produce it free of charge. The station agreed, and two campaign workers recorded the following ad in the station's studio:

Male voice: Five million dollars an hour. That's how much the U.S. and Russia are spending on nuclear weapons.
Female voice: In half an hour these weapons could destroy every city in the Northern Hemisphere.
Male voice: This insane arms race raises our taxes, causes inflation, and produces fewer jobs.
Female voice: We can stop the arms race. The first step is to vote "yes" on Question 7, which calls upon both countries to stop building nuclear weapons.
Radio announcer: Paid for by the "Yes on 7" Committee.

Reproduction of the spot for use by other radio stations cost the price of one blank cassette tape per radio station, plus a small copying fee. The cost of broadcasting in these rural areas was just $7 to $35 per broadcast, depending on the time of day and the size of the audience. In urban areas, where the audience is many times larger, the cost would be proportionately larger also. Still, radio ads are much cheaper than television.

For their television ads, Western Massachusetts Freeze campaign leaders asked friends who do professional video work to volunteer their time. The volunteers, charging only for the use of their equipment and for videocassettes, produced three different ads on a total budget of $400. The cost of airing each ad ranged from $35 to $400 per 30-second broadcast (again, these amounts would be much greater for stations in an urban area).

Each ad consisted of very brief interviews or statements (four to seven seconds each) from a variety of local residents—for instance, an older woman standing outside her home ("*Nobody* would win a nuclear war"), a minister in front of his church ("Nuclear war is the most serious threat humanity has ever faced"), a mother sitting on the grass beside her two children ("I want my kinds to have a future. With the threat of nuclear war hanging over them, there *is* no future"), a dairy farmer feeding his calves ("I guess I'll vote 'yes' on Question 7"). Each spot concluded with a voice saying, "On November fourth, vote 'YES' on Question 7 to stop the nuclear arms race. . . . Paid for by the 'Yes' on 7' Committee."

In a 1982 utility rate reform campaign, Michigan Citizens Lobby Executive Director Joseph S. Tuchinsky produced an even cheaper television ad. After the opposition ran paid ads on one station, Tuchinsky informed the station managers of their responsibility to let his side respond and suggested that they allow him to use their studio to make a short statement. Tuchinsky prepared a 30-second script and delivered his monologue as the cameras rolled. This is known as a "talking head" ad because viewers see only the head and shoulders of the speaker. No expensive on-location shooting is done, so ads of this type are cheap to produce. The station used its own employees and studio during an idle time of the day, so it cost the station only the price of a videocassette.

For a nominal fee, Tuchinsky was able to have his ad copied onto additional videocassettes. These he delivered to other stations, where they were again broadcast free of charge under the Fairness Doctrine. "Talking head" ads are frowned upon by some consultants as too boring to be effective, but Tuchinsky claimed that his ad was as good as anything produced by the $4.4 million opposition campaign. His side won 50.7 percent of the vote, despite being outspent by a ratio of 133 to 1.

If a campaign has enthusiastic supporters who are professional filmmakers, however, they can produce something to compete with Madison Avenue's best. In a 1983 San Francisco campaign managed by Ken Masterton, backers of a ballot measure to restrict smoking in public places created an imaginative ad that evoked memories of the Marlboro men who once galloped across the nation's television screens.

The "Yes on Proposition P" ad featured a cowboy riding a horse through the streets of downtown San Francisco. The camera then focused on the cowboy in a closeup, and he told viewers that people in the West have always liked to make their own decisions. But all this "Vote No" advertising by out-of-state tobacco companies "just makes me mad," growled the cowboy. "Join me in telling the tobacco companies to butt out of San Francisco's business—vote 'yes' on P." The visual then showed a piece of leather being branded with a hot iron that spelled out "Yes on P."

Scheduling advertising. Campaign planners should concentrate radio and television ads in the final two weeks before the election. Listeners are less responsive to, and more forgetful of, ads aired much earlier. Any opposition advertising, however, no matter how early, makes free response time available under the Fairness Doctrine. Initiative sponsors should take advantage of the opportunity.

Hiring a Professional Campaign Consultant

Like professional ad designers, most professional campaign management consultants are priced out of the reach of the typical grassroots Initiative campaign committee. Some may be willing to work at a discount because they support the cause. This is not, by itself, sufficient reason to hire such a person.

Several factors need to be considered. First, is this particular consultant the right person for the job? What is his or her prior experience? Candidate campaign experience is not as valuable as ballot measure campaign experience. Initiative sponsors should scrutinize references and find out what the consultant's previous clients have to say.

Second, even if sponsors intend to hire a consultant, they still need to know their business. One of the best texts on the business is *The Rise of Political Consultants: New Ways of Winning Elections,* by Larry J. Sabato.[6]

Third, sponsors should interview several candidates. Consultants should be able to provide some useful ideas for the campaign during the interview, even if you do not hire them. And by interviewing several, sponsors will find out whether any qualified consultant is willing to work at a lower price. Is any consultant willing to give advice from time to time free of charge? If sponsors cannot afford a full-time or part-time consultant, this may be the best alternative.

Finally, but perhaps most important, sponsors should ask themselves whether their campaign budget can absorb the consultant's fee. If the consultant has fundraising experience, that is a plus. If the consultant's fee is equivalent to more than a tenth of the campaign budget, the campaign cannot afford that consultant.

WHERE TO GET HELP: RESOURCES FOR
BALLOT MEASURE CAMPAIGNS

In addition to works cited in the notes, the following resources may be useful to ballot campaign planners.

The Initiative Resource Center is a clearinghouse for information on I&R campaigns and procedures nationwide. The center, directed by the author, has numerous publications helpful to Initiative activists, including a quarterly newsletter, *Initiative and Referendum: The Power of the People!* For more information, or to get a free sample issue, write to the Initiative Resource Center, 235 Douglass St., San Francisco, CA 94114.

"Be It Enacted by the People: A Citizens' Guide To Initiatives." by Mike A. Males (1981). This 56-page booklet focuses on Initiative procedures and recent Initiative history in Montana, Oregon, Washington, Colorado, Idaho, and Wyoming. Available from the Northern Rockies Action Group (NRAG), 9 Placer Street, Helena, MT 59601.

"The Initiative Process: A Lesson in Citizen Participation for Montana Students" (1984) is a guide to teaching the Initiative process to high school and junior high school students. Although geared to Montana's procedures, it could easily be adapted for any other state by substituting local procedures. This 30-page booklet is available from the Secretary of State, Montana State Capitol, Helena, MT 59620.

"Using Initiatives and Referenda to Protect Open Space: A Survey and Analysis of Northern California's Experience" (1983) is a study of city and county ballot Initiatives aimed at restricting urban sprawl. Includes excellent how-to information and 18 case histories of actual campaigns. Available from the Greenbelt Alliance, 116 New Montgomery St., Suite 640, San Francisco, CA 94105.

"Local Initiative: A Study of the Use of Municipal Initiatives in the San Francisco Bay Area" (1984) focuses on the variations in Initiative procedures in this region of California from 1974 through 1983. Since similar procedures are in use in the rest of the state, this guide is useful throughout California and in fact throughout the nation. The 65-page booklet is available from the Coro Foundation, 1370 Mission Street, San Francisco, CA 94103.

Campaigns and Elections: *The Journal of Political Action.* This is the professionals' slick magazine on the latest techniques in political campaigns. Back issues are available; the annual subscription rate is $48. Published by C & E Inc., 1835 K St. NW, Suite 403, Washington, D.C. 20006.

Appendix I

Initiative and Referendum Election Results, 1987–1988

March 1987		% Yes	% No
N. Dakota	Increase income tax*	52	48

November 1987		% Yes	% No
Maine	Ban nuclear power	42	58
Ohio	Select judges by appointment rather than election	35	65
Washington	Limit doctors' medicare fees	35	65
Wash., D.C.	Require beverage container deposits ("Bottle Bill")	45	55
Wash., D.C.	Require public hearings on school funding	77	23

June 1988		% Yes	% No
California	Require public financing of campaigns, candidate spending limits	53	47

California	Declare AIDS a communicable disease subject to quarantine	32	68
California	Issue $776 million bonds for parks and wildlife	65	35
California	Loosen state/local government spending limit	49	51
California	Exempt highways/transportation from state/local spending limit	38	62
California	Limit state/local candidate campaign contributions	58	42
N. Dakota	Create state lottery	42	58
N. Dakota	Impose sales tax on cable television, video services*	22	78

November 1988		% **Yes**	% **No**
Alaska	Limit civil liability for damages	71	29
Alaska	Separate community colleges from University of Alaska	44	56
Arizona	Make English the official language	51	49
Arkansas	Amend state constitution to ban state-funded abortion	52	48
Arkansas	Require 60% majority of legislature to approve tax changes	38	62
Arkansas	Require financial disclosure for lobbyists, officials	63	37
California	Aid homeless by using fines from housing code violations	45	55
California	Test sex crime suspects on mandatory basis for AIDS	62	38
California	Reinstate Cal. Occupational Health and Safety Administration	54	46
California	Revise spending limit to increase school funding	51	49
California	Increase tobacco, cigarette tax by 25¢ per pack	58	42
California	Regulate auto insurance rates, give good-driver discount	41	59
California	Cut auto insurance rate, limit damages	13	87
California	End AIDS test confidentiality, allow insurers' AIDs test bias	34	66
California	Cut and regulate auto, property, casualty insurance rates	51	49
California	Require no-fault auto insurance, limit damages	25	75
California	Require disclosure to consumers, investors, voters	54	46

California	Limit attorneys' contingent fees in liability lawsuits	47	53
Colorado	Make English the official language	61	39
Colorado	Limit tax increases, cut tax rates	42	58
✗ Colorado	Repeal 1984 Initiative banning state-funded abortions	40	60
Colorado	Require hearing and vote on all bills in legislature	72	28
Florida	Limit non-economic damages to $100,000 in liability lawsuits	43	57
Florida	Make English the official language	84	16
Maryland	Ban sale, manufacture of cheap handguns*	58	42
Mass.	Increase state legislators' pay*	17	83
Mass.	Require humane treatment of farm animals	29	71
Mass.	Repeal "prevailing wage" requirement on government construction	42	58
Mass.	Ban nuclear power	32	68
✗ Michigan	Ban state funding for abortion*	57	43
Missouri	Extend 0.1% sales tax for parks and soil and water conservation	70	30
Missouri	Impose 0.6% earnings tax for health insurance for uninsured	29	71
Montana	Repeal mandatory auto seat belt law	43	57
Montana	Require beverage container deposits ("Bottle Bill")	22	78
Nebraska	Withdraw from interstate compact on low-level nuclear waste	36	64
Nebraska	Add "right to bear arms" to state constitution	64	36
Nevada	Prohibit state personal income tax	82	18
N. Dakota	Require legislature to replenish veterans trust fund	60	40
Oregon	Ban parole for certain repeat felonies	79	21
Oregon	Increase by 1¢ beer can/cigarette pack tax to fund college sports	37	63
Oregon	Ban indoor public smoking	39	61
Oregon	Double river mileage protected by Scenic Rivers System	54	46
✗ Oregon	Revoke governor's ban on discrimination by sexual orientation	53	47
S. Dakota	Allow card game/slot machine gambling in Deadwood	64	36
S. Dakota	Limit and roll back property tax	39	61
S. Dakota	Require restoration of metallic minerals surface-mined land	41	59

S. Dakota	Impose surface mine tax to fund mined-land restoration	35	65
S. Dakota	Deregulate intra-state phone/tele-communications services*	53	47
S. Dakota	Ban corporate hog farms	60	40
Utah	Limit property taxes and state spending	39	61
Utah	Roll back income, sales, fuel, and tobacco taxes	38	62
✗ Utah	Give tuition tax credit for parents of private school students	31	69
Washington	Raise state minimum wage for workers not covered by federal wage	77	23
Washington	Prefer either of two hazardous sub-stance production taxes to fund tox-ics cleanup**	85	15
Washington	Prefer hazardous substance tax ini-tiative (Yes) or legislature's bill**	55	45

*Denotes Referendum on bill passed by legislature and placed on ballot by citizen petitions circulated by opponents of bill.

**Washington State's legislature placed an alternative version of the tox-ics tax on the ballot alongside the Initiative. Voters decided on two ques-tions: 1) whether they preferred either measure (85%) over neither (15%), and 2) whether they preferred the Initiative (55%) or the legislature's bill (45%).

ABOUT THE 1987–1988 RESULTS

The number of Initiatives on state ballots nationwide in the 1987–1988 election cycle was about average in comparison with the previous 12 years, except in California, where six Initiatives on the June 1988 primary ballot combined with 12 on the general election ballot set a new California record of 18. This brought the nation-wide total up to 61 Initiatives, which equalled the 50-year high set in 1982. When the six voter-initiated Referendums (on bills passed by legislatures) are added to the 1988 total, it makes the largest number of voter-initiated state ballot measures—67—since 1932.

The biggest surprises were the success of major insurance rate cuts and a hefty cigarette tax increase in California, and the pas-sage of a handgun control measure in Maryland, despite opposition campaign spending that broke previous state spending records in each case.

In California, voters not only passed the insurance rate-cutting Proposition 103, which was backed by consumer advocate Ralph Nader, but they rejected four competing insurance reform Initiatives backed by insurance companies, trial attorneys, and banks that spent over $70 million. The group backing "103" ("Voter Revolt to Cut Insurance Rates") by contrast spent less than $3 million. Tobacco companies similarly spent about $20 million on an ad campaign to defeat a 25¢-per-pack cigarette and tobacco tax increase, which passed overwhelmingly nevertheless. Medical and health groups backing the tax were outspent by at least a 4 to 1 ratio.

In Maryland, advocates of a Referendum to ban sale and manufacture of cheap handguns also won overwhelmingly despite a massive, $5 million–plus "Vote No" advertising blitz funded primarily by the National Rifle Association. It was the first statewide ballot measure defeat for the immensely influential gun lobby, and gave encouragement to members of Congress pushing for stricter gun control laws.

Meanwhile, voters approved bans on state-funded abortions in Michigan, Colorado, and Arkansas (though the Colorado and Arkansas votes merely reinforced the status quo in those states), and won passage of state constitutional Initiatives in Florida, Colorado, and Arizona to make English the official language.

Nationwide, voters passed 26 of the 61 Initiatives on state ballots, or 43%, just slightly higher than the historical average Initiative success rate of 38%. Of these 26 winning Initiatives, 11 were sponsored by conservative groups, and 12 by liberal-oriented or environmental groups. This showed once again the essentially moderate nature of the American electorate, which has approved virtually equal numbers of liberal-sponsored and conservative-sponsored Initiatives since the mid–1970s.

There was no dominant issue in the 1987–1988 Initiative campaigns analogous to the "Tax Revolt" of 1978–1980 or the "Nuclear Freeze" ballot measures of 1982. Thus, there was no emerging trend for the 1990s as this book went to press, but rather a great diversity of issues that could lead wherever the voters want to go. But one thing the 1988 Initiatives did show, by way of popular support for insurance rate cuts, tobacco tax, and handgun control: when the voters want to pass an Initiative badly enough, no amount of special interest money can stop them.

Appendix II

Development of the Initiative

A STATE-BY-STATE HISTORY OF THE INITIATIVE PROCESS

ALABAMA

The movement for direct democracy was weak in Alabama during the Populist/Progressive era. The only victory recorded by the Initiative and Referendum movement organ *Equity* was a state law giving voters the right of Referendum on ordinances in major municipalities, invoked by petition of 1,000 voters. No provisions for statewide I&R were ever enacted.

ALASKA

Alaska became the 20th state to get a statewide Initiative process at the time of statehood in 1959. However, the procedure does not include the right to make appropriations or amend the state constitution.

In 1974 voters approved an Initiative to relocate the state capital. Without an appropriation, this decision could be implemented only if the legislature acted. Since the legislature failed to respond, voters passed another Initiative in 1978, this time requiring the state government to determine the cost of relocation and stipulating that any bond issue to finance that cost be subject to voter approval. The bond issue went to the voters in 1980, but they rejected it, with the result that Juneau is still the state capital, despite its great distance from the major population center, Anchorage.

In 1976 Alaskans passed an Initiative to abolish one house of their legislature and create a unicameral lawmaking body like Nebraska's. Unfortunately, a constitutional amendment was needed to accomplish this change, and Alaska's Initiative procedure does not allow amendments. Members of the legislature, not wishing to abolish their jobs, predictably ignored the measure. They did pay heed, however, to an Initiative sponsored by the Libertarian Party to abolish the state personal income tax. The Initiative qualified for the November 1980 ballot but was enacted by the legislature on 25 September of that year, thus making a popular vote unnecessary.

ARIZONA

Arizona acquired statewide Initiative, Referendum, and Recall rights at the time of statehood in 1912. *Equity* mentions "Hon. A. C. Baker of Phoenix" as a leader of the local direct democracy movement.

The first Initiative was for women's suffrage, and it passed by a margin of greater than two to one on 5 November 1912. Two years later, in 1914, a total of 15 Initiatives qualified for the Arizona ballot—a record for Initiative use in that state which still stands.

Organized labor that year was successful in passing four Initiatives: one to prohibit blacklisting of union members; a second establishing an "old age and mother's pension"; a third establishing a state government contract system, printing plant, and banking system; and a fourth requiring that businesses limit employment of noncitizens. Voters passed a fifth Initiative barring the governor and legislature from amending or repealing Initiatives.

The legislature responded with a constitutional amendment to make it harder to pass Initiatives. This amendment, however, could take effect only if approved by voters. The Arizona Federation of Labor waged a campaign against the measure, and voters defeated it by a narrow margin in 1916.

Arizona government reforms passed by voter Initiative include changes in reapportionment (1918 and 1932), changes in the court system (1960 and 1974), and the innovative, highly successful voter registration system known as "Motor Voter" (1982), which allows applicants for driver's license renewal to simultaneously register to vote.

Arizonans owe many of their reforms to John Kromko. Kromko, like most Arizonans, is not a native; he was born near Erie, Pennsylvania, in 1940 and moved to Tucson in the mid-1960s. He was active in protests against the Vietnam War and in the 1970s and 1980s has been elected to the lower house of the state legislature several times. By night, he is a computer programming instructor; by day, he is Arizona's "Mr. Initiative."

Kromko's first petition was a Referendum drive to stop a Tucson city council ordinance banning topless dancing. (He explains with a touch of embarrassment that he was fighting for the principle of free speech.) In 1976 Kromko was among the handful of Arizonans who, in cooperation with the People's Lobby Western Bloc campaign, succeeded in putting on the state ballot an Initiative to phase out nuclear power. The Initiative lost at the polls, but Kromko's leadership on the issue got him elected to his first term in the legislature.

Once elected, he set his sights on abolishing the sales tax on food, a "regressive" tax that hits the poor hardest. Unsuccessful in the legislature, Kromko launched a statewide Initiative petition and got enough signatures to put food tax repeal on the ballot. The legislature, faced with the Initiative, acted to repeal the tax.

After the food tax victory, Kromko turned to voter registration reform. Again the legislature was unresponsive, so he launched an Initiative petition. He narrowly missed getting enough signatures in 1980, and he failed to win re-election that year. Undaunted, he revived the voter registration campaign and turned to yet another cause: Medicaid funding. Arizona in 1981 was the only state without Medicaid, since the legislature had refused to appropriate money for the state's share of this federal program.

In 1982, with an Initiative petition drive under way and headed for success, the legislature got the message and established a Medicaid program. Kromko and his allies on this issue, the state's churches, were satisfied and dropped their petition drive. The voter registration Initiative, now under the leadership of Les Miller, a Phoenix attorney, and the state Democratic Party, gained ballot placement and voter approval. In the ensuing four years, this "Motor Voter" Initiative increased by over 10 percent the proportion of Arizona's eligible population who were registered.

Kromko, re-elected to the legislature in 1982, took up his petitions again in 1983 to prevent construction of a freeway in Tucson that would have smashed through several residential neighborhoods. The Initiative was merely to make freeway plans subject to voter approval, but Tucson officials, seeing the campaign as the death knell for their freeway plans, blocked ballot placement through various legal technicalities. Kromko and neighborhood activists fighting to save their homes refused to admit defeat. They began a new petition drive in 1984, qualified their measure for the ballot, and won voter approval for it in November 1985.

Arizona's monied interests poured funds into a campaign to unseat Kromko in 1986. Kromko not only survived but fought back by supporting a statewide Initiative to limit campaign contributions, sponsored by his colleague in the legislature, Democratic State Rep. Reid Ewing of Tucson. Voters passed the measure by a two to one margin.

Kromko's Initiative exploits have made him the most effective Democratic political figure, besides former governor Bruce Babbitt, in this perennially Republican-dominated state. And Babbitt owes partial credit for one of his biggest successes—enactment of restrictions on the toxic chemical pollution of drinking water—to Kromko. Early in 1986 Kromko helped organize an environmentalist petition drive for an anti-toxic Initiative, while Babbitt negotiated with the legislature for passage of a similar bill. When Initiative backers had enough signatures to put their measure on the ballot, the legislature bowed to the pressure and passed Babbitt's bill.

ARKANSAS

The Arkansas Populist Party endorsed Initiative and Referendum in its 1896 state platform; the Democrats followed suit in 1898. But it was not until a decade later that the Democrat George W.

Donaghey won election as governor and, in 1909, successfully shepherded an I&R amendment through the legislature. It won voter ratification on 5 September 1910.

That summer, out-of-state Progressive movement leaders flocked into Arkansas to popularize the amendment. George Judson King of Ohio set up a press bureau to provide newspapers with pro-I&R information. William Jennings Bryan made a whistle-stop tour of the state with Governor Donaghey in a specially chartered train. In five days they covered 1,750 miles and gave 55 speeches to between 75,000 and 100,000 people. The presidents of the state Farmers Union and Federation of Labor were on board to urge their members to support I&R.

On election day voters approved I&R by a greater than two to one margin. In 1912 seven Initiatives qualified for the ballot, of which three passed: one limiting the legislature's session and members' salaries; a second providing for recall of elected officers; and a third authorizing cities and towns to issue bonds for public works. Opponents of the successful Initiatives went to court to overturn them on legal technicalities, and the Arkansas state supreme court encouraged such challenges with a series of decisions that chipped away at Arkansans' rights to self-government, beginning with the recall and bond Initiative votes. I&R supporters fought back with an Initiative to strengthen I&R procedures, only to see it lose with a frustratingly close 48.6 percent of the vote. They tried again by writing I&R provisions into a new constitution proposed by a state constitutional convention in 1917–1918, but that lost also. They tried a third time in 1920 with an Initiative that won the popular vote but lost in court on a legal technicality, and the voters rejected a fourth Initiative in 1922.

Unexpected salvation for I&R advocates came in 1925, when the state supreme court reversed its decision on the 1920 technicality (*Brickhouse* v. *Hill,* 167 Ark. 513 [1925]). Meanwhile, the state Federation of Labor won approval of an Initiative prohibiting child labor (1914), and the local bond authority Initiative won on a second try in 1918. In 1926 voters approved an Initiative to consolidate their state and federal elections, up to that year held on different dates.

Like the legislatures of other southern states, voters in Arkansas enacted several regressive measures: a 1928 Initiative to ban the teaching of evolution in the schools; a 1930 law to require Bible-reading in the schools; and a 1956 Initiative requiring the legislature to use any constitutional means to block school integration. The last won with 56 percent of the vote, thus supporting Gov. Orval Faubus' segregationist policy.

In the same election, however, Arkansans showed a liberal streak by approving, by a nearly three to one margin, an Initiative to increase workmen's compensation (a previous Initiative had authorized workmen's compensation in 1938). In 1964 they voted by a 56 percent majority to abolish the state's poll tax—another liberal move.

CALIFORNIA

Californians rightly credit Progressive-era Gov. Hiram Johnson with leading the successful fight for direct democracy in the Golden State, but few are familiar with the critical groundwork by Dr. John Randolph Haynes. A Philadelphian who held doctorates in both medicine and philosophy, Haynes moved west to Los Angeles in 1887, at the age of 34. He established a successful medical practice, counting many prominent Southern Californians among his patients, invested his profits skillfully in real estate, and eventually became a millionaire.

In 1895 Haynes helped found the California Direct Legislation League, dedicated to winning the rights of Initiative, Referendum, and Recall both statewide and in every local jurisdiction. He won election in 1900 to a Los Angeles "board of freeholders" responsible for drafting a new charter for that city. Haynes used this strategic position to make sure that the board included I&R in the new charter, only to see the entire charter thrown out by the courts on a technicality. A new board, without Haynes, was elected in 1902, but he continued to advocate I&R and brought Eltweed Pomeroy of New Jersey, president of the National Direct Legislation League, from the east coast specifically to address the board. After Pomeroy's speech, the board voted to include Initiative, Referendum, and Recall in the new charter. Voters ratified the charter in 1903.

Haynes then concentrated his efforts on winning I&R statewide. The odds against him were daunting. The entire state government had for decades been under the control of the Southern Pacific Railroad. Bribery was the accepted method of doing business in the state capitol. Realizing the hopelessness of dealing with the current officeholders, Haynes and other reformers began a campaign to get rid of them and remake state government from top to bottom. In May 1907 they founded the Lincoln-Roosevelt League of Republican Clubs, and elected several of their candidates to the legislature. Once elected, these legislators worked for a bill to require nomination of party candidates through primary election rather than the backroom deals of state party conventions. The bill passed, and the League's 1910 gubernatorial candidate, Hiram Johnson, ran in the state's first primary election. Johnson won the primary and the general election and swept dozens of other reformers into the legislature on his political coattails.

Johnson and the new Progressive majority in the legislature made the most sweeping governmental changes ever seen in the history of California. Among these were the introduction of Initiative, Referendum, and Recall at both the state and local levels. Voters ratified these amendments in a special election on 10 October 1911.

Reformers in Los Angeles won voter approval, in December 1911, of a unique local Initiative to create a municipally owned, yet editorially independent, newspaper to compete with the anti-labor, anti-reform *Los Angeles Times* and provide unbiased news and an equal forum for all political views. Each political party was given a column in every weekly edition.

This bold experiment in free speech attracted the state's top newspaper talent and got off to a highly successful start. After less than a year, however, it failed because of harassment of vendors and an advertiser boycott organized by the Los Angeles reformers' arch-enemy, *Times*-owner Harrison Gray Otis.

The first significant statewide Initiative in California abolished the poll tax in 1914; a construction bond Initiative for the University of California also won voter approval that year. Immediately thereafter, anti-Initiative forces launched their first counterattack, in the form of a constitutional amendment passed by the legislature to make it more difficult to pass Initiative bond proposals. Haynes mobilized his pro-Initiative forces and defeated the amendment at the polls in 1915.

Anti-Initiative forces tried again in 1920, this time using the Initiative process themselves to propose a measure that would have made it virtually impossible to put any tax-related Initiatives on future ballots. Haynes mobilized again and defeated the measure at the polls; he won a third, similar contest in 1922. After this he changed the name of his California Direct Legislation League to "the League to protect the Initiative," and for the rest of his life kept close watch over the legislature to make sure that it enacted no laws to restrict I&R procedures. Haynes died on 30 October 1937, at age 84.

On the ballot in 1934 were four successful constitutional Initiatives to revamp the state's law enforcement and criminal justice systems. All four were sponsored by Alameda County District Attorney Earl Warren, who went on to become the state's attorney general in 1938, its governor in 1942, and the Chief Justice of the U.S. Supreme Court in 1953. The principal changes involved procedures for judicial selection and retention, and increasing the woefully inadequate powers and jurisdiction of the office of attorney general. Warren's foresight in revamping the justice system before running for attorney general accounted in no small measure for his effectiveness once elected, which in turn made possible his rise to higher office.

Each decade for the first half of this century, the number of signatures required to put a statewide Initiative on the ballot roughly doubled. It was set at 8 percent of the number of votes cast in the previous gubernatorial election. In 1911 this was 30,481 signatures; in 1930, it was 91,529; in 1939, it was 212,117. The rapid change was due to California's explosive population growth and the increasing participation of women as voters. As petition requirements increased, the number of Initiatives qualifying for the ballot decreased, particularly in the 1940s, 1950s, and 1960s.

The Initiative campaign with the highest stakes, in terms of campaign spending (until the 1988 insurance rate reform struggle—see Appendix I) was the 1956 struggle over changes in state regulation and taxation of oil and gas production. The Initiative was sponsored by one group of oil companies that sought to make their business more profitable, and opposed by another group of oil firms that preferred the existing system. Campaign funds spent by both sides totaled over $5 million—equivalent to over $15 million in 1986 dollars. Until 1988, no Initiative campaign anywhere had exceeded this spending record (see Appendix I). The 1956 Initiative lost: California voters, inundated with conflicting claims about a complex measure, took the cautious route and voted "no."

Almost as expensive was the gargantuan 1958 labor-capital conflict over a "Right to Work" (open shop) Initiative sponsored by employers. This battle, in which about $10 million in 1986 dollars was expended, ended in a double defeat for employers: not only did voters decisively reject the Initiative, but the opposition campaign mobilized Democrats and union members to vote in droves, resulting in the election of Gov. Edmund G. Brown, Sr.—the first Democrat to occupy that office in 16 years.

In the 1960s California liberals soured on the Initiative process as a result of two measures passed by voters in 1964. The first repealed the Rumford Fair Housing Act, which the legislature had passed, and Governor Brown had signed, in 1963. The second banned cable television. That measure was sponsored by theater owners who, fearing competition, advertised the Initiative as guaranteeing "free television" and eliminating the specter of "pay television." Both 1964 Initiatives were later overturned by the courts as unconstitutional.

The California Initiative process gave rise to a new breed of campaign professional: the paid petition circulator. With signature requirements doubling nearly every decade, as we have seen, citizen groups were unable to rely solely on volunteer effort. As early as World War I, Joseph Robinson was offering his organizing services to Initiative proponents. His firm, which paid its employees a fee for each signature brought in, had a virtual monopoly on the petition business from 1920 to 1948–a period during which, Robinson estimated, his firm was involved in 98 percent of the successful statewide Initiative petition drives. Robinson stayed in business into the late 1960s (when he offered his services to Ed and Joyce Koupal), but by then he had competitors. (For a history of California Initiatives in the 1970s and 1980s, see Chapters 3, 4, 6, and 7.)

COLORADO

The effort for I&R in Colorado was started by Dr. Persifor M. Cooke of Denver in the mid-1890s. Cooke and the constitutional lawyer J. Warner Mills of Denver, as secretary and president, respectively, of the Colorado Direct Legislation League, fought for I&R from 1900 until 1910, when Gov. John F. Shafroth called a special session of the legislature to consider the issue. The constitutional amendments passed provided for Initiative, Referendum, and Recall on both state and local levels.

Coloradans set their state's record for Initiative use the first year it was available, in 1912, by putting 22 Initiatives on the ballot, of which nine passed. Among these were laws or amendments establishing an eight-hour work day for workers employed in "underground mines, smelters, mills and coke ovens"; giving women workers an eight-hour day; providing pensions for orphans and for widows with children; establishing juvenile courts in major cities and counties; and granting home rule to cities and towns.

Over the years Colorado voters proved sympathetic to the needs of the aged and infirm, approving Initiatives providing for the treatment of mental illness in 1916 and 1920, relief for blind adults in 1918, pensions for the aged and for indigent tuberculosis sufferers in 1936, and increased pensions adjusted for inflation in 1956. Coloradans also remained friendly to organized labor, approving an Initiative statute changing the workmen's compensation law to benefit employees in 1936, and defeating an employer-backed "Right to Work" Initiative in 1958.

In the early 1970s Coloradans passed environmentalist-backed Initiatives to keep the Winter Olympics from being held in their state (1972) and prohibit underground nuclear explosions except with prior voter approval (1974). Richard Lamm, an obscure state legislator when he sponsored the anti-Olympics Initiative, gained sufficient prestige from his leadership of this campaign to later win election as governor.

In 1984 Colorado became the first state to pass an Initiative banning use of state funds for abortion (the second was Arkansas, in 1988—see Appendix 1). Voters approved the measure by a single percentage point. Less controversial and more popular was the 1984 "Motor Voter" Initiative, which set up a system of voter registration at driver's licensing bureaus. This highly successful program increased the number of registered voters in Colorado by 12.4 percent in the 15 months from July 1985 to October 1986.

CONNECTICUT

Progressive era direct democracy advocates failed to win Initiative and Referendum rights at either state or local levels, except in the city of Bristol. Citizens in many of the state's small towns, however, still enjoy the right to enact ordinances by popular vote in their town meetings.

DELAWARE

Delaware is the only state that not only bars Initiative and Referendum, but does not even allow citizens to ratify amendments to the state constitution. Yet during the Progressive era, the I&R movement publication *Equity* described Delaware as one of 11 states where "the Initiative sentiment is all-powerful."

Delaware's extraordinarily difficult procedure for amending its state constitution stacked the deck against I&R agitators from the start. Under the leadership of Wilmington's Francis I. DuPont (of the well-known chemical company family), I&R advocates persuaded the legislature to schedule a statewide advisory referendum on whether I&R should be added to the state constitution. In the 1906 election voters approved the idea by a landslide six to one margin.

Instead, the legislature passed a bill giving I&R rights to the city of Wilmington only. Voters there quickly used their new rights to put five Initiatives on the city's ballot in early 1907. According to *Equity,* it was "the first use of Direct Legislation on general questions of public policy in an eastern city, and the first among negro voters." Meanwhile, the Delaware Referendum League pressed on for statewide I&R. Twelve years later, in 1919, they still came up short of the necessary two-thirds majority of both houses of the legislature.

In the 1960s State Rep. John P. Ferguson of the town of Churchman's Road sponsored an I&R bill, which he reintroduced in every session. By the mid-1970s, as Speaker of the House, he engineered the amendment's passage by a vote of 33 to 1; it then sailed through the state senate (14 to 3). The state constitution, however, required that a constitutional amendment be approved by two-thirds of both houses a *second* time after the next election. This gave opponents, led by Gov. Pierre S. DuPont IV (who did not have the reformist notions of the earlier DuPont), a chance to organize. On 29 March 1979, the house defeated I&R by 22 to 6, ending all hopes for its passage. Ferguson, frustrated by this defeat after so many years of effort, retired.

In 1980 the police and firefighters' unions collected enough signatures to put an Initiative on the ballot in Wilmington, only to be told that there was no longer an Initiative procedure. The legislature had quietly passed a municipal charter law in 1965 that contained no I&R provision, and this law, state courts ruled, superseded the law that had given Wilmington I&R back in 1907!

Between 1907 and 1987, Delawareans voted on only one statewide ballot question, which the legislature put on the ballot in 1984: should the state allow charities to sponsor gambling games to raise money? Voters said "yes," by a 72 percent majority.

DISTRICT OF COLUMBIA

Home rule bills for the District of Columbia with I&R provisions were introduced in Congress in 1912 by Representatives Tavenner of Illinois and Prouty of Iowa, but neither passed; in fact, Congress refused to grant even partial home rule to the District until 1973.

The first serious attempt to put I&R into the District of Columbia's home rule charter was made by D.C. Council Member Julius W. Hobson, Sr., in 1976. Hobson, representing the District's tiny Statehood Party, had been one of the city's leading civil rights activists in the 1960s, but he was known to have little clout on the council. Hobson's I&R bill benefited from the timely arrival in the District in early 1977 of Roger Telschow and John Forster, field organizers of the 1975–1976 Western Bloc anti–nuclear power Initiative campaigns (see Chapter 4).

Along with Lynne Zamil of the local chapter of Americans for Democratic Action, Sam Newman, and a few others, Telschow and Forster collected 1,230 signatures on a petition demanding I&R in just a couple of weeks. They submitted it to council members at a 1 March 1977 committee hearing on the I&R bill.

Hobson, by this time wheelchair-bound and dying of cancer, lived long enough to see his bill approved unanimously in committee on 16 March. He died a week later. In the full council the bill also passed unanimously, and sympathy for Hobson certainly played a role in its passage. But it was not just sympathy: Telschow had organized a campaign of letters and phone calls from constituents urging their council members to approve I&R. The pressure was so effective that some members admitted in private that they opposed I&R but voted for it because of constituent pressure.

Telschow kept the pressure on through the council's final approval of I&R (17 May) and the mayor's signing of the bill (14 June). One hurdle remained: voter ratification of the charter amendment at the November 1977 election. Telschow laid the groundwork for the campaign by collecting written endorsements of the amendment from council members, other officials, community leaders, and groups.

He and Forster then bought an old school bus to be used as a mobile office and a second-hand electric printing press, which they loaded onto the bus. Pulling up to an outdoor electrical outlet in a suburban parking lot, they plugged in the press, printed 20,000 handbills backing the District of Columbia I&R amendment, and drove off before anyone asked them whether they had permission to do this.

Their campaign committee, Initiative D.C., was a shoestring operation. Lacking money for radio ads, Telschow went to the mayor and other prominent elected officials with a tape recorder, and recorded spoken endorsements. Then he rigged a makeshift tape feed by connecting the tape machine to his telephone with alligator clips and wire. With this apparatus he called radio stations a few days before the election, told them about the I&R ballot question, and fed them the recorded endorsements. Radio stations throughout the city broadcast news stories with the voices of the city's top elected officials urging people to vote for I&R. Voters approved I&R by a greater than four to one margin on 7 November 1977.

Of the eight Initiatives that qualified for District of Columbia ballots in the first half of the 1980s, only one made national news: a 1984 ordinance giving homeless people a legal right to overnight shelter. The sponsoring organization, the Community for Creative Non-Violence, had provided food and shelter to Washington's homeless population since the mid-1970s. Led by the charismatic Mitch Snyder, whose work was portrayed in the 1986 made-for-television movie *Samaritan,* CCNV collected over 32,000 signatures—a record for District Initiatives. Most of the signatures were the result of a one-day effort outside polling places during the 1984 presidential primary. Several CCNV workers, including Snyder, collected over a thousand signatures *each* in that single day.

In the fall of 1984, CCNV's Initiative campaign was just one of the group's several ongoing projects, which included finding food donations to feed up to a thousand people a day, a series of protests at the White House, an 800-bed shelter, and a hunger strike by Snyder and others to get federal aid for the District's homeless. The only two CCNV activists working primarily on the Initiative campaign were Mary Ellen Hombs and Steve O'Neill.

On 11 October, less than a month before the election, the District government announced a lawsuit to knock the measure off the ballot—even though it had already been certified as acceptable by the D.C. Board of Elections—on the grounds that the D.C. charter bars Initiatives that make appropriations. The CCNV Initiative, argued the government, would require money to implement and therefore was invalid.

O'Neill and CCNV attorneys persuaded a D.C. Superior Court judge on 24 October to leave the Initiative on the ballot. Mayor Marion Barry, thwarted in his attempt to prevent a vote, now turned to persuading them to vote "no." District government workers printed up thousands of flyers urging a "no" vote and distributed them at the polling places on election day. But Hombs and O'Neill organized an even bigger volunteer effort to hand out "Vote Yes" flyers there. Voters backed the Initiative by a 72 percent majority.

Mayor Barry, instead of bowing to the people's mandate, fought on in court, winning an initial decision against the validity of the Initiative. On 20 May 1986, however, a three-judge panel of the D.C. Court of Appeals ruled unanimously to uphold the CCNV Initiative. And on 9 October U.S. District Judge George H. Revercomb handed down an order barring city officials from spending public funds to take sides in future Initiative campaigns.

D.C. tenants' rights activists in 1985 successfully petitioned for a Referendum on a bill passed by the city council to weaken the city's rent control ordinance. Voters upheld the stronger rent control provisions by a narrow margin of less than a single percentage point—a victory for tenant activists and a defeat for landlords and Mayor Barry.

FLORIDA

Florida's best known Initiative and Referendum backer of the Progressive Era was retired U.S. senator Wilkinson Call. The closest the Florida legislature came to approving statewide I&R was the state senate's passage, in 1912, of a version so restrictive that it would have made it virtually impossible to put an Initiative on the ballot. The senate quickly rescinded even this weak bill.

In the late 1960s, following the transformation of Florida from a southern state to a sunbelt state populated largely by transplanted northerners, the legislature passed an amendment authorizing Initiative constitutional amendments only—not Initiatives or Referendums on statutes. The new provision was successfully employed for the first time in 1976, when Governor Reuben Askew sponsored an Initiative requiring public disclosure of campaign contributions. After the Initiative passed, infuriated state legislators passed bills banning collection of signatures at polling places and imposing a 10-cent-per-signature "verification fee" to further discourage future Initiative proponents.

Both these laws were thrown out as unconstitutional in a 1984 decision by U.S. District Judge William J. Castagna.

GEORGIA

The I&R movement was never a major force in Georgia politics. *Equity* noted in October 1912 that the gubernatorial candidate Hooper Alexander was an I&R backer, and it was in the years 1911–1913, the high-water mark of the Progressive era nationwide, that the Georgia legislature enacted laws granting Initiative, Referendum, and Recall rights to the residents of four cities, including Atlanta.

HAWAII

Hawaii's territorial Democratic Party convention of 1907 passed a resolution favoring I&R, but the territorial government was dominated by anti-Initiative Republicans until the 1950s. After the Democrats gained power, however, most of them turned against I&R, which was not included in the state constitution when Hawaii became a state in 1959. Initiative advocates were narrowly defeated in their attempt to pass an I&R amendment in the state's 1978 constitutional convention.

Until 1982 the county of Honolulu (island of Oahu) allowed Initiative charter amendments, but not ordinances. State Sen. Mary Jane McMurdo, who routinely sponsored bills in the legislature to get statewide I&R (and won approval for one by the state senate in 1987), led a campaign for a Honolulu Initiative charter amendment to authorize citizens to pass ordinances by Initiative. Voters approved it in November 1982 by a 55 percent margin, despite strong opposition from labor unions. Sen. McMurdo then led a drive for an Initiative ordinance to save a block of moderate-income Honolulu apartments that were slated for destruction by high-rise builders. Voters approved this measure in 1984.

In 1986 McMurdo helped place on the ballot another Honolulu Initiative, this one to prevent conversion of Fort DeRussy's 45 acres of mostly open space into a hotel–convention center complex. After a campaign in which pro-development forces spent $200,000, outspending Initiative backers by a ratio of 20 to 1, voters turned it down. In 1988, Senator McMurdo and conservationists sponsored an Initiative to restrict development at Oahu's Sandy Beach. This time, despite a campaign spending advantage by pro-development forces, voters passed the Initiative.

On the island of Kauai, voters approved a 1980 Initiative to stop construction of a hotel-condominium complex at Nukoli'i Beach, but the developer sponsored another Initiative, which passed in 1984, to authorize completion of the half-built project.

IDAHO

There is no better proof that the price of liberty is eternal vigilance than the history of the statewide Initiative process in Idaho. In 1911, swept up in the reformist spirit of the times, the Idaho legislature approved an I&R amendment to the state constitution, which was approved by voters the following year. But the amendment was flawed: it did not set the number of petition signatures needed to qualify an Initiative for the ballot. This meant that the legislature could set the threshold—and change it—at any time. Nor could any Initiative qualify for the ballot until the legislature passed a bill to set the requirement. This the legislature did in 1915, but Gov. Moses Alexander vetoed the bill because he thought the signature requirement unreasonable. Two decades went by before another such bill passed.

The first Initiative to qualify for the ballot was one to establish the state Fish and Game Commission; it gained three to one voter approval in 1938. In 1954, voters passed an anti-pollution Initiative to ban dredge mining in riverbeds.

In 1974, Idahoans voted for greater disclosure of campaign contributions and expenditures. In 1978, they approved a property tax cut Initiative patterned after California's Proposition 13, but the legislature amended it to tilt the benefits toward businesses, not homeowners.

Idaho homeowners regained their property tax cut with another Initiative on the 1982 ballot, at the same time approving a second allowing denture technicians to compete with dentists in the sale and fitting of dentures and a third supporting the development of nuclear power—the only pro-nuclear statewide Initiative ever to pass.

In early 1984, anti-Initiative forces—primarily timber, mining, and farm interests—persuaded their friends in the legislature to double the number of signatures required to put an Initiative on the ballot. Without a hearing, the bill was introduced, voted on, and sent to the governor's desk within 24 hours. Initiative sponsors, however, got to Gov. John Evans first and persuaded him to veto the bill.

ILLINOIS

Illinois's fight for I&R began in 1897, when 250 delegates met in Chicago to form the Direct Legislation Union. The organization secured endorsements for Initiative and Referendum from the state Democratic Party, and from Gov. John Peter Altgeld in an 1899 Labor Day speech.

The state legislature, seeking to defuse the I&R agitation without giving voters any real lawmaking power, in 1901 passed a "Public Opinion Law" allowing citizens to petition to put nonbinding advisory questions on state or city ballots. It restricted this Initiative power further by setting the signature requirement at a different threshold of 10 percent of the registered voters statewide, and a nearly impossible 25 percent in local jurisdictions. Nonetheless, the Initiative advocates reorganized as the Referendum League of Illinois to put important issues on the ballot and elected Dr. Maurice F. Doty of Chicago as their leader.

The League lost no time in employing the advisory petition as a means for citizens to demand real I&R lawmaking rights. The first two advisory Initiatives on the state ballot called for state and local I&R. Both propositions received a landslide 83 percent favorable vote on 4 November 1902.

In 1904 the League sponsored a statewide advisory Initiative calling for primary elections to replace the smoke-filled rooms of nominating conventions. This too passed by a healthy majority, and the League put more advisory Initiatives on the state ballot in succeeding years, calling for enactment of a law to restrict corrupt political practices (backed by 422,000 to 122,000 in 1910) and another law to create a commission to shorten the long, complicated election ballots (also approved). The legislature, however, acted favorably only on the voters' demand for primary elections.

The League put the I&R question on the ballot a second time in 1910. Leaders in this campaign included Harold L. Ickes, who later became secretary of the interior under Franklin D. Roosevelt, and suffragist Dr. Anna E. Blount. Illinoisans again demanded I&R, this time by a resounding 78 percent, but the legislature again ignored the people's wishes.

In the four decades following World War II, only one advisory Initiative qualified for the state ballot: a measure calling for tax reduction, sponsored by Gov. James R. Thompson in 1978. Thompson, running for re-election, was attempting to capitalize on the nationwide popularity of California's tax-cutting Proposition 13, which passed in June of that year. Illinoisans approved the measure and re-elected Thompson, but no tax cuts resulted.

At the local level, the earliest major I&R battle in Illinois began in 1901 when Progressives took on the "traction trust," as the price-gouging, politician-bribing streetcar companies were known. Ray Ginger, in *Altgeld's America* (see Sources following states listing), gives a detailed account of this convoluted campaign. Between 1902, when the Referendum League put a municipal ownership advisory Initiative on the ballot by petition of 140,000 voters, and 1907, Chicagoans voted on five separate ballot questions regarding city takeover of the streetcar lines. The voters consistently endorsed municipal ownership, but were ultimately forced to settle for a compromise that delayed this goal for 20 years and set up a system of city regulation in the interim.

After a final, unsuccessful struggle by Progressives to win passage of a statewide I&R amendment at a 1920 constitutional convention, Initiative activity was infrequent until the Coalition for

Political Honesty's campaigns in the 1970s and 1980s (see Chapter 5).

INDIANA

The movement for I&R came late to Indiana. After Ohioans approved an I&R amendment in November 1912, the Ohio leaders turned their attention to the state next door. Rev. Herbert S. Bigelow, among others, spoke throughout the state and helped organize a pro-I&R Citizens League. Yet a native Indiana reformer assessed the situation gloomily in 1914: "Indiana, politically, is one of the most backward of our States. It must continue to be, under the ironclad restrictions of the present constitution. . . . The state has remained untouched by the progressive movement in the states around it." I&R advocates' only victory came in 1913, when a Public Utilities Act approved by the legislature included a provision allowing municipal Initiatives to mandate municipal purchase and operation of utilities (Public Service Commission Act of 1913, Sect. 8-1-2-99/100 [54-612, 613]).

State Sen. John Bushemi of Gary waged a long, lonely battle in the late 1970s and 1980s to pass a statewide I&R amendment, but he got scant support from other legislators and constituents.

IOWA

In 1904 I&R advocates began making headway with an endorsement from the Prohibitionist Party, followed in 1906 by the support of the Socialists and Populists, and, in 1910, that of the Democrats. Republican State Rep. David E. Kulp's I&R amendment reached the floor of the lower house of the legislature in 1911, but was defeated 58 to 42.

In the election campaign of 1912, both the Republican Party and its offspring, the Progressive Party, endorsed I&R. The 1913 votes in the legislature for I&R were overwhelming: approval was nearly unanimous in the senate, and there were only 11 negative votes in the house. But ratification by the voters had to wait because the state constitution specified that any amendments had to be cleared by the legislature *twice,* in two successive sessions with an election in between. In 1915 the legislature voted against I&R, and the proposed amendment never went to the voters.

KANSAS

Agitation for Initiative and Referendum in Kansas was well under way in 1900, when the Democratic and Populist parties in the state endorsed the idea. In 1909 Initiative supporters won approval of their amendment in the state's lower house, but suffered an overwhelming defeat in the state senate.

In 1911 Gov. W. R. Stubbs called for enactment of an I&R amendment, and by 1913 all the state's major parties had endorsed it, including Kansas' first state conference of women voters. The nationally known progressive leader William Allen White of Emporia was called Kansas' "foremost champion of Direct Legislation" in a contemporary periodical. Despite all this support, I&R backers never came any closer to passing a statewide I&R amendment. They did, however, push through the legislature a bill establishing I&R in all the state's cities in 1909, and a statewide recall amendment in 1914.

KENTUCKY

Populist State Sen. J. H. McConnell of Otter Pond, Kentucky, successfully pushed a statewide I&R bill through the state senate in 1900, but the measure failed in the house. Kentucky Initiative advocates had to settle for a 1910 state law giving most of the state's major cities an Initiative procedure.

By the 1970s this municipal I&R provision (Kentucky Revised Statutes, Ch. 89) applied to all of the state's 27 largest cities, except Louisville. In 1980, however, the provision was abolished when the legislature passed a new municipal government law.

LOUISIANA

Progressive reformers, never a major force in Louisiana politics, failed to pass a statewide Initiative and Referendum amendment, but they did succeed in passing laws providing for municipal I&R (1912) and for recall of statewide elected officers (1914).

In the mid-1970s backers of a rent control Initiative collected the required 10,000 signatures to put it on the New Orleans ballot, only to be barred by a state supreme court ruling that Initiative charter amendments must be related to matters in the existing city charter. In April 1981 voters passed an Initiative to restrict the city council's power to enact flat-rate taxes on real property and motor vehicles.

The biggest New Orleans Initiative battle in recent years, however, was over the city council's power to regulate electric utility rates. The council held this prerogative until 1982, when voters approved the transfer of this authority to the state public service commission. Little more than a year later, the utility company, New Orleans Public Service, Inc. (NOPSI), asked for a huge rate increase to finance the construction of the Grand Gulf nuclear power plant.

Mayor Ernest Morial and Council Members Joseph Giarusso and James Singleton sponsored a 1983 Initiative to regain the council's rate regulation power. Utility company executives and stockholders raised $800,000 for a campaign to defeat it, an unprecedented amount for a New Orleans election campaign. Backers spent only $35,000 and saw a heartbreakingly narrow defeat on 8 November 1983: 78,746 (49.8 percent) in favor, 79,434 against.

They came back with another Initiative a year and a half later. This time the utilities spent $2 million on their "Vote No" advertising blitz, but it did not sway the voters. On 4 May 1985 New Orleans voted by a two to one margin to regain city control of utility rates.

MAINE

In 1908 Maine became the first state east of the Mississippi to adopt a constitutional provision for statewide Initiative and Referendum. It could not have happened without the work of the state's foremost I&R advocate, Roland T. Patten of Skowhegan.

Patten, editor of the Skowhegan *Somerset Reporter,* was, in the early 1890s, an advocate of municipal ownership of public utilities. "About 1894," he wrote, he "heard something of the idea [of I&R] as made use of in Switzerland," and realized that I&R could be used in the cause of municipal ownership.

A member of the Republican Party, he first pushed for adoption of an I&R resolution at the Republican convention in his county. Failing there, he became a leader of the state's Socialist Party and lobbied all four of the state's major parties—Republican, Democratic, Socialist, and Prohibitionist—to endorse I&R. In 1902 Maine Democrats adopted Patten's I&R resolution verbatim, and in 1903 Democratic State Rep. Cyrus W. Davis of Waterville introduced the first statewide I&R bill.

Meanwhile, Patten had founded the Initiative and Referendum League of Maine and allied with the state Grange and the state Federation of Labor. In 1905 they nearly succeeded: the I&R bill got a tie vote in the state senate. The following year all four parties endorsed I&R, and Davis made it a central issue in his Democratic gubernatorial campaign.

Davis lost to Republican William T. Cobb, who was lukewarm on the issue, but the I&R League succeeded in electing more I&R supporters to the legislature. Despite opposition from banks, timberland owners, and railroads, the legislature passed an Initiative bill without a single dissent. However, it was not exactly what the I&R League wanted: it provided for Initiative statutes, but not constitutional amendments. The Republicans, who controlled both houses of the legislature, forced the Initiative advocates to accept this compromise because they feared that an Initiative constitutional amendment might be used to repeal their state's prohibition amendment.

Governor Cobb signed the I&R amendment on 20 March 1907, but it still had to be ratified by popular vote before taking effect. In the 18 months prior to this vote, most of the state's newspapers reiterated their anti-I&R stands in editorials, and Maine's U.S. Senator Hale sent his constituents copies of a vehement anti-I&R speech by Sen. Henry Cabot Lodge of Massachusetts. Nevertheless, I&R won voter approval by a two to one margin on 15 September 1908.

The first Initiative on the state ballot was a victory for the Progressives: a law mandating nomination of state and county candidates by popular vote in primary elections, rather than party conventions. It passed by a greater than three to one margin on 11 September 1911.

Only seven Initiatives were on the ballot during the first 60 years of the Initiative process, and none during the 1950s and 1960s. The only successful one after the 1911 direct primary law was a 1936 statute "to prevent diversions of the general highway fund" (to uses others than highways).

In the 1970s, as in other states, Maine voters rediscovered their Initiative lawmaking power. In 1972 they approved an Initiative to change the ballot forms to eliminate party columns in order to encourage independent consideration of each candidate by voters.

In the 1970s and 1980s, more than half of Maine's Initiatives were on energy and environmental matters. In 1976, voters enacted a beverage container deposit (Bottle Bill) Initiative and established a state park at Bigelow Mountain; in 1980, 1982, and 1987, they turned down proposed Initiatives to ban nuclear power, following massive "Vote No" ad campaigns paid for by the owners of the Maine Yankee nuclear plant. The Maine Nuclear Referendum Committee, sponsors of the nuclear ban Initiatives, won only one campaign: a 1985 Initiative to require a statewide referendum on any plan to dump low-level radioactive waste.

Consumer advocates in 1986 waged a successful battle against the local telephone company to pass an Initiative outlawing local measured service, whereby callers are charged by the minute for local calls. The company had set a campaign spending record with its "Vote No" ads, which featured former U.S. senator (and 1972 presidential candidate) Edmund Muskie.

MARYLAND

By 1900, reformers had organized a Maryland Direct Legislation League, with A. G. Eichelberger as its president. Ten years later the League claimed "more than 1,000 active, working members." In 1914, the League pushed an I&R bill sponsored by State Sen. William J. Odgen of Baltimore, but the legislature amended it to remove the Initiative provision. This "Referendum only" amendment passed both houses in 1915 and was ratified by the voters.

The following year the League pressed the legislature for an Initiative amendment. Their bill passed the senate with only six dissenting votes, but was tabled (effectively killed) in the house by a 66 to 27 vote. Never again did an Initiative amendment come close to approval. Charles J. Ogle, secretary of the League in 1916, attributed the failure to the committee chairmen, "a very active lobby against" the Initiative amendment, and rural legislators' fear of the Baltimore masses.

Since the Referendum amendment was ratified in 1915, it has been used 13 times by citizens to force a statewide popular vote on unpopular laws passed by the legislature. In 1970, voters vetoed the legislature's bill regarding a Department of Economic and Community Development, and in 1972 and 1974, they vetoed state aid to nonpublic schools. All subsequent Referendum petitions, until 1988, failed because of either insufficient signatures or court decisions barring ballot placement. In that year, however, the legislature passed a bill banning cheap handguns, and gun control opponents responded with a petition drive that put the measure on the ballot. Despite a record-breaking $4-million plus "Vote No" campaign sponsored by the National Rifle Association, voters approved the law by a 58-percent margin.

MASSACHUSETTS

Massachusetts' Populist Party in 1895 adopted a resolution calling for statewide Initiative and Referendum. In 1900, State Rep. Henry Stirling introduced one of the first I&R proposals; Socialist State Rep. James Carey introduced another in 1901. In 1905, Mrs. Ella O. Marshall organized the Massachusetts Referendum League to push for I&R, but results were slow in coming.

After a decade of unsuccessful attempts, the Massachusetts Direct Legislation League hired Henry Stirling to organize support for I&R throughout the state. The Progressive and Democratic parties, by now staunch supporters of I&R, used this issue with some success against the Republicans in the electoral campaigns of 1912.

In 1913 the legislature approved a bill establishing a procedure for advisory Initiatives to be placed on the ballot by voters in any of the state's senatorial or representative districts; I&R advocates used the procedure in 1914, 1915, and 1916 to get "straw votes" throughout the state showing public support for I&R.

The first Irish Catholic elected to statewide office in Massachusetts, Gov. David I. Walsh, a Democrat, in 1915 formed the Union for a Progressive Constitution to push for a state constitutional convention to consider various reforms, with I&R as a priority. In 1916 the legislature passed a bill authorizing such a convention, if the voters approved it—which they did, in November 1916.

The convention met in 1917 and passed the I&R amendment by a vote of 163 yeas, 125 nays, and 30 delegates not voting. Conservative opposition to I&R, led by former state attorney general Albert E. Pillsbury of Wellesley and railroad counsel Charles F. Choate of Southborough, was strong enough to force numerous compromises in the final version—compromises that even today make the Massachusetts Initiative procedure the nation's most cumbersome and complicated. Submitted to the voters for ratification on 5 November 1918, the amendment passed by a narrow margin.

The first Initiative to win voter approval was a 1920 measure defining cider and beer as nonintoxicating liquors, and thus exempt from Prohibition. Other successful early Initiatives included measures to end the ban on Sunday sports events (1928), repeal the state's prohibition law (1930), reform candidate nominating procedures (1932), and regulate animal trapping (1930).

On the 1948 ballot was a controversial Initiative to legalize contraceptives, which was opposed by the Catholic Church, and three labor relations measures sponsored by employers and bitterly opposed by organized labor: a "Right to Work" Initiative, a law regulating strikes, and a third measure regarding the election of union officers. The four Initiatives provoked an extraordinarily heavy Democratic turnout, which not only defeated all the Initiatives but swept Republican incumbents out of office. The Democrats gained a majority in Massachusetts' lower house for the first time in the state's history, tipped the balance of power in the senate, and ousted Republican Gov. Robert Bradford. The Initiative that got the most favorable vote, though it still lost, was on the contraceptive issue; 43 percent of the electorate said "yes."

In 1964, voters passed an Initiative statute reducing the powers of the governor's Executive Council. The state's most famous Initiative was the tax-cutting "Proposition $2\frac{1}{2}$" (See Chapter 6). Dog and cat lovers made successful use of the Initiative process in 1983 by proposing a measure to ban research on these animals. The legislature, responding to an Initiative petition signed by a record 145,170 voters, passed the Initiative in December of that year, thus eliminating the need for it to go on the 1984 ballot.

A 1986 Initiative mandating cleanup of toxic waste dumps, sponsored by the Massachusetts Public Interest Research Group (Mass-PIRG), became the most popular Initiative in the state's history, garnering 73 percent approval.

MICHIGAN

Agitation for Initiative and Referendum in Michigan started with the formation of the state's Direct Legislation Club in 1895 by George F. Sherman and David Inglis, both Detroit physicians. Inglis was 45 years old, a distinguished professor at the Detroit Medical College. Sherman and Inglis led I&R efforts in Michigan for over a decade without success, despite support from the noted reformer, Detroit mayor, and later Michigan governor Hazen S. Pingree. In 1900 S. D. Williams of Battle Creek cited the legislature's Republican majority as the major obstacle.

The reformers won passage of an I&R amendment at the state constitutional convention of 1907. It was ratified by the voters in 1908, but the victory turned out to be hollow. The amendment proved so restrictive that citizens were unable to place a single Initiative on the ballot.

Michigan I&R advocates resumed lobbying the legislature for a better amendment and gained the support of Gov. Chase S. Osborn, a Progressive elected in 1910. The legislature initially rejected Osborn's plea, but relented in 1913 during the administration of Governor Ferris, another I&R supporter.

Under the new provisions, it took 39,000 signatures to put a constitutional amendment Initiative on the 1914 ballot. The first two Initiatives to win voter approval, however, were on the ballot in 1932: a measure to establish a liquor control commission passed overwhelmingly, and an amendment to limit property taxes won 51.1 percent of the vote.

In 1938, voters passed an amendment to make sure that gas and vehicle weight taxes were used for roads and streets; the following year, in an April special election, they approved a system for the nonpartisan election of judges. In 1946, voters enacted an Initiative to ensure that part of the state's sales tax revenues were returned to the municipalities; in 1948, they modified the property tax limitation.

The Initiative for which Michigan is most famous is the Bottle Bill, approved by a two to one margin in 1976, that put a 10-cent deposit on bottles and cans.

MINNESOTA

The Minnesota legislature in 1897 struck a death-blow to the Initiative process without meaning to. The legislators' actual objective was to block passage of a Prohibition amendment, which was bitterly opposed by brewery interests. In 1897 the question of Initiative and Referendum had not even been seriously discussed. It was still two years before Gov. John Lind called for I&R in his message to the legislature, and eight years before the Minnesota suffragist Mrs. Eugenia Farmer helped found the state's I&R League.

The 1897 "Brewer's Amendment," sponsored by state representative (and Hamm Brewing Co. attorney) W. W. Dunn, proposed changing the ratification threshold for state constitutional amendments: instead of requiring ratification by majority popular vote *of those voting on each individual amendment,* as was then the case (and is now the case in most states), they would require a majority of *all votes cast in the election.* In effect, under this system those who do not vote on a particular question are counted as voting against it.

Dunn's amendment passed both houses and was placed on the ballot for ratification by the voters in 1898. The amendment could not have passed under its own standard for voter ratification, but it did pass under the old standard. Of those who voted on the question, 68 percent favored it—but less than one-third of those voting in the election voted on this question.

The first Minnesota I&R amendment to get through the legislature was on the ballot in 1914 and was approved by a three to one margin, but lost because the "yes" votes were still less than a majority of all the votes cast in the election. In 1916, the legislature passed an I&R amendment again, and voters supported it by a margin of nearly four to one, but those voting in favor turned out to be only 45 percent of all voters at the polls, so it lost again. The Progressives decided the following year that the "supermajority" requirement was an "unsurmountable obstacle," and apparently gave up.

Sixty years later, the newly elected liberal State Sen. Robert Benedict of Bloomington renewed the fight for statewide Initiative. By late April 1978 the three leading candidates in that year's gubernatorial election had endorsed I&R—but trouble for the amendment was brewing elsewhere. On 25 April, in a special state election in St. Paul, voters approved an Initiative to repeal a city ordinance banning discrimination on the basis of "affectional or sexual preference"—a stunning defeat for gay rights advocates and the entire liberal community. Christian fundamentalists sponsoring the Initiative had shrewdly petitioned for a low-turnout special election; such elections tend to favor conservatives, who turn out to vote in greater numbers than liberals.

Republican Al Quie, elected governor in 1978, made I&R the centerpiece of his legislative agenda and by April 1980 had pushed it through the legislature. The state senate approved it 47 to 13; in the house the vote was 86 to 47.

Lobbyists and attorneys for the beverage industry were the first to organize a campaign against voter ratification of the I&R amendment. Just as in 1897, they wanted to prevent Minnesotans from voting on *any* Initiative that might qualify for the ballot, in order to ensure that one specific proposal—in this case, a Bottle Bill—could never pass. The industry lobbyists maintained a low profile and encouraged allies from liberal groups (who were upset about the 1978 gay rights vote in St. Paul) to lead the "Vote No" campaign.

The opposition group was co-chaired by Wayne Popham, a former Republican state senator and vice president of the Minneapolis Chamber of Commerce, and Treva Kahl, who headed the state AFL-CIO's political department. Popham's group made Harriette Burkhalter, president of the state League of Woman Voters, the most visible anti-I&R spokesperson.

On 4 November 1980 the election returns showed 53.2 percent in favor and 46.8 percent against—not enough to win. Of the total who turned out to vote, 12 percent had failed to mark "yes" or "no" on I&R. With these added to the "no" side, the amendment lost.

Former governor Elmer Anderson and Governor Quie had run a lackluster pro-Initiative campaign, but a University of Minnesota political scientist, Charles H. Backstrom, identified another reason for the loss: many voters failed to cast ballots on the I&R question because they were not tall enough to see it on their voting machines. This factor alone, Backstrom found, could have changed the outcome of the election.

The long-dead legislators of 1897, combined with a voting machine arrangement designed for tall people, defeated the efforts of Minnesotans to get I&R.

MISSISSIPPI

Mississippi is the only state that once had a statewide Initiative process but lost it—not because the people rejected it, but because the state supreme court in 1922 decided on the basis of a legal technicality to throw the I&R provision out of the state constitution.

Agitation for I&R in Mississippi achieved partial success for the first time in 1912, the peak year for I&R success nationwide. Mississipians approved an I&R amendment by a nearly two to one margin, but the measure failed because of the state's requirement that a "supermajority" of all votes cast in the election, rather than a simple majority of votes on the I&R question, ratify it. This was the same requirement that defeated Minnesota's I&R amendment three times.

In Mississippi, after the initial defeat, I&R forces under the leadership of State Reps. N. A. Mott of Yazoo City and Frank Burkitt of Okalona succeeded in pushing their proposal through the legislature a second time, and it was on the ballot again in 1914. This time it passed by a *greater* than two to one margin, though it barely squeaked by the supermajority requirement.

In 1916 voters successfully petitioned for a Referendum on a bill passed by the legislature appointing a certain Z. A. Brantley to the office of game and fish commissioner, and then rejected the law by popular vote. Brantley took the case to court, charging that the I&R amendment was not valid.

On 26 March 1917 the state supreme court upheld the Referendum and the I&R process (*State* v. *Brantley,* 113 Miss. 786, 74 South, 662, Ann. Cas. 1917E, 723). An elated Assistant Attorney General Lamar F. Easterling, who defended the I&R process in the case, wrote the following day that the decision "settles the matter finally in this state."

Easterling's assessment proved premature. Five years later, a citizen group backing an Initiative to change the salary of the state revenue agent turned in petition signatures sufficient to qualify the measure for the November 1922 ballot. Stokes V. Robertson, the revenue agent, went to court to prevent ballot placement, again attacking the validity of the I&R amendment.

The state supreme court, reversing its 1917 judgment, held that Initiatives or Referendums on statutes are one thing, but Initiative constitutional amendments are another, and thus the constitutional Initiative power should have been approved in 1914 in a separate amendment. And because it was not, the entire I&R provision was held unconstitutional. The court abolished the people's right to self-government by I&R, finding that: "The Constitution is the product of the people in their sovereign capacity. It was intended primarily to secure the rights of the people against the encroachments of the legislative branch of the government" (*Power v. Robertson*, 130 Miss. 188, 93 So. 769). In effect, the court said that it had to destroy the people's rights to self-government in order to save them. The legislature could have remedied the situation by approving two new amendments, one covering statutory, and the other constitutional, Initiatives. But it took no such action.

For over half a century, the issue lay dormant, until in 1977 Upton Sisson of Gulfport took up the cause of I&R. Sisson, who served as state representative from 1956 to 1960, was a civil rights attorney who had argued one of the landmark "one man, one vote" reapportionment cases in the U.S. Supreme Court. At age 70 and in failing health, Sisson returned to the legislature to lobby for I&R.

Although unsuccessful, his efforts sparked enough interest in the subject that State Attorney General Bill Allain, running for governor in 1983, pledged to work for passage of an I&R amendment if elected. Allain won, but as of 1988 Mississippians were still waiting for him to make good on his promise.

MISSOURI

Initiative and Referendum became part of Missouri's constitution primarily as the result of a decade of work by three people: St. Louis attorney Silas L. Moser, William Preston Hill, M.D., Ph.D., and Anna Beard, Dr. Hill's assistant.

Moser, as president of the Missouri Direct Legislation League, brought an I&R bill to a vote in the lower house of the state legislature in 1900. A majority of legislators wanted to be recorded as voting in favor of it—which is not to say that it passed, for after the roll call showed a majority in favor, enough legislators switched their votes to make the bill lose by one vote. In 1904 the legislature approved I&R, but Missouri voters rejected it by a 53,000-vote margin.

Refusing to accept defeat, the I&R leaders persuaded the legislature to pass another I&R amendment in 1907. To avoid a repeat of the 1904 disaster, they embarked on a year-long voter education campaign. They engaged the Illinois Progressive leader John Z. White to criss-cross the state making four speeches a week for the entire year before the vote. Dr. Hill prepared a three-piece mailer and sent it to all 60,000 names listed in telephone directories throughout the state. The effort paid off when Missouri's voters backed I&R by a 35,868-vote majority.

Missouri's most notable Initiative was probably the 1940 constitutional amendment to establish a nonpartisan system for the nomination, appointment, and retention elections of judges. This was copied by several states and is now known as the "Missouri Plan" for judicial selection.

The first Initiative to pass was a 1920 statute requiring that a new state constitution be drawn up. The next was a 1924 measure to provide funding for the maintenance and construction of the state's highways, followed in 1928 by a $75 million bond issue for further construction. Also approved in 1924 was an Initiative to allow voters in the city of St. Louis and St. Louis County to consolidate their local governments.

In the 1930s Missouri voters enacted Initiatives to allow public employee benefits and to create a Conservation Commission to manage fish, game, and forest resources.

MONTANA

Montana's Populist governor Robert B. Smith, elected in 1896, and his successor, Joseph K. Toole, elected in 1900, both called for I&R, but neither made much headway until December 1903, when the reformer F. Augustus Heinze organized an "Anti-Trust Democratic Party" and an "Anti-Trust Republican Party." These groups, combining their efforts with those of the very vocal "seven or eight men" from the state's Direct Legislation League, were able to push an I&R amendment through the legislature. The bill did not include the right to pass state constitutional amendments by Initiative.

The I&R amendment, on the 1906 ballot, won by a six to one margin, including majorities in every single county. Montanans added the right of constitutional Initiative to their constitution at the 1972 state constitutional convention, 66 years later.

Montanans first used I&R in 1912, when voters approved four out of four Initiatives on the ballot. One required primary elections to nominate state and local candidates; the second established a presidential preference primary; a third called for direct election of U.S. senators; and the fourth limited candidates' campaign expenditures.

The reformers' goal for the 1912 election, which was to "Put the Amalgamated [Copper Company] out of Montana politics," proved to be an elusive one. The legislature and the governors of the World War I era continued to do the company's bidding. Even after the election of Joseph M. Dixon as governor in 1920, a victory for the reformers, Amalgamated continued to dominate the legislature. Near the end of his term, Dixon and the reformers turned to the Initiative process.

Dixon selected as his key issue the undertaxing of Amalgamated: in 1922 the production of Montana's metal mines was $20 million, but the state got less than seven-hundredths of one percent of that in taxes. To remedy the situation, Dixon drew up Initiative 28, which proposed no taxes on mines with annual production of $100,000 or less, but taxed larger mines at up to 1 percent of the value of their production. The Initiative qualified for the ballot in 1924, the same year Dixon was up for re-election.

During that campaign, observed K. Ross Toole in his history of Montana, "The people heard little from Dixon himself because he had no medium for expression. The press was controlled [by Amalgamated], and there were no radios." Amalgamated

attacked Dixon's policies and Dixon himself, and they defeated him by a plurality of 15,000 votes. But in their attacks on Dixon they overlooked Initiative 28, and it passed. . . . A year later, under the new tax, called confiscatory and ruinous by the Company, its net profit for 1925 was . . . nearly three times its net for 1924. And the state of Montana . . . received $300,000.

This was 22 times as much as the $13,559 the state took in from its metal mines tax prior to the Initiative. Toole considered Initiative 28 the most significant reform won by Montana's Progressive movement.

In 1920, voters approved a 1.5 mill property tax for maintenance of the state university, and on the same ballot passed an Initiative issuing $5 million in bonds to fund school construction. In 1926, they passed a three-cent-per-gallon gasoline tax to fund road construction, and they approved more highway funding in a 1938 Initiative vote.

NEBRASKA

Nebraska's legislature in 1897 became the first in the nation to pass a bill allowing Initiative and Referendum—but only in municipalities, not on the state level. This bill was the Sheldon-Geiser Act, sponsored by state legislator A. E. Sheldon.

Walter Breen of Omaha led early efforts for I&R in Nebraska. Breen, a native of London, emigrated to the United States at age 17 and lived in Lincoln, Nebraska, before settling in Omaha. He became a successful real estate salesman and was among the initial organizers of the Populist Party. By 1897 he had become secretary of the Omaha Direct Legislation League, as well as a member of the seven-man executive committee of the National Direct Legislation League—all by the age of 30.

Since Nebraska did not have prohibition, the prohibitionists favored I&R, but liquor interests blocked it until 1911. I&R finally made it through the legislature with the support of the orator and presidential candidate William Jennings Bryan, H. Mockett, Jr., president of the Nebraska Direct Legislation League, and Prof. F. E. Howard of the state university. Bryan, who spoke on behalf of I&R throughout the nation, wrote in a 1909 letter: "I know of nothing that will do more than I&R to restore government to the hands of the people and keep it within their control."

In 1912 Nebraska voters approved I&R by a thirteen to one margin. It helped that under Nebraska's constitutional amendment ratification procedure, blank ballots were counted as "yes" votes— the opposite of the system that doomed I&R in Minnesota.

Nebraska's most famous Initiative was the successful 1934 amendment to create the nation's only unicameral state legislative body. U.S. Sen. George Norris, who is best known for his bill creating the Tennessee Valley Authority, led the unicameral campaign. Another highlight of Nebraska Initiative history was the passage, in 1982, of a constitutional amendment prohibiting farm buy-outs by corporations—the toughest statewide anti–corporate farm legislation in the nation.

Nebraskans have been infrequent Initiative users, placing only 27 such measures on state ballots in 70 years—an average of less than one per election. The first was a 1914 women's suffrage Initiative, defeated by a 52.4 percent negative vote of the then-all-male electorate. Nebraskans in 1930 approved authorization for municipally owned electric utilities to extend their lines. In 1966 they voted by a narrow margin to prohibit property taxes.

NEVADA

The Nevada legislature approved, and voters ratified by a five to one margin in 1905, an amendment giving themselves a statewide Referendum power. The Initiative came later.

By 1909 Initiative backers included acting governor Denver S. Dickerson and U.S. Sen. Francis G. Newlands, architect of the Newlands Reclamation Act of 1901, which set up the federal Bureau of Reclamation and provided for construction of dams and canals to irrigate the arid lands of the western states. The amendment passed the legislature and was approved by Nevada voters in 1912.

The first Initiative to pass was a prohibition statute, approved by a 59 percent majority in 1918. In 1922, a change in the divorce law was initiated by petition, sparking the legislature to place its own alternative on the ballot also. The legislature's version passed, and the Initiative lost. In 1936, Nevadans rejected by a nearly three to one margin a pension Initiative, but changed their minds eight years later, approving by a 53.5 percent margin another Initiative to increase the state's old-age benefits. During the 1950s business interests and labor unions clashed in three successive elections over the "Right to Work" issue. The loser in all three battles was organized labor.

The battle began in 1952, when voters approved a "Right to Work" measure by a slim 50.7 percent margin. Labor unions fought back with a 1954 Initiative to repeal the new law; Nevadans rebuffed it by a narrow 51.4 percent margin. A second union-spon-sored repeal Initiative on the 1956 ballot was rejected by a 53.9 percent margin. Another union-backed Initiative on the same ballot sought to amend the state constitution to prohibit "Right to Work" laws, but was rejected by an even more decisive 57 percent margin.

In 1958, business interests responded with their own Initiative to end the dispute in employers' favor, simply by making it more difficult to put Initiatives on the ballot, and more difficult to pass them. Approved by a 61.9 percent majority, the new provision required that Initiative petitions meet signature quotas in three-quarters of the state's 75 counties. No more could Initiative proponents get all the signatures they needed from the heavily populated Las Vegas and Reno areas. Another new requirement specified that Initiative constitutional amendments be approved by voters twice, in two successive elections, before taking effect. Nevada is the only state with such a requirement. These procedures proved so discouraging that it was 18 years before another Initiative qualified for the state ballot.

In 1982 an Initiative spurred the legislature to pass a bill creating a consumer advocate's office to deal with utility matters. Both measures were on the ballot, but Initiative sponsors liked the legislature's version so much that they campaigned against their own! Not surprisingly, the legislature's measure won voter approval.

NEW HAMPSHIRE

Initiative and Referendum advocates were defeated at New Hampshire's 1902 constitutional convention by an overwhelming 250 to 40 vote of the delegates. George H. Duncan of East Joffrey, secretary of the New Hampshire Direct Legislation League in 1912, led an effort to pass I&R at the next state constitutional convention, but lost again by a 166 to 156 vote. Duncan attributed the defeat to the fact that "officials of the Concord and Montreal Railroad, a subsidiary of the Boston and Maine [Railroad], were using railroad money to defeat us."

NEW JERSEY

It is ironic that New Jersey, the state where the national Initiative and Referendum movement originated (see Chapter 1), never adopted provisions for I&R. Certainly it was not for lack of enthusiasm among New Jersey's I&R supporters, including AFL founder Samuel Gompers. At that time the New Jersey branch of the federation, which endorsed I&R, represented 20,000 workers.

In December 1900 the *Direct Legislation Record* published the gloomy prediction of Clarence T. Atkinson that the reform had "no chance of success until the evil of bribery is abolished." By 1907, after 14 years of effort, the New Jersey Direct Legislation League had despaired of passing an amendment to give voters actual lawmaking power and instead sponsored a bill allowing voters to put nonbinding, advisory Initiatives on the state ballot. That proposal too failed again and again. In 1911 the I&R movement's journal *Equity* explained New Jersey's failure in terms of its being "the Trust State"–the nation's biggest businesses were chartered there, and they were the major source of opposition to I&R.

A second attempt to adopt I&R was made at the state's 1947 constitutional convention, strongly backed by organized labor, but again without success. Interest revived, however, during the mid-1970s, when the state chapters of Common Cause and the League of Women Voters began supporting I&R.

Initiative advocates in 1981 won state senate approval of an I&R bill by a 30 to 3 vote, but Democratic Party leaders in the assembly kept the bill bottled up in committee. In 1983, the same thing happened: 32 to 4 approval in the senate; no vote at all in the assembly. In 1986, I&R advocates, led by Republican assemblyman (and former state Common Cause director) Richard Zimmer, pushed their bill through the assembly for the first time, but lost in the senate.

NEW MEXICO

In 1910 statehood was just around the corner, and New Mexicans elected delegates to a convention that drew up a constitution for the proposed new state.

Of the 100 delegates, Initiative and Referendum supporters included 23 Democrats, 19 Democrat-Populist "Fusionists," and at least a dozen independent Republicans—a majority of at least 54 percent. The *Albuquerque Journal* noted, however, that "every one of the candidates whom the *Journal* attacked as bosses, railroad attorneys, and corporation lawyers have [*sic*] been elected to the Constitutional Convention."

The Republican Party, which dominated the convention with 58 delegates, set up procedures so that its leaders—the anti-I&R "Old Guard"—ran the meeting. The independent Republicans were enticed to drop their push for I&R by a promise of support for their pet proposal, a constitutional provision mandating popular election of state supreme court justices and corporation commissioners. Once this was done, the Democrats and Fusionists knew that the Republican leaders could prevent I&R from even coming up for a vote. Rather than lose on *both* Initiative and Referendum, the Democrats and Fusionists decided to drop Initiative and push for a Referendum provision alone.

The Referendum provision passed by a vote of 65 to 25 in October 1910. A month later the convention approved the entire constitution, which was then sent to the voters for ratification. It passed, though there was much public dissatisfaction with the lack of an Initiative provision.

George Judson King, a leader of the national I&R movement who visited New Mexico while the convention was in progress, described the situation as typical: "It is the same story here as in every state, people for it, corporations against it, politicians trying to straddle the issue and save their scalps."

Between 1912 and 1988 only two Referendums qualified for the ballot (in 1950 and 1964). Both were sponsored by citizen groups seeking to overrule laws regarding state nominating conventions. In both cases the majority of voters cast their ballots to uphold the enactments of the legislature.

NEW YORK

The I&R movement organ *Equity* in 1911 explained the failure to win Initiative and Referendum rights in New York:

> No Direct Legislationist has expected New York State to come into the fold until about the last. The 'interests' are so strong, so thoroly intrenched [sic], and have so much at stake in that state, that it is expected that their strongest fight against real popular control of public affairs will be made there.

In 1907 the attorney and "prominent club woman" Mrs. Harriet M. Johnston-Wood of New York City had helped organize the state

Direct Legislation League. Hamilton Holt was elected President of the group. The League proved ineffective. In July 1909 *Equity* reported: "The introduction of I&R in the New York legislature seems to have been taken as a joke. It was referred to committee, and we find no other allusion to it."

In 1914 *Equity* told its readers that Tammany Hall's recent electoral defeat should help I&R, but later reported that despite the decline of New York City's machine, "the legislature in Albany was still sufficiently in the control of reactionary leaders not to take any definite action in favor of I&R."

By mid-1917 Buffalo's Referendum provision was the only example of direct legislation in the state. Over the years the legislature proved willing to allow limited I&R in local jurisdictions, but never at the statewide level. The most important such I&R provision is the section of the New York City charter that allows voters to propose a charter amendment by petition of 50,000 registered voters—about 2 percent of the city's voters.

It was last successfully used in 1966 when police officers petitioned for—and voters approved—an amendment giving the police more control over the Civilian Review Board that had been set up to investigate citizens' complaints about the police. New Yorkers petitioned in the late 1960s for an anti–Vietnam War Initiative and, in 1985, for an Initiative to prohibit harboring ships with nuclear weapons, but state courts ruled against ballot placement on the ground that these were not proper subjects to go into the city charter.

NORTH CAROLINA

Though unsuccessful at the state level, Initiative and Referendum backers managed by 1917 to persuade the legislature to grant local I&R powers to the citizens of nine North Carolina cities.

In 1977 voters in Charlotte passed an Initiative sponsored by civil rights activists to change the system of at-large city council elections (which had previously guaranteed domination of the council by white businessmen) to one of district representation. In Wilmington, voters put an Initiative on the ballot for the first time in a special election held 29 June 1982. By a nearly two to one margin, they approved an ordinance to change the zoning laws to prohibit construction of a planned coal storage facility.

NORTH DAKOTA

The father of the North Dakota Initiative process was L. A. Ueland of Edgely, a state legislator who served on the executive committee of the National Direct Legislation League from its founding in 1896. If Ueland was the father, however, Katherine King of McKenzie was the midwife. Mrs. King, married to Royal V. King, in 1902 organized a state chapter of the League. Mrs. King's League won passage of Ueland's I&R bill through both houses of the legislature in 1907, despite opposition from prohibitionists, who feared the possibility of an Initiative to repeal the state's anti-liquor amendment.

The 1907 I&R amendment needed approval by the legislature twice, in two successive sessions with an election in between. In 1909 the legislature reversed itself and killed I&R. Mrs. King and Ueland pressed on nonetheless, and won the necessary legislative approvals in 1911 and 1913. The I&R amendment finally went to the voters for ratification in 1914 and passed.

The watershed event in North Dakota's century of statehood was the agrarian revolt of 1915–1916, which spawned the Non-partisan League, one of the most successful state-level reform organizations in the nation's history. In that revolt, which was dramatized in the 1979 movie *Northern Lights,* farmers united against an unresponsive state government controlled by banks, railroads, and big grain dealers.

The League put seven constitutional amendment Initiatives on the 1918 ballot. All seven passed by similar majorities of about 58 percent. Taken together, they brought about a revolutionary change in state government by

• Reducing the number of signatures required for Initiative petitions
• Forbidding the legislature to exempt any bills from Referendum petitions
• Abolishing the requirement that proposed constitutional amendments be approved in two successive legislatures (in favor of a single approval)
• Authorizing the legislature to classify personal property for purposes of tax exemptions
• Authorizing the legislature to impose an acreage tax on land to ensure crops against hail damage

• Authorizing the state to issue up to $10 million in bonds rather than the existing $200,000 limit; allowing mortgages on state industries

• Authorizing the state, counties, and cities to engage in business activities, thus clearing the way for bills that set up the state-owned bank, mill, and grain elevator, which continue to operate to the present day. Considered "socialistic" enterprises by critics, they provided a model for President Franklin D. Roosevelt's Tennessee Valley Authority.

Bankers and grain dealers sponsored an Initiative backlash against the state-owned industries in 1920, gaining voter approval of measures requiring public audits of such industries, banning real estate loans by the state bank, and limiting state bank deposits to the assets of the state, rather than including local governments' assets. But North Dakotans in 1921 defeated four Initiatives to further restrict the operations of state-owned industries, including one that would have abolished the state bank outright. In 1922 voters again confirmed their support for the state bank by approving an Initiative doubling the state's bonded indebtedness limit so that the bank could make more farm loans.

A state record of 18 Initiatives qualified for the ballot in 1932. Among the measures passed by voters were Initiatives reducing property taxes, prohibiting crop mortgages, banning corporations from farming, reducing salaries of judges and state and local elected and appointed officials, reducing officials' travel expenses, and abolishing the requirement of published, public notice regarding auction of land to pay delinquent taxes.

In 1938, North Dakotans passed an Initiative providing for pensions for senior citizens, and in 1940, they approved measures earmarking sales tax revenues for schools and welfare and increasing funding for financially distressed schools. In 1944, the voters initiated over $12 million worth of bonds to match federal funds for highway construction, and in 1948, they voted to ban parking meters. Notable Initiatives passed in the 1950s include a conflict-of-interest measure prohibiting legislators from doing over $10,000 worth of business annually with the state or local governments (1954), and an Initiative that set up a $1 million college student loan fund from state bank profits (1955). In 1962 voters struck a blow for ballot-box freedom by passing an Initiative abolishing the requirement that they publicly state their party affiliation when they vote.

In 1963 Robert P. McCarney, a Bismarck auto dealer, sponsored three petitions for Referendums to block tax increase bills just approved by the legislature. Although the state's voters upheld each of the bills, McCarney was not about to give up. Years earlier, as chauffeur to Non-partisan League Governor (and later U.S. senator) William ("Wild Bill") Langer, McCarney had learned the value of tenacity in politics. Over the next 17 years, he sponsored 10 successful petition drives for Initiatives or Referendums on tax issues. In 1978 his Initiative to lower the North Dakota income tax on individuals, but raise it for corporations, won—the capstone of his activist career. It is still said in state government circles that North Dakota's tax structure is more a product of McCarney than of the legislature.

In 1980, before he was elected to Congress, Byron Dorgan sponsored an Initiative to more than double the tax on oil production (from 5 percent to 11.5 percent). Despite strong opposition from oil companies, it passed with 56 percent of the vote.

The other most hotly contested Initiative of the state's recent history was a 1978 measure to establish a state agency to regulate health care costs. Sponsored by state Insurance Commissioner Byron Knudsen, it provoked intense opposition from hospitals' and doctors' organizations, which raised $175,000 for the effort—a huge amount by North Dakota standards. Voters rejected the Initiative by a three to one margin.

OHIO

When the founding convention of the National Direct Legislation League met in St. Louis in 1896, it elected 56 vice presidents, of whom four were Ohioans. None of the other 36 states represented provided so many.

The leader who guided Ohio Initiative and Referendum forces to victory was the Reverend Herbert S. Bigelow of Cincinnati's Vine Street Congregational Church. Church members disapproving of his political work quit in droves; his salary diminished to the point that he and his wife had to take in boarders to make ends meet. When he invited the I&R advocate and prohibitionist R. S. Thompson to speak to the congregation, the church's trustees locked the doors. Later, the trustees filed formal charges of heresy against Bigelow before a church court, but he was never tried. Eventually, Bigelow's supporters won control of the board of trustees and helped him make Vine Street a nerve center of the state's Progressive movement.

When the Ohio state senate approved an I&R amendment in 1906, Bigelow sensed that success was near and took a leave of absence from the church, with his congregation's consent, to work full time for I&R, "for a time, perhaps two or three years." In 1908, despite opposition from Governor Grosvenor, "the well-known machine representative," (as *Equity* called him), the I&R bill passed both houses, but was killed by legislators voting secretly in a conference committee. I&R backers charged that "the Republican bosses and their tools in the state senate" were responsible.

The Progressives finally got their I&R amendment, not through the legislature, but in a state constitutional convention, along with some 41 other amendments, which were submitted for voter approval in a special election held 3 September 1912. A contemporary account of the campaign called it

> the most bitter and momentous struggle known in the state for a generation. Every ruse and trick known to Big Business politicians was employed to frighten the people of Ohio from adopting the I&R. The whole corporate power of the state backed by Wall Street money and influence was thrown into the fight. The Catholic Church stood against the people's power measures and issued printed instructions to their members, at the Sunday services, on how to vote.
>
> The fight for the I&R and other vitally important amendments was led by [Reverend] Bigelow, ably assisted by Mayor [Brand] Whitlock of Toledo, [and] Mayor Baker of Cleveland.

The I&R amendment passed with 57.5 percent of the vote.

The first Initiatives to win voter approval were a prohibition measure and a law, later ruled unconstitutional, to allow voters to veto the legislature's ratification of a federal constitutional amendment (1918).

Voters in 1933 approved aid to the aged, and, in 1936, overwhelmingly passed an Initiative banning taxes on food. In 1949 they dealt a serious blow to political machines in the state, abolishing the voting-booth system of electing an entire party slate of candidates with the flick of a single lever. Henceforth, voters decided the merits of each candidate independently.

During the next 39 years, voters rejected all but one Initiative put before them. The exception was a 1977 vote to repeal a law, approved only months previously by the legislature, that allowed people to register to vote at the polls on election day.

OKLAHOMA

Oklahoma's earliest Initiative and Referendum advocate was Theodore L. Sturgis of Perry, who founded the territory's Direct Legislation League in 1899—eight years prior to statehood. The I&R movement soon picked up a formidable champion: Robert Latham Owen, who became the state's U.S. senator. Through the efforts of Sturgis' growing League, 102 of the 112 delegates elected in 1906 to Oklahoma's founding constitutional convention were committed in writing to supporting I&R. In early 1907 the convention voted 80 to 5 to include I&R in the constitution. Oklahoma's I&R provision, however, contained a quirk that was to cause Initiative proponents endless headaches: it required that for any ballot measure to pass, it must be approved not just by a majority of the ballots cast on the proposition, but by a majority of all ballots cast in the election.

The state's first successful Initiative, on the ballot in a 11 June 1910 special election, proposed two questions in one: (1) Shall a permanent state capitol be established, and (2) if "yes" on the first, shall the capitol be at (a) Guthrie, (b) Oklahoma City, or (c) Shawnee? It passed, and voters chose Oklahoma City by a wide margin, but the state supreme court overruled their decision owing to the ballot's deviation from the single-question, "yes or no" norm. Nevertheless, Oklahoma City ultimately became the permanent state capital.

In the August 1910 primary, Oklahomans passed an Initiative requiring a literacy test as a qualification for voting, and including a "grandfather clause" making it apply solely to blacks. The U.S. Supreme Court (223 U.S. 347) struck down the measure as unconstitutional. Yet the election had been unfair for another reason as well: racist state officials, instead of printing "yes" and "no" on ballots, printed in small type: "For the amendment." Anyone wishing to vote against it was supposed to scratch out those words with a pencil. If they left their ballot as it was, it was counted as a vote in favor. In some precincts voters were not even provided with pencils. Casting further doubt on the accuracy of the 1910 vote count was a "literacy test" measure placed on the ballot by the legislature in the 1916 primary, six years later: voters rejected it by a 59 percent margin.

On the 1910 ballot they rejected an Initiative to allow liquor sales in cities, Oklahoma having prohibited them in its original constitution. It was the first of several prohibition-repeal Initiatives. The Oklahoma humorist Will Rogers would later say that "Oklahomans vote dry as long as they can stagger to the polls." Indeed, liquor was so plentiful that voters in 1914 passed an Initiative to make "drunkenness and excessive use of intoxicating liquors" cause for impeachment of elected officials.

In 1912 majorities of voters favored one Initiative to require direct election (by the people, instead of by state legislators) of U.S. senators, and another to move the state capital to Guthrie. The first was superseded by passage of the Seventeenth Amendment to the U.S. Constitution, ratified the following year; the second failed to win a majority of all ballots cast in the election.

The saddest victim of the supermajority requirement was the 1914 gubernatorial candidate Charles West, who sponsored four Initiatives: one to reduce the number of appellate courts, a second to reduce the property tax by 29 percent, a third to tax oil and gas production, and a fourth to abolish the state senate, thereby creating a unicameral legislature. All four garnered majorities of ballots cast on each proposition, but not majorities of the total cast in the election—and therefore failed.

In 1916 this unfair requirement brought down two more Initiatives, to the chagrin of their Socialist sponsors. Ironically, the measures were designed to ensure the fairness of elections. One proposed voting registration procedures; the other would have created a state election board composed of three members, one appointed by each of the state's three major political parties (the Socialists were the third-largest party at that time).

In the 1920s corruption in state government prompted an Initiative to establish a procedure to convene the legislature promptly to investigate such problems; it passed by a nearly three to one margin but was thrown out by the state supreme court, which ruled that it was not the proper subject of a constitutional amendment. When the court threw out a 1926 Initiative that would have established a procedure for contesting property tax levies, however, sponsors persisted: they rewrote their Initiative in conformance to the court's complaints, and voters passed it the second time in 1928 by a nearly five to one margin.

The Great Depression hit Oklahoma hard, and Oklahomans turned to the Initiative process to propose economic reforms. Among these were a 1935 Initiative establishing a state welfare program and appropriating $2.5 million in relief for it (passed by a 65 percent margin); a 1936 Initiative increasing the automobile tag and sales taxes to provide assistance to needy elderly and disabled persons and children (approved by a 60 percent margin); and a 1936 constitutional amendment authorizing the latter Initiative statute (passed by a 62 percent margin).

In the 1940s Oklahomans passed Initiatives that provided retirement pensions for teachers (1942), allowed local property tax increases to aid schools (1946), and allowed the legislature to raise additional school funds(1946).

The only Initiative to gain approval in the 1950s was a 1956 reapportionment measure; despite a four to three margin in favor, it failed to get a majority of those voting in the election. In the 1960s two more Initiatives failed for the same reason: a 1962 reapportionment proposal, and a 1964 measure changing the property tax limits. In 1974 the state constitution was finally amended so that an Initiative would win if a majority of those voting on the individual Initiative approved it.

OREGON

Oregon holds the records for the most statewide Initiatives (239 from 1904 to 1986), the highest average Initiative use (5.5 per general election), and the most statewide Initiatives on the ballot in a single year: 27 in 1912.

Historians identify one man as the driving force behind I&R: William Simon U'Ren, known as early as 1898 as "Referendum U'Ren" for his single-minded devotion to the cause. U'Ren was born on 10 January 1859 in Lancaster, Wisconsin, the son of a blacksmith who, with his wife, had emigrated from Cornwall in England. Young U'Ren accompanied his family westward to Nebraska, then to Colorado, learning the blacksmith's trade from his father. In 1885, at age 26, he earned a law degree in Denver, then moved to Iowa, Hawaii, and California before settling in Milwaukie, Oregon, in 1889. By this time he had been a miner, newspaper editor, and Republican Party worker, in addition to practicing law.

In 1892 he was forced to give up his law practice as a result of an asthma attack and, having no family in the area, was nursed back to health by the Lewellings, a local family of fruit growers. The Lewellings were also reformers, "good government being to us what religion is to most people," wrote the lady of the house. Albert Lewelling brought U'Ren a copy of James W. Sullivan's then-new book, *Direct Legislation,* and U'Ren, at age 33, found his life's work. As he later told an interviewer:

> Blacksmithing was my trade and it has always given color to my view of things. I wanted to fix the evils in the conditions of life. I couldn't. There were no tools. We had tools to do almost anything with in the blacksmith shop; wonderful tools. So in other trades, arts and professions . . . in everything but government.
>
> In government, the common trade of all men and the basis of social life, men worked still with old tools, with old laws, with institutions and charters which hindered progress more than helped. Men suffered from this. There were lawyers enough, many of our ablest men were lawyers. Why didn't some of them invent legislative implements to help people govern themselves: Why had we no tool makers for democracy?"

U'Ren, with the financial support of the Lewellings, took it upon himself to forge the tools of democracy: Initiative, Referendum, and Recall. He brought together representatives of the state Farmer's Alliance and labor unions to form the Oregon Direct Legislation League, of which he was named secretary.

In 1894 U'Ren was elected chairman of the state's Populist Party convention, and won approval of an I&R platform plank. That same year the League published a pamphlet explaining I&R and distributed it throughout the state—50,000 copies in English, and 15,000 in German.

In 1896 U'Ren won a seat in the state's lower house and in 1897 worked the legislature—without success—to gain approval for I&R. Warned that he might go to purgatory for his wheeling and dealing, U'Ren replied thunderously: "I'd go to hell for the people of Oregon!"

Following the 1897 defeat, U'Ren reorganized the League to broaden the base of I&R support. In addition to farmers and labor unionists, the new 17-member executive committee included bankers, the president of the state bar association (such attorneys' associations were notorious during the Progressive era for opposing I&R), and Portland *Oregonian* editor Harvey W. Scott.

U'Ren ran for the state senate in 1898 and lost, but nevertheless won passage of his I&R amendment the following year. Under Oregon's constitution, amendments had to be approved by two successive sessions of the legislature. In 1901 I&R passed with a single dissenting vote and a year later voters ratified it by an eleven to one margin.

U'Ren joined other reformers in sponsoring dozens of Initiatives during the next two decades. In 1906, he was among the sponsors of an Initiative to ban free railroad passes, which the railroads routinely handed out as gifts to politicians, and which he himself had once received. In 1908, he proposed Initiatives to make Oregon the first state with popular election of U.S. senators and to reform election laws. Both passed by overwhelming margins. In 1910, Oregonians passed an Initiative to establish the first presidential primary election system in the nation. The margin was small (43,353 to 41,624), but two dozen other states copied it within six years.

The closeness of the 1910 vote showed that the voters were not quite as ready for reform as was U'Ren; they rejected his 1912 Initiative proposing a unicameral legislature by a greater than two to one margin.

Other early Initiatives that bear the mark of U'Ren were a 1906 constitutional amendment extending I&R powers to local jurisdictions, approved by three to one, and a 1908 amendment that gave voters power to recall elected officials.

And these were just the beginning, for U'Ren associated himself with many more Initiative efforts before his death, at age 90, in Portland on 8 March 1949. In Oregon, I&R had worked just as its early advocates said it would: this one reform opened the door to all the others.

As Progressive reformer and practitioner of Initiative and Referendum campaigns, U'Ren had no equal in any state. Lest he get all the credit for establishing I&R in Oregon, however, another man must be mentioned as the state's number two I&R advocate: Max Burgholzer of Buxton (near Eugene), Oregon, whom some contemporaries claimed deserved equal credit.

Oregon is one of two states (the other is Arizona) where women gained the right to vote by an Initiative. But it lost on the first try in 1906, and by an even bigger margin in 1908. In 1910 suffragists tried a different approach: an Initiative giving only female *taxpayers* the right to vote, a compromise that was rejected by about the same margin as the 1908 suffrage amendment. Finally, in 1912, suffragists led by Abigail Scott Duniway won their long struggle—61,265 in favor to 57,104 against.

Leading the fight against women's suffrage were the liquor and saloon interests, which (rightly, in this instance) feared women would vote for prohibition. In 1914, the first year Oregon women voted, a prohibition Initiative passed by a wide margin. Women also provided the slim 157-vote victory margin (out of over 200,000 votes cast) for a 1914 Initiative constitutional amendment abolishing the death penalty in Oregon. In 1912 a similar Initiative had failed, 41,951 to 64,578.

Labor unions won approval of a 1912 Initiative establishing an eight-hour day for workers on public works projects, and two others prohibiting private employers from hiring convicts from state or local jails.

Some of the most innovative Oregon Initiatives of the early days were those that failed to pass. One was a 1914 full-employment Initiative sponsored by the Socialist Party. The proposal would have set up a job creation fund derived from an inheritance tax on estates worth more than $50,000 (a huge fortune in those days); the state labor commissioner would then have the duty to employ any citizen demanding work in a "Department of Industry and Public Works." The measure failed 57,859 to 126,201.

In 1930, another unique proposal—a state constitutional amendment to ban cigarettes—was put on the ballot by citizen petition. By a three to one margin, Oregonians rejected the idea. They did, however, approve an Initiative amendment that year establishing a procedure to set up independent, locally owned "People's Utility Districts" to market water and power. In 1938, Oregonians approved the "Townsend Plan" old-age pension Initiative. The idea was the brainchild of Dr. Francis E. Townsend of Long Beach, California, who proposed making monthly payments to senior citizens if they promised to spend their entire allotment each month and thus stimulate the economy. Also on the ballot that year was an Initiative to clean up the Willamette River, which was heavily polluted by pulp and paper mills and sewage. The measure had been passed by the legislature in 1937 but vetoed by Gov. Charles Martin. Voters passed the Initiative by a wide margin.

In the late 1940s a University of Oregon at Eugene student, Clay Myers, a leader of the campus Young Republicans, began a movement for reapportionment of the state's legislative and congressional districts, whose boundaries had not been redrawn for over 50 years. Rebuffed by the legislature, Myers sponsored an Initiative constitutional amendment specifying that if the legislature failed to reapportion the state during its first six-month session after the census data are released every ten years, the secretary of state would do the job. Voters approved the Initiative by a nearly two to one margin in 1952. Myers went on to reapportion the state himself during his 1967–1977 term as secretary of state.

In the 1960s, Oregonians put only seven Initiatives on the state ballot in five elections, far below their average. In 1960, scenery-conscious citizens sponsored an Initiative to limit billboards through the state, but the electorate rejected it by a nearly two to one margin. In the 1970s, however, leading the national trend, Initiative use rebounded, with 17 qualifying for the ballot. Among those approved was a "denturism" Initiative (1978) that broke dentists' monopoly by allowing denture technicians to sell and fit dentures at a lower cost. This Initiative was championed by Ron Wyden, a young lobbyist for senior citizens. Dentists opposed the measure with a saturation advertising campaign that voters found so obnoxious that they approved the Initiative by a seven to two margin. Voter interest ran so high that the number of ballots cast on the "denturism" question was only a tenth of a percent less than the number cast for gubernatorial candidates. For Wyden, the Initiative was a starting point for his successful 1980 campaign to win election to Congress.

All this could not have occurred had it not been for the work of William Simon U'Ren. U'Ren is perhaps the only person to be honored by a monument commemorating his Initiative work. The monument can be found in front of the Clackamas County Courthouse, on Main Street in Oregon City. The bronze plaque reads: "In honor of William Simon U'Ren, author of Oregon's constitutional provisions for initiative, referendum, and recall, giving the people control of law making and law makers and known in his lifetime as father of Oregon's enlightened system of government."

PENNSYLVANIA

Among the earliest Pennsylvania Initiative and Referendum advocates was Charles Fremont Taylor, M.D., of Philadelphia. Dr. Taylor, one of the movement's most successful publicists, edited and published its periodical *Equity* (originally *Equity Series*) for over a decade. Taylor collaborated with Prof. Frank Parsons of Boston in publishing several of Parson's reformist works. Parsons' *The City for the People,* a guide to the reform of city government, included a 132-page chapter on Initiative, Referendum, and Recall, which they later published separately.

Although Taylor's publications had a nationwide impact, efforts for I&R foundered in his own state. Under the leadership of Finley Acker of Philadelphia and Clarence Van Dyke Tiers of Pittsburgh, the Pennsylvania Direct Legislation League waged an unsuccessful, 20-year battle against "the rule of the corporation machine," headed by Republican boss Boies Penrose. In July 1909 State Rep. Hyatt M. Cribbs wrote that the state house of representatives "is so overwhelmingly machine that I have little hope of ever getting my [I&R] bill out of committee."

The I&R advocates' biggest victory came in 1914, when they succeeded in persuading the legislature to pass a law allowing I&R in third-class cities—a category that included most of the major cities of the state, *except* the two biggest, Philadelphia and Pittsburgh.

Few Initiative campaigns in Pennsylvania have attracted much attention outside the local jurisdictions in which they have taken place. One exception was the May 1983 vote in Bucks County (an elite rural area just north of Philadelphia) to block construction of a massive pump that would have drawn water from the Delaware River. The project drew opposition from environmentalists and voters, who passed the anti-pump Initiative by a 56 percent margin. The Philadelphia Electric Company, which wants the water to cool a nuclear plant, fought a five-year legal battle to build the pump anyway, and won a state ruling in its favor in 1988.

RHODE ISLAND

By 1917 Rhode Island was one of only four states in the Union where the state legislature had completely blocked Initiative and Referendum for both the state and local governments. Like Pennsylvania, Rhode Island was controlled from the Civil War to the Great Depression by a Republican Party machine allied with the state's big industrialists, in this case textile mill owners.

Foremost among its I&R advocates was Lucius F. C. Garvin, a state legislator elected governor in 1902. Garvin called for passage of an I&R bill in his 1903 message to the legislature and continued pushing for I&R after his term was over. Lewis A. Waterman, Democratic candidate for governor in 1910, also called for I&R, but to no avail.

In the 1980s agitation for I&R resumed under the leadership of Marilyn Hines, director of the state chapter of Common Cause. The group won approval of a statewide Initiative amendment in a state constitutional convention in 1986, but voters, probably not comprehending its meaning due to a lack of publicity on the issue, rejected it by a narrow margin.

SOUTH CAROLINA

South Carolina Initiative and Referendum advocates' only victory in the Progressive era was the enactment of a state law allowing I&R at the municipal level in 1910.

SOUTH DAKOTA

South Dakota, the first state to adopt Initiative and Referendum on a statewide level, did so in 1898. The *Direct Legislation Record* for December of that year gave credit for this achievement to the organizing efforts of Walter E. Kidd of Brown County. Kidd, born in Michigan in 1849, spent "half his mature years" in farming and the other half in "newspaper work" as publisher of the *Dakota Ruralist*, whose front-page motto was "Socialism in Our Time." Kidd claimed that it was the "only daily paper in the county advocating socialism." He had served as chair of the Populist Party State Central Committee, and as state representative from his district.

South Dakota was also the only state in which the I&R idea orig-inated on home soil. According to an article by a Mr. Doane Robin-son, originally published in the *St. Paul Pioneer Press* and re-printed in the October 1910 *Equity Series*, I&R

> originated in the fertile mind of Rev. Robert W. Haire, a Catholic cler-gyman of Aberdeen. . . . With him the plan was pure invention, for he had not heard of the Swiss I&R when in 1885 he proposed a people's legislation embodying the features of the present constitutional provi-sion. Father Haire was active in the Knights of Labor and he exploited his scheme widely through the literature of that organization.
>
> Later the Farmers' Alliance took it up. . . . The populists, too, stood for the measure, and when they secured control of the legislature in 1897 they submitted an [I&R] amendment. Hon. H. L. Loucks, widely known as the father of populism, was most earnestly for the amend-ment. . . . at the general election that fall [1898] it was adopted by a vote of 23,816 to 16,483.

South Dakotans in 1912 passed a primary election Initiative known as the "Richards primary election law," and a further stat-ute on the same subject, by the same author, in 1918. These were the only statewide Initiatives approved by South Dakota voters for the next 60 years.

South Dakota saw a revival of Initiative use in 1978–1984, when 10 Initiatives qualified for ballot placement, a tally equal to the total number of Initiatives on the ballot during the previous 55 years.

TENNESSEE

The Progressives and labor unions never won enactment of state-wide Initiative and Referendum rights, and had to settle for a 1913 law granting such rights to residents of a few municipalities.

TEXAS

The founders of the Texas Initiative and Referendum movement were two ministers: Rev. A. B. Francisco of Milano and Rev. B. F. Foster of Galveston. Also important in Texas I&R leadership before 1900 was Judge Thomas B. King of Stephenville, county judge of Erath County.

The movement was slow to catch on in Texas. By 1912 Congressman (later U.S. Senator) Morris Shepard had declared himself in favor of I&R; in 1913 the legislature passed a bill allowing I&R as an option for home rule cities, and a state constitutional amendment providing for statewide I&R.

The latter amendment would have required more petition signatures to put an Initiative on the ballot than were needed in any other state: 20 percent of the number of ballots cast in the previous election. When the amendment was put on the ballot for voter ratification in 1914, voters rejected it, to the delight of some I&R advocates, who believed that they could get the legislature to pass a better version. They were unable to do so.

After a hiatus of more than half a century, Texans' interest in getting statewide I&R revived when Californians approved their electrifying Proposition 13 tax cut Initiative in 1978. Leading the movement was Republican State Sen. Walter Mengden of Houston, who had pushed unsuccessfully for I&R at the state's 1974 constitutional convention and in the legislature until his retirement in 1982. Within a month of the California vote, Gov. Dolph Briscoe and gubernatorial candidate William Clements had announced their support for statewide I&R.

Clements reiterated his commitment once elected, telling the legislature on 25 May 1979: "I have made it absolutely clear to everyone that if I do not get I&R passed, I will call a special session." But Clements failed to carry out his threat. Leading the charge for the opposition was the Houston lobbyist James K. Nance, whose law firm represented such major corporate clients as Union Carbide, DuPont, Houston Power and Light, Pennzoil, and United Texas Gas Transmission.

In 1980 the state's Republicans put an I&R question on their 2 May statewide primary election ballot, and party members endorsed it by a seven to one margin. Initiative advocates lost a strong ally when Senator Mengden retired, however, and the effort for statewide I&R seemed to be running out of steam. Nevertheless, Texas Republicans put the I&R question on their primary ballot again on 6 May 1982; party voters favored it by a five to one margin.

UTAH

Utah was the second state to win statewide Initiative and Referendum, passing its amendment through the legislature in 1899, and ratifying it by popular vote in 1900. The man most responsible for this early victory was State Rep. Sherman S. Smith of Ogden, the legislature's "lone populist." But another I&R advocate, Henry W. Lawrence of Salt Lake City, wondered whether the legislature would pass reasonable implementing legislation: "The great trouble now will be to get the Legislature to adopt legislation to . . . make it [I&R] effective, as our Legislature will be Republican and no doubt generally opposed to the principle."

Lawrence's concern was on target. Sixteen years later, I&R advocates were still waiting for the legislature to pass an implementing law. Finally, in 1916, they organized the Popular Government League of Utah to lobby for such a law. Its officers were Parley P. Christensen, president; Dr. Grace Stratton-Airey, vice president; and Parker B. Cady, secretary-treasurer.

The legislature reluctantly passed an implementing bill, but it was worthless: among other restrictions, it specified that anyone signing a petition to put an Initiative on the ballot had to sign *in the office and in the presence* of an officer competent to administer oaths" (italics added). The reformers were outraged. The law effectively prohibited Initiative sponsors from circulating petitions. After World War II the restrictions finally were eased, but it was still not easy to put an Initiative on the ballot.

In 1960 Utahans approved a statewide Initiative for the first time. It established a merit system procedure for hiring and employing county deputy sheriffs, thus ending the corrupting patronage system.

VERMONT

Winston Allen Flint, writing in *The Progressive Movement in Vermont,* noted that "no serious attempt was ever made in Vermont" to get a statewide Initiative process: "there is little evidence to show that it was given any important recognition in Vermont by party platforms, legislators, press, or public opinion."

In 1981 and 1982, however, Vermonters exercised their local Initiative process in over 200 town meetings to approximate a statewide vote on a resolution calling for a U.S.–Soviet nuclear arms freeze. More than 160 towns backed the Freeze.

VIRGINIA

While the Populist call for "more democracy" was gaining strength throughout most of the nation, Virginia's ruling Democratic Party was giving its citizens less. In May 1901 voters elected 100 delegates to a state constitutional convention, 89 of them Democrats. The new constitution they approved included a poll tax and a literacy test, both designed to prevent poor whites and blacks from voting. The delegates did not even submit the new constitution to the voters for ratification, having it take effect instead "by [their own] proclamation." In this context, it is surprising not that Virginia's Progressives failed to amend their state constitution to include I&R, but that they even tried.

The Progressives' hopes for a statewide I&R amendment ran highest in 1914, when state Attorney General John Garland Pollard was elected president of the newly formed Progressive Democratic League, which included I&R on its reform agenda. That same year the House of Delegates approved an I&R amendment by a lopsided 64 to 24 vote, but the measure died in the senate.

The next serious discussion of a statewide I&R amendment came 50 years later, in 1969, when Norfolk state senator (and unsuccessful 1977 gubernatorial candidate) Henry Howell and Fairfax delegate Vincent Callahan proposed it—again without success.

In 1980, three northern Virginians—Gwendolyn F. Cody, James W. Roncaglione, and Harley M. Williams—organized Virginians for Initiative and Referendum. In 1981, both houses passed a bill adding I&R provisions to the city charter of Hampton, which were approved by voters of that city by a greater than three to one margin. Cody won election to the House of Delegates; I&R endorser Charles Robb became governor. But Cody was unable to get the statewide I&R bill out of committee, and Robb did nothing to support it. Prospects dimmed further with the death of Williams in 1986.

WASHINGTON

In 1897 State Rep. L. E. Reeder of Ollalla introduced an Initiative and Referendum constitutional amendment that passed the lower house by a 63 to 12 vote, but failed in the state senate. Influential in that partial victory was House Speaker Charles E. Cline of Olympia, who became secretary of the state's Direct Legislation League.

Another state legislator, George F. Cotterill of Seattle, had become president of the League by 1900. By this time, however, Cline was no longer Speaker, and the I&R movement stagnated.

In 1907 the state's organized labor and farm groups cooperated with the Direct Legislation League in deluging the legislature with petitions calling for statewide I&R. Soon after, the I&R bill introduced by State Rep. Glen Rauck of Vancouver passed the lower house 66 to 26, but the state senate defeated it 25 to 15. An I&R sympathizer noted that "just two forces" opposed I&R: "special privileged corporation interests and the organized liquor traffic," the latter because it feared voters would enact a prohibition Initiative.

The state Federation of Labor, whose president was Charles Case, and the state Grange, whose "master" (i.e., president) was C. B. Kegley, formed a Joint Legislative Committee that finally got the I&R amendment through both houses of the legislature in 1911. The version passed by the legislature did not, however, allow voters to initiate state constitutional amendments, because certain state senators, with the active support of Governor Hay, wanted to require that for a constitutional Initiative to pass, at least 60 percent of the voters participating in a general election must vote on it. The pro-I&R committee refused to accept this compromise, and over 70 years later, there is still no provision for constitutional Initiatives in Washington. Voters ratified the statutory I&R bill by a five to two margin in 1912. In the same election, George Cotterill was elected mayor of Seattle.

The farmer-labor Joint Legislative Committee put the voters' newly established lawmaking powers to use immediately. They circulated petitions to put seven Initiatives on the 1914 ballot, of which five qualified, though only one was approved by voters: a measure to abolish private employment agencies. The intent behind this law was to stop the well-documented exploitation of unemployed workers, particularly lumberjacks, by such agencies.

A statewide Prohibition Initiative also passed in 1914, just as the liquor interests had feared. The following year anti-Initiative forces in the legislature—which was "dominated by the whiskey, lumber, and fish interests," according to Grange Master Kegley— struck back by passing a bill (deceptively titled "An Act to Facilitate the Operation of the Initiative and Referendum") that would have made it virtually impossible to get an Initiative on the ballot.

Progressive forces used the Referendum power to stop the bill from going into effect. They quickly circulated petitions to block it until voters could reject it in the November 1916 election (which they did, by a three to one margin).

The legislature soon found a way to obstruct the Referendum provision: by attaching an "emergency clause" to a bill, they could cause it to take effect immediately and thus make it invulnerable to Referendum petitions. Eventually, in 1929, the state supreme court ruled that the legislature could not add an "emergency clause" to a bill in the absence of a real emergency (*State ex. rel. Satterthwaite* v. *Hinkle,* 152 Wash. 221 [1929]).

Property tax limitation Initiatives were on the ballot five times between 1924 and 1938. The proposals, which sought to limit the tax levy on real and personal property to 40 mills, were passed by voters in 1932, 1934, 1936, and 1938, before the legislature acted to make the tax limit permanent by putting it into the state constitution, a move approved by voters in 1940.

Washington State voters twice approved redistricting Initiatives, once in 1930 and again in 1956. The latter Initiative was sponsored by the state League of Women Voters. Another successful election reform passed by voter Initiative was permanent voter registration, enacted in 1932.

In the years of the Great Depression, economic concerns frequently became the subject of Washington State Initiatives. Voters passed an Initiative authorizing creation of public utility districts in 1930, a measure that helped make possible the state's current system of locally controlled, publicly owned electric utilities.

Perhaps the most innovative Initiative of the 1930s was the 1936 "Production for Use" proposal. "Production for Use" was conceived by Upton Sinclair, the Socialist author of *The Jungle,* who turned Democrat in 1934 in order to run for California's governorship. This economic recovery plan called for the government to acquire idle production facilities such as factories, hire the unemployed to work in them, and promote sales of the goods through cooperatives. After Sinclair lost in California, his Washington State admirers decided to give the concept a second chance by putting it on the ballot there in 1936. The Washington Commonwealth Federation, which sponsored the Initiative, was split by internal dissension that year, so little was accomplished to promote the measure's passage. It lost by a nearly four to one margin.

Washington State voters turned generous in 1948, when they approved Initiatives granting a bonus to veterans and increasing Social Security benefits. In 1954 they rejected by a three to one margin an Initiative to restrict advertising for alcoholic beverages on television—a unique proposal that, like "Production for Use" in 1936, never appeared on any other ballot in the nation.

One of the most important postwar reforms accomplished by voter Initiative was the state's civil service system, approved by the electorate in 1958 for county sheriff employees, and in 1960 for state employees. Prior to this, the "patronage" or "spoils system" had filled bureaucracies with incompetent party hacks.

In 1968, the Washington State Medical Association sponsored an Initiative requiring drivers stopped by police for driving under the influence of liquor to submit to breath tests. Voters approved it by a two to one margin. That same year they approved a measure putting a lid on interest rates paid by retail credit customers.

In 1970, environmentalists launched a petition drive for an Initiative to restrict shoreline development, more than a year before California ecology groups launched their drive for a similar Initiative. The Washington State petition qualified for the ballot and prompted the legislature to propose an alternative bill, which was on the 1972 ballot alongside the Initiative measure. The legislature's bill received more votes, and therefore took effect instead of the Initiative. In 1988, however, when the choice was between an environmentalist-backed toxic waste tax and cleanup Initiative and the legislature's version, voters chose the Initiative. (See Chapters 4 and 6 for more details on Washington State's environmental and tax Initiatives of the 1970s and 1980s.)

WEST VIRGINIA

In 1907, a state senator (Campbell) introduced an Initiative and Referendum bill; in 1908, a state delegate (Williams) introduced one; both were defeated. In 1915, Governor Hatfield called for I&R in his annual message to the legislature, but his words went unheeded.

The biggest obstacle to I&R in the Progressive era was probably the corporate-backed Republican Party's domination of West Virginia politics, which lasted from 1896 to 1932. Still, the state's I&R advocates were not without success, for a 1917 chart in the I&R movement organ *Equity* indicated that the legislature had passed "special acts" granting I&R rights to residents of some (unidentified) local jurisdictions.

WISCONSIN

The name Wisconsin is practically synonymous with Progressivism, yet this state has never had a statewide Initiative and Referendum process. Indeed, it is one of only three states where voters turned down their opportunity to get it (Texas and Rhode Island are the others). The circumstances were as follows.

In 1907 Lieut. Gov. W. D. Connor and State Sen. W. D. Brazeau took up the cause and secured approval in the state senate by a 19 to 5 vote, but lost in the lower house. The Progressive reformers had been in power since 1900, and had enacted a host of reforms, but I&R was apparently not a priority.

Any state constitutional amendment needed to pass both houses by a three-fifths majority in two successive sessions of the legislature, with an election in between. Only then, after two years or more, could it be put on the ballot for ratification by the voters. The I&R amendment finally passed both houses in the 1911–1912 legislature with the support of Gov. Francis E. McGovern, U.S. Sen. Robert M. La Follette and his Progressive Republican followers, and the state's Socialists. It passed again in the 1913–1914 legislature, and was placed on the November 1914 ballot.

After 13 years in power, the Progressives had become overconfident. In the 1913 legislature, they passed a series of big tax increases to finance an ambitious public works program, as well as giving final approval to a constitutional amendment raising their salaries. It went on the November 1914 ballot along with the I&R amendment and eight others, including one to allow recall of all state elected officers except judges.

After paying the higher taxes in 1914, the voters had had their fill of the liberal reformers and all their works. The amendments on the 1914 ballot offered an easy target for the voters' wrath. Leading candidates of both major parties damned all the amendments, without informing voters that the Initiative, Referendum, and Recall amendments offered just the mechanism they needed to block legislation they deplored. The state Democratic convention that year disapproved I&R in its platform; Republican gubernatorial candidate Emmanuel L. Phillipp also urged voters to reject I&R.

On election day all 10 amendments were defeated overwhelmingly. The voters discriminated hardly at all between them: the least popular amendments won 26 percent approval; the most popular, 38 percent. The I&R amendment and the recall amendment were approved by 36 percent. Because they decided to vote "no" on everything, Wisconsin voters in 1914 denied themselves, and all Wisconsin voters for the next 75 years, the right to vote on issues of their choice.

WYOMING

Wyoming's Initiative and Referendum pioneer was State Rep. L. C. Tidball of Sheridan. In the early 1890s Tidball was one of the first state legislators in the nation—possibly the first—to introduce a bill to amend a state constitution to provide for statewide I&R.

The Wyoming legislature waited 19 years before finally taking favorable action on an I&R bill in 1912, after all the surrounding states had already put I&R into their constitutions. It was favored by a six to one margin of the voters who cast ballots on its ratification. It still failed to take effect, however, because Wyoming constitutional amendments required ratification by a "supermajority" of all the voters casting ballots in the election, which made blank ballots count as "no" votes. By this standard, the I&R amendment narrowly failed.

Finally, in 1968, Wyoming's legislature passed an I&R amendment, and it won voter ratification. But the procedures, specified by the legislature, included the most difficult petition requirement for Initiative state laws in the nation—15 percent of the number of ballots cast in the preceding gubernatorial election. And it did not allow voters to propose or vote on Initiative constitutional amendments at all.

Though several attempts were made, only one Initiative qualified for the ballot in 20 years: a proposed law, titled "In-stream Flows," that would allow the state's fish and game department to claim water rights on behalf of fish and wildlife, so that future development—and particularly energy projects like a proposed water-guzzling coal slurry pipeline—would not drain essential water sources. The backers' first petition drive, in 1981, fell 1,000 names short, and they were forced to start again. By early 1986 they had finally qualified their measure for the November 1986 ballot. The legislature enacted it in March 1986, making a citizen vote on the measure unnecessary.

SOURCES FOR INITIATIVE HISTORY IN THE 50 STATES

Acena, Albert. Doctoral diss. on Washington Commonwealth Federation, University of Washington, Seattle (WASHINGTON).

Allain, Bill. "Fighting and Winning for a Responsive and Responsible State Government: An Action Plan." Campaign position paper, July 1983 (MISSISSIPPI).

Back, Edith Bierhorst. "Sisson Prepares Proposals to Give Mississippians Direct Political Voice." Gulfport *Sun-Herald,* 27 August 1978 (MISSISSIPPI).

Backstrom, Charles H. "Popular Vote on Populist Amendments." Paper delivered to the convention of the American Political Science Association, Denver, 2 September 1982, pp. 9–16 (MINNESOTA).

———. "Public Attitudes Toward Initiative and Referendum." Paper delivered to the 1983 National Seminar on the Initiative, Washington, D.C., 21 January 1983, p. 2; response to questions and spoken remarks.

Bass, John H. "The Initiative and Referendum in Oklahoma." *Southwestern Political and Social Science Quarterly,* 1, no. 2 (1920), pp. 130, 138, 141–43, 145 (OKLAHOMA).

Bergford, John, Citizens for Representative Government. "Statewide Citizens' Coalition Formed to Oppose Amendment Authorizing Initiative and Referendum." News release, 30 September 1980, St. Paul (MINNESOTA).

Brown, Jeffrey. "I&R After the Fact." *Twin Cities Reader,* 26 November 1980 (MINNESOTA).

Chrislock, Carl H. *The Progressive Era in Minnesota, 1899–1918.* St. Paul: Minnesota Historical Society, 1971.

Cowan, Ruth. "The N.Y. Civilian Review Board Referendum of 1966: A Case Study of Mass Politics." Ph.D. diss., New York University, 1970 (NEW YORK).

Crouch, Winston W. *The Initiative and Referendum in California.* Los Angeles: Haynes Foundation, 1950, p. 14 (CALIFORNIA).

————. "John Randolph Haynes and His Work for Direct Government." *National Civic Review,* September 1938, pp. 435–36 (CALIFORNIA).

Direct Legislation Record, ed. Eltweed Pomeroy:

December 1895, p. 27 (MICHIGAN);

March 1896, p. 10 (COLORADO);

September 1896, p. 2 (NORTH DAKOTA);

September 1896, pp. 25–26 (OHIO);

September 1896, p. 26 (IOWA, TEXAS);

March 1897, p. 6 (WASHINGTON STATE);

December 1897, p. 75 (NEBRASKA);

March 1898, (TEXAS);

March 1898, p. 19 (OREGON);

September 1898, p. 68 (OHIO);

March 1899, p. 1 (PENNSYLVANIA);

June 1899, p. 17 (COLORADO);

June 1899, p. 25 (OKLAHOMA);

June 1899, p. 26 (MICHIGAN);

June 1899, p. 29 (UTAH);

December 1899, p. 88 (ILLINOIS);

March 1900, p. 11 (WASHINGTON STATE);

May 1900, (WASHINGTON STATE);

September 1900, p. 50 (PENNSYLVANIA);

December 1900 (ILLINOIS, KANSAS, KENTUCKY, MARYLAND, MICHIGAN, MISSOURI, TEXAS).

Smith, Sherman S., quoted in December 1900, p. 69 (UTAH).

Dornfeld, Steven. "Perpich Favors Law on Voter Initiative," *Minneapolis Tribune,* 25 April 1978 (MINNESOTA).

Easterling, Lamar F. Letter to Charles Fremont Taylor, 27 March 1917 reprinted in *Equity,* July 1917, p. 87 (MISSISSIPPI).

Eaton, Allen H. *The Oregon System, The Story of Direct Legislation in Oregon.* Chicago: A. C. McClurg & Co., 1912. (OREGON).

Eggleston, W. G. Article in *Equity Series,* January 1913 (MONTANA).

Equity, ed. Charles Fremont Taylor:
January 1907, p. 16 (HAWAII, NEW YORK);
January 1907, p. 20 (OHIO);
January 1907, p. 22 (OKLAHOMA);
April 1907 (OKLAHOMA, WISCONSIN);
April 1907, p. 12 (DELAWARE, NEW JERSEY, NORTH DAKOTA);
April 1907, pp. 13–14 (RHODE ISLAND, WASHINGTON STATE);
April 1907, p. 15 (WEST VIRGINIA);
July 1907, pp. 1, 15 (DELAWARE, NORTH DAKOTA);
October 1907, p. 1 (WASHINGTON STATE);
October 1907, p. 2 (MISSOURI);
October 1907, p. 6 (WISCONSIN);
January 1908, p. 14 (DELAWARE);
January 1908, p. 16 (OHIO);
January 1908, p. 19 (MISSOURI);
April 1908, p. 42 (PENNSYLVANIA, WEST VIRGINIA);
July 1908, p. 71 (OHIO);
July 1908, p. 77 (OREGON);
January 1909, p. 3 (MISSOURI);
April 1909, (RHODE ISLAND);
April 1909, p. 35 (KANSAS);
April 1909, pp. 46, 59 (NEVADA);
April 1909, p. 56 (NEW JERSEY);
July 1909, p. 87 (KANSAS);
July 1909, p. 92 (NEW YORK);
July 1909, p. 94 (NORTH DAKOTA);
July 1909, p. 95 (OHIO);
July 1909, p. 100 (PENNSYLVANIA);
January 1910, (MASSACHUSETTS, NEW HAMPSHIRE);
January 1910, p. 39 (NEBRASKA);
July 1910, p. 101 (MISSOURI);
July 1910, p. 104 (ILLINOIS);
October 1910, p. 136 (ARIZONA, ILLINOIS);
October 1910, p. 158 (RHODE ISLAND);
January 1911, (WISCONSIN);
January 1911, p. 14 (ARIZONA);
January 1911, p. 23 (ILLINOIS);

January 1911, p. 26 (MARYLAND);
January 1911, p. 29 (NEBRASKA, NEW JERSEY);
January 1911, p. 31 (NEW YORK);
October 1912, p. 143 (INDIANA, KANSAS);
October 1912, p. 147 (OHIO);
October 1912, p. 149 (TEXAS);
January 1913, p. 18 (COLORADO);
January 1913, p. 35 (NEBRASKA, NEVADA);
January 1913, p. 43 (MISSISSIPPI);
October 1913, p. 217 (IOWA);
January 1914, p. 31 (DISTRICT OF COLUMBIA);
January 1914, p. 36 (NEW YORK);
April 1914, p. 60 (NEW YORK);
April 1914, p. 89 (MARYLAND);
April 1914, p. 93 (MISSISSIPPI);
April 1914, p. 100 (VIRGINIA);
October 1914, p. 179 (INDIANA, MISSISSIPPI);
October 1914, p. 188 (OREGON);
October 1914, p. 191 (WISCONSIN);
January 1915, pp. 37–38 (ARIZONA);
January 1915, p. 39 (ARKANSAS);
January 1915, p. 56 (OREGON);
January 1915, p. 59 (TEXAS);
January 1915, p. 60 (WISCONSIN);
April 1915, p. 114 (IDAHO);
April 1915, p. 126 (WEST VIRGINIA);
April 1916, p. 69 (OREGON);
July 1916, p. 142 (MARYLAND);
January 1917, p. 27 (ARIZONA);
January 1917, p. 40 (UTAH);
January 1917, p. 89 (NEW HAMPSHIRE);
January 1917, p. 95 (UTAH);
July 1917, p. 88 (MISSISSIPPI);
July 1917, pp. 132–33 (COLORADO);
July 1917, p. 133 (IDAHO, IOWA, KANSAS, KENTUCKY, LOUISIANA, NEW YORK, NORTH CAROLINA, NORTH DAKOTA, PENNSYLVANIA, RHODE ISLAND, SOUTH CAROLINA, TENNESSEE, TEXAS, WEST VIRGINIA);
July 1917, p. 148 (MINNESOTA);
July 1917, p. 201 (NEBRASKA);

April 1919, p. 61 (DELAWARE).

Farmer, Rod. "Direct Democracy in Arkansas, 1910–1918." *Arkansas Historical Quarterly* 40 no. 2 (Summer 1981), pp. 99–118.

———. "The Maine Campaign for Direct Democracy, 1902–1908." *Maine Historical Society Quarterly,* Summer 1983, pp. 15–19, 24 (MAINE).

Flint, Winston Allen. *The Progressive Movement in Vermont.* Washington, D.C.: American Council on Public Affairs, 1941, p. 72 (VERMONT).

Forster, John. Telephone interview with the author, 28 December 1984 (DISTRICT OF COLUMBIA).

Gaillard, Frey, "Martin Luther King Liberated My City from Its Bonds." *Washington Post,* 19 January 1986 (NORTH CAROLINA).

Ginger, Ray. *Altgeld's America.* Chicago: Quadrangle Books, 1965, pp. 275–303 (ILLINOIS).

Gottlieb, Robert, and Wolt, Irene. *Thinking Big: The Story of the Los Angeles Times.* New York: Putnam, 1977, p. 66 (CALIFORNIA).

Graham, Virginia. *A Compilation of Statewide Initiative Proposals Appearing on Ballots Through 1976.* Washington, D.C.: Congressional Research Service, 1978:
ARIZONA, pp. 4–12;
COLORADO, pp. 67–83;
IDAHO, p. 88;
MAINE, p. 92;
MICHIGAN, pp. 101, 103–4;
MONTANA, pp. 118–20 (Montana Initiatives 1912–1976, excluding the metal mines tax);
NEBRASKA, pp. 122–23;
NEVADA, pp. 124–27;
NORTH DAKOTA, pp. 129–44;
OKLAHOMA, pp. 153, 160–82;
OREGON, pp. 187–202 (Initiatives 1904–1976);
UTAH, p. 207;
WASHINGTON STATE, pp. 214–20.

Hobson, Council Member Julius, sponsor. District of Columbia Bill 1-256, 1976 (DISTRICT OF COLUMBIA).

Initiative News Report, ed. David D. Schmidt:

17 November 1980, p. 8 (NORTH DAKOTA);
9 August 1982, p. 5 (IDAHO);
23 August 1982, p. 5 (OKLAHOMA);
12 November 1982, p. 7 (IDAHO);
12 November 1982, p. 8 (OKLAHOMA);
2 June 1983, p. 2 (PENNSYLVANIA);
10 February 1984, (MASSACHUSETTS);
24 February 1984, p. 3 (INDIANA);
4 May 1984, pp. 2–3 (IDAHO);
10 August 1984, p. 2 (IDAHO);
29 July 1983, p. 5 (HAWAII);
18 November 1983, pp. 9–10 (LOUISIANA);
10 February 1984, p. 1 (HAWAII);
24 February 1984, p. 4 (RHODE ISLAND);
4 May 1984, p. 4 (RHODE ISLAND).

Johnson, Alvin W. *The Unicameral Legislature.* Minneapolis: University of Minnesota Press, 1938, p. 136 (NEBRASKA).

Johnson, Claudius O. "The Adoption of the Initiative and Referendum in Washington." *Pacific Northwest Quarterly* 35 (October 1944), pp. 302–3 (WASHINGTON STATE).

Johnson, Claudius O. "The Initiative and Referendum in Washington," *Pacific Northwest Quarterly* (January 1945), pp. 29–62 (WASHINGTON STATE).

Kenney, David. *Basic Illinois Government.* Carbondale: Southern Illinois University Press, 1974, pp. 414–17 (ILLINOIS).

King, Wayne. "Oklahomans Are Voting on Sale of Liquor in Bars." *New York Times,* 18 September 1984 (OKLAHOMA).

Kromko, John, Telephone interviews with the author from 1980 to 1986, particularly one in March 1984 (ARIZONA).

Legislative Research Council. *Report Relative to Revising Statewide Initiative and Referendum Provisions of the Massachusetts Constitution, House No. 5435.* Boston: Commonwealth of Massachusetts, 1975, pp. 57–67, 86–88.

Lobingier, Charles S. *The People's Law.* New York: Macmillan, 1909, pp. 322–25 (VIRGINIA).

Marcus, Ruth. "D.C. Campaign to Fight Referendum Held Illegal." *Washington Post,* 9 October 1986 (DISTRICT OF COLUMBIA).

McBee, Susanna. "N.D. Medical Groups Decry Initiative on Setting Rates for Health Services." *Washington Post,* 2 November 1978 (NORTH DAKOTA).

McCall, Tom. *Tom McCall: Maverick.* Portland, OR: Binford and Mort, 1977, p. 179 (OREGON).

McCauley, David. "The Nuclear Arms Freeze at Vermont Town Meeting '82." *Freeze Newsletter* (published by National Nuclear Weapons Freeze Clearinghouse), April 1982, p. 5 (VERMONT).

McWilliams, Carey. *California: The Great Exception.* New York: Current Books, 1949, p. 207 (CALIFORNIA).

Martin, Jim. "Oregon System's Founder Always Put the People First." *Oregon Territory* (Sunday magazine section of *Portland Oregonian*), 17 June 1979 (OREGON).

Middaugh, David A. "The Defeat of North Dakota's Health Plan." In *Political Action Report,* (March). Washington, D.C.: Tyke Research Associates, 1979, p. 11 (NORTH DAKOTA).

Narus, Bob. "The Liberals' Dilemma." *New Jersey Reporter,* October 1981, p. 5 (NEW JERSEY).

"Origin of U'Renism." *Oregon Voter,* 18 March 1916, p. 213 (OREGON).

Patten, Roland T. "How We Did It in Maine." *Equity Series,* April 1909, pp. 43–45 (MAINE).

Peirce, Neal R., and Hagstrom, Jerry. *The Book of America: Inside Fifty States Today.* New York: Norton, 1983, pp. 102, 187, 558, 579, 824 (NEBRASKA, NORTH DAKOTA, OREGON, PENNSYLVANIA, RHODE ISLAND, WEST VIRGINIA).

"Petition for Referendum on Center Is Rejected." *Washington Post,* 26 October 1978 (DISTRICT OF COLUMBIA).

"Political Dean W. S. U'Ren Succumbs Here at Age 90." *Portland Oregonian,* 18 March 1949 (OREGON).

Pollock, James K. *The Initiative and Referendum in Michigan.* Bureau of Government, University of Michigan, 1940, pp. 2, 9, quoting "The Referendum and Initiative in Michigan." *Annals of the American Academy of Political and Social Sciences* 43 (1912): 150 (MICHIGAN).

Potter, Edwin S. "Letting the People Rule." *Equity,* 1914, p. 123 (PENNSYLVANIA).

"Pull the Plug on NOPSI." *Power Line,* May–June 1985, p. 10 (LOUISIANA).

Referendum News, ed. George Shibley:
  November 1905, (COLORADO);
  December 1905, p. 11 (MASSACHUSETTS);
  December 1905, (PENNSYLVANIA);
  December 1905, p. 11 (NORTH DAKOTA);
  May 1906, (OREGON);
  August 1906, p. 3. (MINNESOTA);
  Rhodes, Jack. "Constitution Proposal Turns Politics Upside Down." *St. Paul Sunday Pioneer Press,* 5 October 1980 (MINNESOTA).

Rosenberg, M. P. "The People, Yes—Or Maybe." *Texas Observer,* 13 March 1981, p. 5 (TEXAS).

Sabato, Larry J. *The Rise of Political Consultants.* New York: Basic Books, 1981, pp. 11–12 (CALIFORNIA).

Samuelson, Eric, and Mitcham, David. *Referendum Blues.* Austin: Public Research Institute, 1981, p. 2 (TEXAS).

Scannell, Nancy. "Citizens Launch Drive for Ballot Questions." *Washington Post,* July 1980; pamphlet soliciting "charter members" of the Virginians for Initiative and Referendum (VIRGINIA), c. 1980.

Schafer, J. "Oregon as a Political Experiment Station." *American Monthly Review of Reviews,* 34 (1906), p. 172 (OREGON).

Schmidt, David D., "New Jersey Initiative Bill Faces Last Chance for '83 Ballot." *Initiative News Report,* 29 July 1983; see also Ibid., 1 July and 15 July 1983; 24 February and 29 June 1984 (NEW JERSEY).

Schmidt, David D., "New Jersey State Senate Rebuffs Leader; Passes Initiative Amendment in 30–3 Vote." *Initiative News Report,* 13 July 1981, p. 3 (NEW JERSEY).

Schmidt, David D. Records for Initiatives 1978–1984, published in *Initiative News Report,* July 1980–December 1984 (OREGON).

Schwaneberg, Robert. "Referendums in the Works on Amendments to State Constitution." *Star-Ledger,* 26 June 1983 (NEW JERSEY).

Stumph, Roy C. "History of the Referendum in New Mexico." Master's thesis, University of New Mexico, Albuquerque, 1941, pp. 30–33, 35–36, 41, 49–50 (NEW MEXICO).

Sutton, Robert P., ed. *The Prairie State: Civil War to the Present—A Documentary History of Illinois.* Grand Rapids, Mich.: Eerdman's, 1976, pp. 173–74; passage from Bogart, Ernest L., and

Mathews, John M., *The Modern Commonwealth, 1888–1918*. Chicago: n.p., 1920, pp. 354–80 (ILLINOIS).

Taylor, Charles Fremont. Editorial in *Equity,* July 1917, quoting C. J. Buell of Minneapolis, article in (Chicago) *Public,* 8 January 1915 (MINNESOTA).

Taylor, Charles Fremont. "Victory in Maine." *Equity Series,* October 1908, pp. 97–98 (MAINE).

Telschow, Roger. Telephone interview with the author, 1 July 1984 (DISTRICT OF COLUMBIA).

Texas Election Bureau. Republican Primary Election Results, 2 May 1980.

Tindall, George Brown. *America: A Narrative History.* New York: Norton, 1984, pp. 856, 1078 (OHIO, OREGON).

Toole, K. Ross. *Montana: An Uncommon Land.* Norman: University of Oklahoma Press, 1959, pp. 223–26 (MONTANA).

"A Tribute to W. S. U'Ren, Father of the Oregon System of Government." Unsigned article published by the U'Ren Memorial Bicentennial Committee, a project of the Hilltop Boosters of Oregon City (OREGON).

U'Ren, William S. "The Results of the Initiative and Referendum in Oregon." *Proceedings of the American Political Science Association* 4 (1907), p. 193 (OREGON).

Van der Zee, J., *Direct Legislation in Iowa.* Iowa City: State Historical Society, 1914, pp. 39–40 (IOWA).

Weikert, G. R. "Dr. David Inglis." *Direct Legislation Record,* December 1897, p. 76 (MICHIGAN).

Weiser, Benjamin. "City Acted Properly On Center, Appeals Court Rules Referendum Not Vital." *Washington Post,* 9 October 1981 (DISTRICT OF COLUMBIA).

White, G. Edward. *Earl Warren: A Public Life.* New York: Oxford University Press, 1982, pp. 33–34 (CALIFORNIA).

Williams, Harley M. "A Brief History of Initiative, Referendum and Recall in the U.S. and Virginia and the Current Status of These Processes." Merrifield, Va.: Virginians for Initiative and Referendum, 1981. (VIRGINIA).

Appendix III

Statewide Initiatives Passed by Voters, 1970–1986

In the results shown, percentages have been rounded to the nearest full point except in cases where the result was extremely close.

Alaska		% Yes	% No
1974	Relocation of state capital	57	43
1974	Disclosure of candidates' personal finances	67	33
1976	Unicameral legislature (nonbinding)	52	48
1978	Relocation of state capital	56	44
1978	State's rights over federal land[a]	57	43
1982	State's rights over federal land[a]	71	29
1984	Abolition of state regulation of transportation	59	41
1986	Nuclear weapons freeze (nonbinding)	58	42

Arizona

		% Yes	% No
1972	Pre-emption by state of luxury, income taxes	53	47
1974	Judicial reform	54	46
1980	State lottery	51	49
1982	"Motor Voter" (voter registration reform)	54	46
1986	Limitation of campaign contributions to candidates	65	35

Arkansas

		% Yes	% No
1972	Repeal of railroad "full crew laws," retention of employees	63	37
1984	Four-year terms for state elected officials	64	36
1986	Change in requirements for bond approval in counties	54	46

California

		% Yes	% No
1972	Death penalty reinstatement[a]	67	33
1972	Coastal zone conservation	55	45
1972	Opposition to public school busing[a]	63	37
1974	Political reform (disclosure of campaign finances, etc.)	70	30
1978	Property tax cut (Proposition 13)	65	35
1978	Death penalty reinstated	71	29
1979	State spending limit	74	26
1982	Abolition of state inheritance tax[b]	62	38
1982	Abolition of state inheritance tax[b]	64	36
1982	Indexing of state income tax	63	37
1982	"Victims' Bill of Rights" (criminal law, sentencing)	57	43
1982	Nuclear weapons freeze (nonbinding)	52	48
1984	Reform of internal rules of legislature[a] ⌅	53	47
1984	Establishment of state lottery	58	42
1984	Establishment of English as official language (nonbinding)	71	29
1986	Change in requirements for voter approval of local taxes	58	42
1986	Establishment of English as official language	73	27
1986	Restriction of toxic pollution; "right to know" about toxics	63	27
1986	"Deep Pockets": limitation of joint and several liability	61	39

Colorado

		% Yes	% No
1972	Political ethics; campaign finance disclosure	60	40
1972	Ban on use of state funds for Winter Olympics	59	41
1974	Local government annexation requirements	58	42
1974	Restriction of public school busing	69	31
1974	Establishment of reapportionment commission	60	40
1974	Requirement of voter approval for under-ground nuclear explosions	58	42
1974	Death penalty for certain crimes	61	39
1980	Requirement of voter approval for local annexation	57	43
1980	Requirement of popular election of transportation board	56	44
1984	Ban on use of state funds for abortion	50.4	49.6
1984	"Motor Voter" (voter registration reform)	61	39

District of Columbia

		% Yes	% No
1980	Lottery	64	36
1980	Statehood constitutional convention	60	40
1982	Mandatory sentencing for gun, drug crimes	72	28
1982	Nuclear weapons freeze (nonbinding)	72	28
1983	Advisory commission to save historic Rhodes Tavern	60	40
1984	Right to overnight shelter for homeless	72	28
1987	Public hearings on education budget	77	23

Florida

		% Yes	% No
1976	Campaign finance disclosure	79	21
1986	State lottery	64	36

Idaho

		% Yes	% No
1970	Limitation on legislators' salaries	59	41
1974	Political ethics, campaign finance disclosure	77	23
1978	Property tax cut	58	42
1982	Property tax shift; partial exemption for homeowners	56	44
1982	Requirement of voter approval for any law restricting nuclear power	61	39

| 1982 | Legalization of sale, fitting of dentures by denture technicians | 65 | 35 |
| 1986 | State lottery | 64 | 36 |

Illinois		**% Yes**	**% No**
1980	Reduction of state representatives; single-member districts	68	32

Maine		**% Yes**	**% No**
1972	Elimination of party column on ballots	63	37
1976	Establishment of a state park on Bigelow Mountain	51	49
1976	Bottle Bill (five-cent beverage container deposit)	57	43
1977	Change in property tax classifications	57	43
1982	Partial indexing of state income tax	57	43
1985	Restriction of low-level nuclear waste disposal	50.3	49.7
1986	Ban on local measured telephone rate	58	42

Massachusetts		**% Yes**	**% No**
1974	Disclosure of campaign finances	65	35
1974	Use of highway revenue for public transportation	58	42
1980	Property tax cut (Proposition 2½)	60	40
1982	Restriction of nuclear power, nuclear waste disposal	67	33
1986	Limitation of government spending growth	55	45
1986	Toxic waste cleanup	73	27

Michigan		**% Yes**	**% No**
1972	Daylight savings time	55	45
1974	Repeal of sales tax on food and prescription drugs	56	44
1976	Bottle Bill (10-cent beverage container deposit)	64	36
1978	Limitations on parole	75	25
1978	Increase in minimum age for liquor purchases	57	43
1978	Limitation of state spending growth	53	47
1978	Establishment of collective bargaining for police	56	44

Statewide Initiatives

| 1982 | Abolition of utility rate "pass-through" clause | 51 | 49 |
| 1982 | Nuclear weapons freeze (nonbinding) | 57 | 43 |

Missouri		% Yes	% No
1974	Campaign finance disclosure	77	23
1976	Ban on "Construction Work in Progress" utility surcharge	63	37
1976	⅛-cent sales tax for wildlife programs	51	49
1980	Limitation of state spending growth	55	45
1982	One-cent sales tax for school funding, property tax relief	53	47
1984	Legalization of pari-mutuel betting	60	40

Montana		% Yes	% No
1974	Establishment of 90-day biennial legislative sessions	51	49
1976	Recall of elected officials	57	43
1976	Tax relief for owner-occupied homesteads	71	29
1978	Restriction of pornography[a]	53	47
1978	Requirement of voter approval for nuclear power/nuclear waste	65	35
1978	Wine sales in grocery stores	60	40
1980	Ban on disposal of low-level nuclear waste	51.1	49.9
1980	State income tax indexing	69	31
1980	Lobbyists' financial disclosure	78	22
1982	For nuclear weapons freeze, against MX missile (nonbinding)	57	43
1982	Investment of coal tax revenue in state economy	71	29
1984	Sale/fitting of dentures by denture technicians	53	47
1986	Limits on liability to be imposed by legislature	56	44
1986	Freezing of property taxes at 1986 levels	55	45

Nebraska		% Yes	% No
1982	Ban on corporate takeover of farms	56	44

Nevada		% Yes	% No
1982	Ban on personal property tax	76	24
1982	Office of utility consumer advocate	43	57[d]

North Dakota

		% Yes	% No
1976	Cut in sales tax from 4% to 3%; cut in vehicle tax	58	42
1978	State and local revenue sharing	72	28
1978	Income tax cut for individuals, increase for corporations	65	35
1978	Funding increase for fish and game department	68	32
1980	State housing loan program	60	40
1980	Increase in oil well production tax	56	44
1982	Nuclear weapons freeze (nonbinding)	58	42
1984	Addition of "right to bear arms" to state constitution	80	20

Ohio

		% Yes	% No
1977	Repeal of law allowing election-day voter registration	62	38

Oklahoma

		% Yes	% No
1978	Auto registration and tax payment by mail	64	36
1982	Legalization of pari-mutuel betting	58	42
1984	Legalization of sale of liquor "by the drink"	52	48

Oregon

		% Yes	% No
1970	Scenic waterways (ban on dams on certain rivers)	65	35
1972	Repeal of governors' retirement act	66	34
1972	Change in line of succession to office of governor	82	18
1974	Ban on purchase and sale of steelhead trout	63	37
1978	Sale/fitting of dentures by denture technicians	78	22
1978	Reinstatement of death penalty[a]	64	36
1978	Ban on "Construction Work in Progress" utility surcharges	69	31
1980	Requirement of voter approval for new nuclear power plants	53	47
1982	Nuclear weapons freeze (nonbinding)	62	38
1984	Citizens Utility Board (consumer advocacy group)	53	47
1984	Zero-emission standard for radioactive waste disposal	55	45

1984	Amendment of state constitution to allow lottery	66	34
1984	Establishment of state lottery	66	34
1984	Amendment of constitution to allow death penalty	56	44
1984	Requirement of death penalty for certain crimes	75	25
1986	Ban on local measured telephone rates	80	20
1986	Victims' rights, criminal law reform	75	25
1986	Voter registration deadline 21 days before election	70	30

South Dakota	**% Yes**	**% No**
1978 Ending of state regulation of milk prices	55	45
1982 Change from multiple- to single-member senate districts	52	48
1984 Change in opening/closing dates of public schools	50.2	49.8
1984 Requirement of voter approval for low-level radioactive waste disposal	62	38
1986 Fixing of Memorial Day to make 3-day weekend	59	41

Utah	**% Yes**	**% No**
1976 Ban on compulsory fluoridation of water	50.2	49.8

Washington	**% Yes**	**% No**
1972 Regulation of shoreline development[c]		
1972 Property tax limitation	76	24
1972 Political ethics, campaign finance disclosure	72	28
1973 Limitation of salary increases for judges and other officials	80	20
1975 Requirement of death penalty for certain crimes[a]	69	31
1977 Restriction of pornography[a]	55	45
1977 Repeal of sales tax on food	55	45
1978 Restriction of school busing[a]	66	34
1979 Tax limitation	68	32
1980 Ban on importation of nuclear waste[a]	75	25
1981 Requirement of voter approval for public power plant building bonds	58	42

1981	Repeal of state inheritance tax	66	34
1984	Sales tax exemption for value of trade-in items	69	31
1984	Ending of Indians' special fishing rights	53	47

[a]Initiative passed but later invalidated (wholly or in major part) by court ruling(s).

[b]Two similar Initiatives on same ballot; the one getting more votes took effect.

[c]See state of Washington Appendix II. A measure similar to the Initiative was sponsored by the state legislature, and the legislature's version took precedence because it received more votes.

[d]See state of Nevada in Appendix II. This Initiative is recorded here as a "winning" Initiative because proponents accomplished their objective, even though their measure did not receive a majority of the vote.

Appendix IV

Petitioning:
A State-by-State Guide
to Rights and Requirements

THE RIGHT TO PETITION

Before starting any petition drive, readers should confirm the requirements listed here with state or local election officials.

As noted repeatedly above, shopping malls are the best place to circulate petitions. A study of shopping mall patronage in the late 1970s showed that during an average 30-day period, 87 percent of all adults living in the San Jose, California, metropolitan area made one or more visits to one or more of the area's 15 largest shopping centers. Unfortunately, most shopping malls are on private property, and mall managers often deny Initiative petition circulators access.

The U.S. Supreme Court in the early 1970s denied any *federal* right to free speech in malls, but later decided to uphold a *California* ruling guaranteeing mall access for petition circulators (*Pruneyard Shopping Center* v. *Robins,* 447 U.S. 74, 64 L. Ed. 741, 100 S. Ct. 2035 [1980]). Next, Washington State Initiative petition circulators won access to malls in the case of *Alderwood Associates* v. *Washington Environmental Council* (69 Wn. 2d. 230 [1981]).

Courts in Oregon (*Lloyd Corp.* v. *Whiffen,* 1988), Massachusetts and Bergen County, New Jersey, have also upheld petitioners' rights to free speech in malls. But state supreme courts have ruled against petition circulators' mall access in Connecticut, North Carolina, Michigan (1985), and New York (1985). Lower courts in Maryland and Florida have followed this trend.

In 1986 the Pennsylvania Supreme Court struck a compromise on mall access. In the case of *Western Pennsylvania Socialist Workers Party* v. *Connecticut General Life Insurance Co.,* the court ruled that malls that allow access to any solicitors (such as the March of Dimes or Salvation Army) must also allow access to political petitioners. But malls that deny access to all solicitors may continue to do so.

In states where courts have ruled against mall access, free speech advocates are trying a new strategy: legislation. In Michigan, State Rep. Perry Bullard in 1986 introduced a mall access bill, H.B. 5449, with backing from the Michigan Citizens Lobby. In New York, similar bills backed by the state chapter of the American Civil Liberties Union were introduced in 1986 by Assembly Speaker Stanley Fink (A-10512) and State Sen. John Marchi (S-8844).

The right to circulate petitions on public sidewalks and other public places with unrestricted access has long been guaranteed by the U.S. Supreme Court (*Hague* v. *CIO,* 307 U.S. 496 [1939]). In California, even the right to solicit signatures door-to-door is guaranteed by the state supreme court's ruling in *Van Nuys Publishing Co.* v. *City of Thousand Oaks* (5 Cal. 3d. 817 [1971]).

STATEWIDE INITIATIVE & REFERENDUM PETITION REQUIREMENTS

State	Initiative Statutes		Constitutional Amendments		Nos. Given Valid Until	Referendum
	%	No.	%	No.		%
Alaska	10 TV	20,343	—	—	1991	10 TV
Ariz.	10 GV	86,699	15 GV	130,048	1991	5 GV
Ark.	8 GV	55,081	10 GV	68,851	1991	6 GV
Calif.	5 GV	372,174	8 GV	595,479	1991	5 GV

State	Initiative Statutes %	Initiative Statutes No.	Constitutional Amendments %	Constitutional Amendments No.	Nos. Given Valid Until	Referendum %
Colo.	5 SV	50,668	5 SV	50,668	1991	5 SV
D.C.	5 RV	15,000[a]	—	—	1989[a]	5 RV
Fla.	—	—	8 PV	363,886	1993	—
Idaho	10 GV	38,743	—	—	1991	10 GV
Ill.[b]	10 RV	600,381	8 GV	180,813	1991	—
Maine	10 GV	42,686	—	—	1991	10 GV
Mass.[c]	3 GV	50,525	3 GV	50,525	1991	2 GV
Md.	—	—	—	—	—	3 GV
Mich.	8 GV	191,725	10 GV	239,656	1991	5 GV
Mo.	5 GV	104,296	8 GV	166,874	1993	5 GV
Mont.	5 GV	18,351	10 GV	36,702	1993	5 GV
Neb.	7 GV	39,510	10 GV	56,442	1991	5 GV
Nev.	10 TV	35,426	10 TV	35,426	1991	10 TV
N. Dak.[d]	2 pop.	13,055	4 pop.	26,110	1991	2 pop.
N. Mex.	—	—	—	—	—	10 TV
Ohio	3 GV[e]	91,999	10 GV	306,662	1991	6 GV
Okla.	8 TV	93,683	15 TV	175,656	1991	5 TV
Oreg.	6 GV	63,578	8 GV	84,770	1991	4 GV
S. Dak.	5 GV	14,723	10 GV	29,444	1991	5 GV
Utah	10 GV	64,911	—	—	1993	10 GV
Wash.	8 GV	150,001	—	—	1993	4 GV
Wyo.	15 TV	27,962	—	—	1991	15 TV

Abbreviations:

GV = Total votes cast for office of governor at preceding gubernatorial election.

PV = Total votes cast at preceding presidential election.

RV = Registered voters.

SV = Total votes cast for office of secretary of state at previous election for that office.

TV = Total votes cast at preceding general election for state officer receiving highest number of votes.

[a]Since the District of Columbia's petition requirement is based on the number of registered voters as of 30 days before petition drive begins, it is constantly changing.

[b]Illinois statutory Initiatives are nonbinding—that is, they cannot be used to enact legislation and merely function as advice to the legislature. Illinois constitutional Initiatives *are* binding, but their subject matter is so restricted that only one such Initiative has ever qualified for the ballot (see Chapter 5).

Requirements, continued

cProponents of Massachusetts statutory Initiatives must submit petitions with an additional 0.5 percent of the GV (8,421 signatures) seven months after completing their initial petition drive. Massachusetts constitutional Initiatives are hampered by the legislature's prerogative to block them from the ballot. In no other state does the legislature have this power.
dNorth Dakota's petition requirement is based on a percentage of the state's total population, as recorded in the decennial census.
eProponents of Ohio Initiative statutes must submit petitions with signatures equal to 3 percent of the GV before the legislature convenes and another set of petitions (with an equal number of additional signatures) after it adjourns.

SUMMARY OF LOCAL INITIATIVE AND REFERENDUM PROCEDURES

ALABAMA

State law (Code of Alabama 1975, Sec. 11-44-105) allows Initiative ordinances in cities with an "Option A" commission form of government by petition of 25 percent of the registered voters. As of 1981, Mobile was the only city with this form of government.

ALASKA

All Alaska cities and boroughs (counties) allow Initiative ordinances and Referendums, and, in cities with charters, Initiative charter amendments. Petition requirements vary. In Anchorage the requirement for all types of voter-initiated ballot measures is signatures equal to 10 percent of the number of ballots cast in the previous mayoral election.

ARIZONA

All municipalities and counties allow Initiative ordinances, Referendums, and, in chartered cities, Initiative charter amendments. In most jurisdictions the petition requirement is 15 percent of registered voters for Initiative ordinances or charter amendments, 10 percent for Referendums.

ARKANSAS

All municipalities allow Initiative ordinances and Referendums by petition of voters equal to 15 percent of the number of ballots cast in the previous mayoral election. For counties, the requirement for Initiative ordinances and Referendums is 15 percent of the vote total in the previous election for circuit clerk.

CALIFORNIA

All municipalities and counties allow Initiative ordinances, Referendums, and, were there are charters, Initiative charter amendments. Petition requirements vary but are usually reasonable. In San Francisco and Los Angeles, petition quotas for Initiative ordinances as of 1988 are approximately 12,000 and 70,000, respectively.

COLORADO

All municipalities allow Initiative ordinances, Referendums, and, in home rule cities, Initiative charter amendments. Petition requirements vary. Denver requires signatures equal to 5 percent of the previous mayoral vote total for Initiative ordinances and charter amendments, and 5 percent of the local gubernatorial vote for Initiative charter amendments.

CONNECTICUT

Initiative ordinances can be proposed in any of the roughly 80 non-chartered towns. The petition requirement is 200 voters, or 10 percent of the registered voters, whichever is less.

DELAWARE

Initiative ordinances can be proposed only in a handful of towns, like Arden, that still govern themselves by town meeting.

FLORIDA

All municipalities allow Initiative charter amendments by petition of 10 percent of the registered voters. The state's home rule counties also allow Initiative charter amendments: Broward (Fort Lauderdale), Dade (Miami), Jacksonville, Pinellas (St. Petersburg), Sarasota, and Volusia (Daytona Beach). Petition requirements vary from 7 percent of the number of votes cast in the previous general election (Broward) to 10 percent of registered voters (Dade, Jacksonville, Pinellas). Dade and Broward counties also allow Initiative ordinances, by petition of 4 percent of registered voters in Dade, and 7 percent of the previous general election vote total in Broward.

GEORGIA

State law provides for Initiative charter amendments and Referendums in all municipalities. Petition requirements are set by Georgia Code Annotated Sec. 36-35-3. For cities with population over 100,000, the requirement is 15 percent of registered voters. The state constitution (Art. 9, Sec. 2, Para. 1) sets out petition requirements for Initiative charter amendments in all counties (10 percent of registered voters in counties with a population over 50,000). Atlanta is one of the few cities that provide for Initiative ordinances. The petition requirement is 15 percent of registered voters.

HAWAII

Initiative ordinances and charter amendments are allowed in all four of Hawaii's island counties: Hawaii, Oahu, Kauai, and Maui. Referendums are also allowed. Petition requirements vary from 5 percent of the mayoral vote (for Initiative ordinances in Kauai) to 20 percent of registered voters (for Initiative charter amendments in Hawaii, Maui, and Kauai). Cities do not have governments separate from the counties.

IDAHO

All cities and counties allow Initiative ordinances and Referendums by petition of 20 percent of registered voters. Some local charters also provide for Initiative charter amendments.

ILLINOIS

Nonbinding advisory Initiatives can be placed on ballots in all municipalities by petition of 10 percent of registered voters. In addition, Illinois's 1970 constitution (Art. 7) provides for Initiatives to "alter, amend, or repeal" the form of municipal government by petition of voters equal to 10 percent of the total vote in the previous general election.

INDIANA

Provision for Initiative is limited to a narrow range of specified purposes. One is municipalities' purchase and/or operation of a local utility, and creation of utility service board to run the utility. Petitions proposing such Initiatives must be signed by at least 5 percent of the registered voters. This provision does not apply to cities with populations over 150,000 (see Indiana Statues, Title 8, Transportation and Public Utilities, Art. 1, Public Utilities, Chap. 2, Public Service Commission Act of 1913, Sec. 8-1-2-99 and 100). There is also a Referendum provision for rules changes adopted by local school boards (see IC 20-4-10.1-8[d]).

IOWA

Only Iowa City has a provision in its charter for Initiative ordinances and Referendums. State law provides for Initiatives to change the form of city government in any city (by petition of voters equal to 25 percent of ballots cast in previous general election), but options are limited to five specific forms of government. State law also provides for local Initiatives on a narrow range of specified subjects, such as enactment of sales and services, hotel/motel and vehicle taxes, and property tax levies to fund local libraries or (musical) bands (see Iowa Code Ch. 422[a] and 422[b], Iowa Code Sec. 362.4 and 384.12).

KANSAS

All cities and counties have home rule, and therefore their provisions for I&R vary widely. State law sets out provisions for Initiatives on a narrow range of subjects (for example, municipal

Initiative charter amendments are limited to proposals to change the form of city government). Local charters may include broader provisions.

KENTUCKY

The only jurisdiction with full-fledged I&R is the city and county of Lexington. Citizens may propose Initiative ordinances or Referendums by petition of 25 percent of the number of voters casting ballots in the previous mayoral election; the requirement for Initiative charter amendments is 10 percent. State law allows Initiatives elsewhere only on a limited range of subjects: local option on liquor sales, changes in cities' form of government; Referendums are allowed on some local tax increases.

LOUISIANA

New Orleans does not allow Initiative ordinances or Referendums, but provides for Initiative charter amendments by petition of 10,000 voters. Most of the state's most populous areas provide for Initiative charter amendments; petition requirements vary. Shreveport and Jefferson Parish (Metairie) have provisions for Initiative ordinances and Referendums by petition of 10 percent of the registered voters. State law also allows Initiatives on a narrow range of subjects (like local option on liquor sales) in all parishes (equivalent to counties).

MAINE

State law provides for Initiative charter amendments in all chartered jurisdictions by petition of voters equal to 20 percent of ballots cast in the previous gubernatorial election (see Maine Revised Statutes Annotated, Title 30, Sec. 1914). Most major cities have provisions for Initiative ordinances and Referendums; petition requirements vary. A few (Bangor, Lewiston, Portland) have the peculiar restriction that petitions cannot be circulated: they may be signed by voters only at the city hall. In towns governed by town meetings, voters may put Initiative ordinances on the town meeting warrant (agenda) by petition.

MARYLAND

State law provides for Initiative charter amendments in Maryland's 150 chartered cities by petition of 20 percent of the registered voters, and in the eight chartered counties by petition of 10,000 voters, or 20 percent of registered voters, whichever is less. These counties are Anne Arundel (Annapolis), Baltimore, Harford, Howard, Montgomery, Prince Georges, Talbot, and Wicomico. These counties, plus Allegany, Kent, and Worcester counties, provide for Referendums by petition of 5 to 10 percent of registered voters (requirements vary). See Annotated Code of Maryland, Art. 23A and 25A.

MASSACHUSETTS

State law provides for Initiative ordinances and Referendums in cities that have adopted government plans A through F (see General Laws, Chap. 43, Sec. 37-44). Most of the State's major cities, with the exception of Boston, have provisions for Initiative ordinances and Referendums. Springfield and Worcester allow Initiative charter amendments; most other large cities do not. State law provides for nonbinding advisory Initiatives in all state house and senate districts. The petition requirement is 1,000 voters for state senatorial districts; 200 voters for state house districts.

MICHIGAN

State law provides for Initiative charter amendments in all cities with charters by petition of 5 percent of the registered voters. Most major cities provide for Initiative ordinances and Referendums; petition requirements vary. The easiest such requirement is Detroit's: 3 percent of the number of ballots cast in the previous mayoral election. County charters must provide for I&R, but the only chartered county is Wayne (Detroit).

MINNESOTA

State law provides for Initiative charter amendments in all 104 chartered cities by petition of 5 percent of the registered voters. Of these cities, 69 also provide for Initiative ordinances and Referendums. St. Paul is one of the 69, but its twin—Minneapolis—is not. A chart listing petition requirements in all 104 cities is available from the League of Minnesota Cities, 480 Cedar St., St. Paul, MN 55101. Petition requirements generally range from 5 to 10 percent of registered voters.

MISSISSIPPI

There are 23 cities with charters: some of these may have I&R provisions. In addition, state law provides for Initiatives on a narrow range of subjects (like changing the form of municipal government) in all municipalities. For details, see Mississippi Annotated Code, Title 21, Sec. 21-8-1 et. seq.

MISSOURI

All of the state's chartered cities and counties provide for Initiative ordinances and charter amendments and Referendums. There are approximately 25 chartered cities (including most of the state's largest cities) and two chartered counties: St. Louis and Jackson (Kansas City). Petition requirements vary, but most range between 5 percent of the previous mayoral vote, and 10 percent of the registered voters.

MONTANA

All municipalities and counties provide for Initiative ordinances and Referendums by petition of 15 percent of registered voters. Municipal Initiative charter amendments are allowed by petition of 15 percent of registered voters, but are limited to the single purpose of changing a city's form of government.

NEBRASKA

All cities and towns provide for Initiative ordinances and Referendums. In Omaha, the petition requirement is 15 percent of the ballots cast in the previous mayoral election; in Lincoln it is 5 percent of registered voters for Initiative ordinances, 6 percent for Referendums. In all other cities and towns it is 15 percent of registered voters. Omaha and Lincoln also provide for Initiative charter amendments.

NEVADA

All cities and counties provide for Initiative ordinances and Referendums by petition of 15 percent and 10 percent, respectively, of total votes in the previous general election. Chartered cities also provide for Initiative charter amendments.

NEW HAMPSHIRE

In all towns, Initiative ordinances may be proposed for town meeting or town ballot by petition of 5 percent of registered voters (see New Hampshire Revised Statues Annotated, Chap. 4 A : 2). In all incorporated cities and towns, charter amendment Initiatives may be proposed by petition of voters equal to 20 percent of ballots cast in the previous gubernatorial election (see NHRSA 49 B : 5II). Of the state's four largest cities, only Nashua provides for Initiative ordinances—by petition of voters equal to 5 percent of the previous gubernatorial vote.

NEW JERSEY

Most of the state's large cities have provisions for Initiative ordinances and Referendums under the Optional Municipal Charter Law of 1950, under which 100 local jurisdictions now operate, including Newark, Elizabeth, Camden, Passaic, New Brunswick, Trenton, Jersey City, Paterson, Atlantic City, and the suburban townships of Cherry Hill and Hamilton. There are 35 additional jurisdictions with Initiative ordinance and Referendum provisions set out in the Commission Form of Government Law of 1916. Petition requirements range from 15 percent of the number of ballots cast for state legislative seats in the previous election (in the most populous jurisdictions) to 25 percent of the registered voters.

NEW MEXICO

All counties, as well as cities with a commission-manager form of government (including Albuquerque), provide for Initiative ordinances and Referendums, by petition of voters equal to 20 percent of the ballots cast in the previous general election. Commission-manager cities also provide for Initiative charter amendments by petition of 5 percent of registered voters, as does Gallup. Los Alamos provides for Initiative ordinances and Referendums by petition of voters equal to 15 percent of the general election vote; Gallup's petition requirement for these is 20 percent of the gubernatorial vote.

NEW YORK

In New York City, Initiative charter amendments can be proposed by petition of 50,000 registered voters. In the other 62 chartered cities, Initiative charter amendments can be proposed by petition of 30,000 voters, or voters equal to 10 percent of the previous gubernatorial vote, whichever is less (see Municipal Home Rule Law, Art. 4, Sec. 37). State law limits Initiative and Referendum in towns and villages to a narrow range of specified subjects, such as establishment of public parks, playgrounds, and airports.

NORTH CAROLINA

State law provides for Initiative charter amendments in all 450 municipalities by petition of 5,000 voters or 10 percent of the registered voters, whichever is less (see NC General Statutes, 160A-101 to 110). In all cities and counties, certain types of bond issues are subject to Referendum upon petition of 10 percent of the registered voters (see NC General Statutes, Secs. 159–60). Some municipal charters provide for Initiative ordinances (including those of Asheville, Greensboro, Raleigh, and Wilmington) and Referendums (all of the above except Wilmington). Petition requirements range from 10 percent (Raleigh) to 25 percent (Greensboro and Wilmington) of the votes cast in the previous municipal election. Asheville's requirement is a flat 1,000 registered voters.

NORTH DAKOTA

All North Dakota cities with commission or home rule charter forms of government allow Initiative ordinances and Referendums. These include about 38 of the state's most populous cities:

Fargo, Grand Forks, Bismarck, Minot, Jamestown, Williston, Dickinson, and others. Petition requirements vary, but the standard is 15 percent of the previous mayoral vote. County Initiatives are limited to a narrow range of subjects specified by state law. Small towns provide for nonbinding advisory Initiatives to be proposed by citizen petition.

OHIO

All municipalities allow Initiative ordinances and Referendums; most provide also for Initiative charter amendments. Among the major cities, petition requirements are easiest in Cleveland (5,000 signatures to propose an Initiative ordinance) and Columbus (5 percent of the number of votes cast in the previous general election). The most difficult big-city petition quota is Dayton's—25 percent of registered voters to propose an Initiative ordinance (though Dayton charter amendments require only 10 percent). State law provides for Referendums in all counties, but only on bills to establish or increase taxes. The petition requirement for these is 10 percent of the ballots cast in the previous gubernatorial election.

OKLAHOMA

All municipalities provide for Initiative ordinances, charter amendments, and Referendums proposed by petition; signatures equal to 25 percent of the votes cast in the preceding general election are required.

OREGON

All Oregon cities and counties provide for Initiative ordinances, charter amendments, and Referendums. The petition requirements for counties is 6 percent of the number of ballots cast for governor in the preceding election for ordinances and charter amendments, and 4 percent of that number for Referendums. For cities, the state constitution sets a maximum signature requirement at 15 percent of the registered voters for Initiative ordinances and charter amendments, 10 percent of the voters for Referendums. Requirements are lower in most of the large cities.

PENNSYLVANIA

State law provides for Initiative charter amendments in all 53 jurisdictions (cities, boroughs, townships, etc.) with home rule charters, except Philadelphia. The petition requirement is 10 percent of the number of ballots cast for governor at the preceding election. Of these 53 jurisdictions, 35 provide for Initiative ordinances and Referendums. Scranton's petition requirement for these is 15 percent of the votes cast in the preceding mayoral election. In 49 additional cities, state law provides for Initiative ordinances and Referendums proposed by petition of voters equal to 20 percent of the mayoral vote (see Third Class City Code, Sec. 1030 and 1050). For details, order the free booklet "Citizen Referenda in Local Government" from the Information Services Center, Department of Community Services, P.O. Box 155, Harrisburg, PA 17120.

RHODE ISLAND

Of the state's major cities, only a few have I&R provisions. Providence provides for Initiative ordinances proposed by 5 percent of the registered voters. Newport provides for Initiative ordinances and Referendums proposed by 20 percent of the voters. North Kingstown allows Initiative ordinances by petition of 10 percent of the voters.

SOUTH CAROLINA

All cities and counties provide for Initiative ordinances and Referendums by petition of 15 percent of the registered voters (see South Carolina Code, Sec. 5-17-10, 5-17-20, 4-9-210, and 4-9-230).

SOUTH DAKOTA

All cities allow Initiative ordinances and Referendums by petition of voters equal to 5 percent of the votes cast at the previous gubernatorial election. All counties allow Initiative ordinances by petition of 10 percent, and Referendums by petition of 5 percent, of the gubernatorial vote.

TENNESSEE

Provisions for I&R are found only in some of the municipalities with home rule charters. Among the state's most populous jurisdictions, Memphis has no I&R provisions; Chattanooga and Knoxville allow Initiative ordinances, charter amendments, and Referendums (by petition of 25 percent of the mayoral vote in Chattanooga, and 25 percent of the vote for judicial offices in Knoxville); Nashville-Davidson County allows Initiative charter amendments proposed by petition of voters equal to 10 percent of the ballots cast in the preceding general election.

TEXAS

All 217 cities with home rule charters and more than 5,000 residents (including all major Texas cities) provide for Initiative charter amendments by petition of 5 percent of the registered voters or 20,000 voters, whichever is less. Most cities provide for Initiative ordinances and Referendums. Petition requirements range from 5 percent to 10 percent of registered voters. County bond issues and local property tax increases are subject to Referendums proposed by 5 percent and 15 percent, respectively, of the registered voters (Texas Property Tax Code, Sec. 2607, 1980 Supplement, originally passed by the legislature and signed by Governor Clements in 1979 as Senate Bill 621).

UTAH

All municipalities provide for Initiative ordinances and Referendums. Petition requirements are based on a sliding scale that ranges from 10 percent of the gubernatorial vote (in cities where more than 10,000 votes for governor were cast) to 30 percent of the gubernatorial vote (in towns where fewer than 250 gubernatorial votes were cast). In the state's two chartered cities, Tooele and Ogden, petition requirements for Initiative charter amendments are based on the same scale.

VERMONT

State law provides for Initiative ordinances and Referendums in all municipalities by petition of 5 percent of registered voters (see

Vermont Statutes Annotated, Title 17, 2642[a]). In all of the roughly 50 chartered jurisdictions, Initiative charter amendments can be
proposed by petition of 5 percent of the registered voters (see VSA,
Title 17, 2645).

VIRGINIA

State law limits city and county Initiatives to a narrow range of
specified subjects, including local option on liquor sales, and Sunday closing of businesses ("blue laws"). Four major cities have their
own I&R provisions. Hampton, Norfolk, and Portsmouth provide
for Initiative ordinances and Referendums (the petition requirement is 25 percent of the municipal vote in Hampton and Norfolk;
30 percent of the gubernatorial vote in Portsmouth). Richmond
provides for Initiative charter amendments and Referendums on
bond issues by petition of voters equal to 10 percent of the most
recent presidential vote.

WASHINGTON

All major cities have provisions for Initiative ordinances and Referendums; most also provide for Initiative charter amendments.
Only five counties have I&R provisions: King, Snohomish, What-
com, Clallam, and Pierce. Petition requirements range from 5 percent of the mayoral vote (for Initiative ordinances in Spokane) to
25 percent of the mayoral vote (for Initiative ordinances and Referendums in Olympia). Seattle's requirements for Initiative ordinances, charter amendments, and Referendums are 10 percent, 15
percent, and 8 percent, respectively, of the mayoral vote.

WEST VIRGINIA

State law provides for Initiative charter amendments in all
chartered cities by petition of 15 percent of the registered voters in
Class 1 and 2 cities, and 20 percent of the registered voters in Class
3 cities (see West Virginia Code, Chap. 8, Art. 4, Sec. 7). Most of the
major cities have provisions also for Initiative ordinances and Referendums—as do Charleston, Morgantown, Parkersburg, and
Wheeling. Petition requirements range from 10 percent of the
mayoral vote (to propose Initiative ordinances in Charleston) to 15

percent of the registered voters (to propose Initiative charter amendments in all four cities).

WISCONSIN

State law provides for Initiative ordinances in all cities, proposed by petition of voters equal to 15 percent of the ballots cast in the most recent gubernatorial election. In towns, voters can petition to put Initiative ordinances on the town meeting agenda.

WYOMING

As of 1988 Wyoming has no Initiative and Referendum provisions at the local level.

Notes

Preface

1. Joshua Meyrowitz, *No Sense of Place: The Impact of Electronic Media on Social Behavior* (New York: Oxford University Press, 1985).

Chapter 1

1. Charles S. Lobingier, *The People's Law* (New York: Macmillan, 1909), p. 229.

2. Ibid., p. 155.

3. Ibid., pp. 166–67.

4. Ibid., p. 190.

5. Ibid.

6. Ibid., p. 229.

7. Ibid.

8. Ibid., p. 340.

9. Doane Robinson, untitled article in a September 1910 issue of the St. Paul *Pioneer Press,* reprinted in *Equity Series,* October 1910, p. 159; J. W. Arrowsmith, "The Direct Legislation Movement in New Jersey," *Direct Legislation Record,* May 1894, p. 2.

10. Andreas Gross, "Die direkte Gesetzgebung durch das Volk: Die Utopie des Karl Buerkli (1823–1901)" (Ph.D. diss., University of Lausanne, 1983).

11. Edwin S. Potter, "Letting the People Rule," *Equity,* April 1914, p. 121.

12. Arrowsmith, "Direct Legislation Movement."

13. Ibid.

14. Ibid.

15. George Brown Tindall, *America: A Narrative History* (New York: Norton, 1984), p. 775.

16. *Direct Legislation Record* September 1896, pp. 25–26.

17. Potter, "Letting the People Rule," pp. 122–23.

18. John D. Hicks, *The Populist Revolt* (Minneapolis: University of Minnesota Press, 1931), p. 408.

19. Jim Martin, "Oregon System's Founder Always Put the People First," *Oregon Territory* (Sunday magazine section of the *Portland Oregonian*), 17 June 1979.

20. William S. U'Ren, "Initiative and Referendum in Oregon," *Arena* 32 (1904), p. 28.

21. Eltweed Pomeroy, "March of Direct Legislation," *Arena* 35 (1906), p. 271; William S. U'Ren, "The Results of the Initiative and Referendum in Oregon," *Proceedings of the American Political Science Association* 4 (1907), p. 193.

22. Charles F. Taylor, "Steps Toward Pure Democracy," *Equity Series,* January 1909, p. 1.

23. Richard Hofstadter, *The Age of Reform* (New York: Vintage Books, 1956), pp. 131, 167.

24. Ibid., p. 97.

25. Theodore Roosevelt, "Charter of Democracy" (speech to 1912 Ohio constitutional convention), quoted in *Equity,* January 1913, p. 18.

26. Woodrow Wilson, quoted in *Equity,* January 1913, p. 18.

27. *Equity,* July 1917, pp. 132–33.

28. Hicks, *Populist Revolt,* pp. 263, 337.

29. Hofstadter, *Age of Reform,* pp. 163–64.

30. Ibid., pp. 139–40.

31. Tindall, *America: A Narrative History,* p. 703; Hofstadter, *Age of Reform,* p. 185.

32. Hofstadter, *Age of Reform,* p. 185.

33. Quoted in Tindall, *America: A Narrative History,* p. 793.

34. Carey McWilliams, *California: The Great Exception* (New York: Current Books/A. A. Wynn, 1949), p. 95.

35. *Equity Series,* October 1908, p. 120.

36. Arthur A. Ekirch, Jr., *Progressivism in America* (New York: New Viewpoints, 1974), pp. 20–24.

37. *Equity,* January 1911, p. 19.

38. Hicks, *Populist Revolt,* p. 253.

39. Charles F. Taylor's *Equity* repeatedly mentions these as the most active and widespread opponents of the Initiative process.

40. See Virginia Graham, *A Compilation of Statewide Initiative Proposals Appearing on Ballots Through 1976* (Washington, D.C.: Congressional Research Service, 1978). See also Appendix II below.

41. Graham, *Compilation.*

Chapter 2

1. Kelly Jenkins, quoted in *Initiative News Report* 4, no. 20 (28 October 1983).

2. Dennis Jensen, "Computers, Control and Communication: How 30,000 Volunteers Beat the Gun Initiative," *Campaigns and Elections* 4, no. 3 (1983).

3. Personal recollection of the author.

4. Fred Sollop and Susan Nicholls, *Motor Voter: Toward Universal Registration* (Washington, D.C. and New York: Initiative Resource Center and Human SERVE Fund, 1986).

5. Jane Metzinger, telephone interview with the author, 20 January 1984. Metzinger was a researcher at the Washington, D.C., headquarters of Common Cause.

6. California Fair Political Practices Commission, *FPPC Bulletin* 12, no. 4.

7. Michael Isikoff, "Subsidized-Farm-Loan Plan Falls Flat in Virginia," *Washington Post,* 30 May 1983. See also Martha M. Hamilton, "States, Cities Use Bonds for New Purposes," *Washington Post,* 1 January 1984.

8. Sandra Boodman, and Michael Isikoff, "Pandemonium Is a Way of Life in Virginia's Lawmaking Process," *Washington Post,* 7 February 1983.

9. Tom Sherwood, and Sandra Sugawara, "Committee Kills Bills by the Dozen: Richmond's Night of the Long Knives," *Washington Post,* 13 February 1984.

10. *Initiative News Report* 6, nos. 6, 7, 8, 9, and 10; 4, no. 23; 3, nos. 8 and 10.

11. The studies analyzed voter participation in: 1) California general elections in 1970–1982 (David Magleby, *Direct Legislation* [Baltimore: Johns Hopkins University Press, 1984], pp. 84–85); 2) Colorado's 1976 general election (John Shockley, *The Initiative Process in Colorado Politics* [Boulder: University of Colorado Bureau

of Governmental Research and Service, 1980], p. 3); 3) the 1984 general elections in Oregon (Secretary of State, *1984 Election Results*) and the 1984 general election in Washington (Secretary of State, *1984 Election Results*).

12. Thomas Jefferson, letter to James Madison, 20 December 1787, reprinted in Richard Hofstadter, ed., *Great Issues in American History* (New York: Vintage Books, 1958), p. 115.

13. George Gallup, Sr., telephone interview with the author, 20 January 1984.

14. Woodrow Wilson, quoted in *Equity,* January 1913, p. 18.

Chapter 3

1. Joyce Koupal, letter to the author, 23 October 1983.

2. Lynn Lilliston, "One Man's Family in Pollution War: Smog Vote Petition Battle," *Los Angeles Times View,* 30 July 1971.

3. Ibid.

4. Joyce Koupal, telephone interview with the author, 15 August 1983.

5. Koupal interview.

6. California Constitution, Art. 4, Sec. 1, 22, 23; Art. 23, Sect. 1, 2, 7.

7. John Forster, interview with the author, 3 September 1983.

8. Ibid.

9. Ibid.

10. "500,000 Signatures Claimed in Move to Recall Reagan," *Los Angeles Times,* 30 May 1968.

11. Lou Cannon, telephone interview with the author, 10 October 1983.

12. "Threats Cited in Drive to Recall Reagan," *Los Angeles Times,* 19 July 1968.

13. "Recall Drive Comes to End, Reagan Hails Apparent Failure," *Los Angeles Times,* 1 August 1968.

14. J. Koupal letter to author.

15. Ibid.; Koupal interview.

16. Lilliston, "One Man's Family."

17. Koupal interview.

18. Lilliston, "One Man's Family."

19. Koupal interview.

20. Los Angeles County Board of Supervisors, resolution com-

mending People's Lobby, 24 December 1974; "Supervisors Kill Resolution That Lauded Oil Firm," *Los Angeles Times,* 25 December 1974.

21. John Forster interview, 1983.

22. Laura Tallian, *Direct Democracy* (Los Angeles: People's Lobby Press, 1977), pp. 102–3.

23. Ibid.

24. Lilliston, "One Man's Family."

25. James R. Oakley, Office of the Attorney General, Memorandum to Governor Earl Warren, 27 April 1943, quoted in Tallian, *Direct Democracy,* p. 98; see also pp. 101–5.

26. Lilliston, "One Man's Family."

27. Dwayne Hunn, "Ed Koupal: 'Dream Bigger!' " printed eulogy, copy in the possession of the author, April 1976.

28. J. Koupal letter.

29. S. Prakash Sethi, "The Selling of an Idea—In the Public Interest: The California Campaign to Enact Proposition 9, the Clean Environment Act of 1972," in his *Advocacy Advertising and Large Corporations* (Lexington, Mass.: Lexington Books, 1977), pp. 179–234.

30. Ibid., pp. 195–96, 215 (People's Lobby, newspaper advertisement for Clean Environment Initiative), 188–89.

31. James L. Wanvig, Memorandum to O. N. Miller, 4 June 1971; Whitaker and Baxter, "Preliminary Plan of Campaign Against the People's Lobby Initiative," 1 June 1971. Both in People's Lobby, *Proposition 9, the Political Reform Act: A Fact for California, a Proposal for America* (Los Angeles: People's Lobby Press, 1974), pp. 57–64.

32. Sethi, *Advocacy Advertising,* pp. 212–22.

33. Ibid., p. 196.

34. Ibid., p. 206; see also Chapter 4 herein on anti–nuclear power Initiatives.

35. Daniel H. Lowenstein, "Campaign Spending and Ballot Propositions," paper delivered to the annual meeting of the American Political Science Association, New York City, 5 September 1981, p. 34, Published as "Campaign Spending and Ballot Propositions: Recent Experience, Public Choice Theory, and the First Amendment," *UCLA Law Review* 29, no. 505 (1982).

36. Forster interview, 1983.

37. J. Koupal letter.

38. People's Lobby, *Political Reform Act of 1974* (Los Angeles: People's Lobby Press, 1974), p. 25.

39. Ibid., p. 10.

40. Koupal interview.

41. Al Martinez, "Proposition 9: Its Birth Pangs Nearly Killed It," *Los Angeles Times,* 21 June 1974.

42. Personal recollection of the author.

43. Martinez, "Proposition 9."

44. People's Lobby, *Political Reform Act,* p. 8.

45. Ibid.

46. "Bradley Criticized for State-Paid Aide," *San Jose Mercury,* 7 March 1974.

47. "COPE Delegates Hit Prop. 9 as Anti-Labor Measure," *California AFL-CIO News,* 12 April 1974.

48. George Skelton, "People's Lobby Sues Top Foe of Political Reform Measure," *Los Angeles Times,* 23 April 1973.

49. "People's Lobby Head Starts State Walk," *Sacramento Bee,* 8 March 1974.

50. Forster interview, 1983.

51. "Standard Oil's Family Probe," *San Francisco Examiner,* 21 January 1975; "People's Lobby Founders Sue Standard Oil, Others," *Sacramento Bee,* 20 January 1975.

52. Mervyn M. Dymally, letter to Joyce Koupal, 12 February 1974; Mervyn M. Dymally, letter to Edwin Koupal, 19 April 1974; both reprinted in People's Lobby, *Political Reform Act,* p. 29.

53. "2 Democratic Candidates Lose Support of COPE," *Sacramento Union,* 15 May 1974.

54. "SF Ad Firm Puts Together Campaign Against Prop. 9," *Sacramento Bee,* 14 May 1974.

55. People's Lobby, *Politician Reform Act,* p. 28.

56. Lowenstein, "Campaign Spending."

57. "Prop. 9 Wins," *Los Angeles Times,* 5 June 1974.

58. Quoted in Hunn, "Ed Koupal."

59. Martinez, "Proposition 9."

60. The idea was for city electric customers to purchase their power at lower cost directly from the city government, which owns the massive Hetch Hetchy Dam and Power Plant in the Sierra Nevada. "We're going to vote them out of existence," Koupal threat-

ened, with a backward glance toward PG&E headquarters ("We've Come to Buy the PG&E," *San Francisco Examiner,* 20 June 1974).

People's Lobby did not follow through on this proposed Initiative, but it helped renew interest in the issue, which led to the formation of San Franciscans for Public Power, a group that sponsored a successful petition drive to put the Initiative on the November 1982 ballot. PG&E successfully defended its monopoly on city power sales with a campaign that broke the previous city record for ballot measure spending. The company spent $562,000—57 times what proponents spent. The measure lost by a five to three margin.

61. *Time,* 26 August 1974.

62. *San Francisco Chronicle,* 25 September 1974; People's Lobby, *Newsletter,* December 1974–January 1975.

63. People's Lobby, *Newsletter,* December 1974–January 1975.

64. *Fresno Bee,* 13 September 1974.

65. People's Lobby, "Petition for National Initiative and Vote of Confidence (Recall)" (Los Angeles: People's Lobby Press, 1974).

66. Quoted in *Initiative and Vote of Confidence (Recall)* (Los Angeles: People's Lobby Press, 1974), inside front cover page.

67. Edwin A. Koupal, Jr., quoted in Tiffany Communications Bureau pamphlet (Los Angeles, 1975) advertising Koupal as a paid speaker.

68. People's Lobby, *Newsletter,* May–June 1975, p. 2.

69. Ibid., December 1974–January 1975.

70. Ibid., March–April 1975.

71. Edwin A. Koupal, Jr., letter to People's Lobby activists and contributors, 4 September 1975.

72. Roger Telschow, interview with the author, 16 October 1983.

73. People's Lobby, *Newsletter,* May–June 1975; Dick Nolan, column in *San Francisco Examiner,* 10 August 1975; *Political Animal* (Los Angeles newsletter), 25 August 1975.

74. Forster interview, 1983.

75. "Ed Koupal of People's Lobby Dies," *San Francisco Examiner,* 30 March 1976.

76. Forster interview, 1983; Telschow interviews, 1983.

77. See David D. Schmidt, *Ballot Initiatives: History, Research and Analysis of Recent Initiative and Referendum Campaigns* (Washington, D.C.: Initiative News Service, 1983), pp. 7–10.

78. Ralph Nader, quoted in program for Koupal's funeral service, 3 April 1976.

79. Quoted in Hunn, "Ed Koupal."

Chapter 4

1. Lee Dye, "Atomic Plant Built Near Quake Fault," *Los Angeles Times,* 24 November 1973.

2. Lee Dye, "Initiative to Put Curbs on Atom Plants Started," *Los Angeles Times,* 12 March 1974.

3. The following endorsers were listed prominently on each petition for this Initiative: Ralph Nader, Jack Lemmon, Steve Allen, Federation of American Scientists, People's Lobby, Friends of the Earth, Sierra Club, California Citizen Action Group.

4. Personal recollection of the author.

5. "Press and Public Reactions to Resignation of Nuclear Engineers," *Project Survival News,* March–April 1976.

6. "Rock on 15," *Project Survival News,* May–June 1976.

7. People's Lobby, "People's Lobby Warns Nuclear Industry: No Business As Usual Under Prop. 9," news release, 22 April 1975. Included with the release was a copy of a letter from Michael R. Peevey, director of the California Council for Environmental and Economic Balance, to L. T. Klein of the NUS Corporation office in Sherman Oaks, Calif., advising Klein that Winner/Wagner Associates had been retained to direct the "Vote No" campaign. The letter was dated 4 March 1975—15 months before the election.

8. Personal recollection of the author.

9. The federal government's inflated cost estimates were used in a mass-produced letter by S. L. Sibley, chairman of the board of PG&E, to stockholders, 7 April 1976. The letter urged stockholders to oppose the Initiative.

10. Federal government involvement in the "No on 15" campaign is documented in *Federal Attempts to Influence the Outcome of the June 1976 California Nuclear Referendum,* Report to the Senate Committee on Energy and Natural Resources by the Comptroller General of the United States (Washington, D.C.: General Accounting Office), 27 January 1978, EMD-78-31.

11. Faith Keating and Joyce Koupal, *Success Is Failure Analyzed: A Proposal for Winning Initiative Campaigns* (Los Angeles: Western Bloc, 1976), p. 35. See also full-page ads in the *San Francisco Chronicle,* 26 May 1976 and 4 June 1976; Project Survival

leaflet "Yes on Prop 15 / How Safe Is Nuclear Power?" in files of the author.

12. Brown said this in a speech a few days before the June 1976, election at De Anza College in Cupertino, Calif., at which the author was present. See also Jerry Gilliam, "Brown Qualifies Stand in Backing 3 A-Plant Bills," *Los Angeles Times,* 12 May 1976, and the same journalist's "Three Nuclear Plant Safety Bills Revived," ibid., 13 May 1976.

13. Dwight Cocke and Ken Masterton, undated 1981 fundraising letter to members of Californians for Nuclear Safeguards.

14. Roger Telschow, interview with the author, 25 March 1985.

15. John Forster, interview with the author, 20 March 1985.

16. Telschow interview, 1985.

17. Forster interview, 1985.

18. Telschow interview, 1985.

19. Forster interview, 1985.

20. Vote Yes For Lower Utilities, "Campaign Volunteer Walks 140 Miles to Columbus to Support State Utility Issues," news release, mid-October 1976.

21. Robert H. Snyder, "4 Utility Issues Stay On Ballot, Court Says," (Cleveland) *Plain Dealer,* 23 September 1976; "Utility Court Suit Threatens Ohioans' Right to Vote on Issues" (editorial), *Dayton Daily News,* 3 October 1976.

22. These same slogans were repeated in leaflets and other literature issues throughout the campaign by the utilities' "Committee for Safe, Lower Cost Electricity."

23. Common Cause/Ohio, "Good Government *Is* Worth Two Cents, Says Common Cause/Ohio," news release, 21 September 1976.

24. Forster interview, 1985.

25. Wes Hills, "Issue 4 Lowers Bills, Foe Admits," *Dayton Daily News,* 12 October 1976.

26. Vote Yes for Lower Utilities, "Partial List of Supporters," October 1976.

27. Citizens for Safe, Lower Cost Electricity, "Nuclear Energy—The Lower Cost Fuel of the Future," *Coalition News Service,* June 1976. (*Coalition News Service* was a glossy foldout newsletter published by CSLCE.)

28. Thomas J. Quinn, "1,488 Defects Found in Ohio Nuclear Plant," (Cleveland) *Plain Dealer,* 18 March 1976.

29. Vote Yes for Lower Utilities, news release, 31 October 1976.

30. Telschow interview, 1984.

31. William R. Diem, "CEI Treats 1,000 to Meal for Fighting Utility Issues," (Cleveland) *Plain Dealer,* undated clipping, November or December 1976.

32. Kay Drey, telephone interview with the author, 3 April 1985. Drey, an environmental activist, participated in the 1976 and 1980 Missouri Initiative campaigns. She lives in University City, Missouri.

33. Ibid.

34. Ibid.

35. Mike A. Males, telephone interview with the author, 10 November 1978.

36. Nuclear Vote, "Your Right to Choose," pamphlet published by proponents of Montana Initiative, 1978.

37. Steven D. Lydenberg, *Bankrolling Ballots: The Role of Business in Financing State Ballot Question Campaigns* (New York: Council on Economic Priorities, 1979), pp. 52–53.

38. See news coverage of these campaigns in *Initiative News Report* 1, nos. 1–9 (July–December 1980).

39. Ibid.

40. Steven D. Lydenberg, *Bankrolling Ballots Update 1980* (New York: Council on Economic Priorities, 1981), pp. 106–10.

41. Ibid., pp. 94–98, 103–6.

42. *Initiative New Report* 3, no. 8 (19 April 1982).

43. Steve Zemke, interviews with the author, 9–10 July 1982.

44. Don't Bankrupt Washington, "Fact Sheet on I-394," winter/spring 1981.

45. Zemke interviews.

46. Ibid.

47. Joe Ryan, interview with the author, 2 July 1982. Ryan led the abortive 1980 petition drive for the Initiative to require voter approval of government-funded energy projects.

48. Zemke interviews.

49. *Initiative News Report* 1, nos. 1, 2, 7 (1980).

50. *Initiative New Report* 2, nos. 7, 12, 14.

51. Zemke interviews.

52. Ibid.

53. Ibid.

54. Don't Bankrupt Washington, news release, 14 August 1981.

55. *Initiative News Report* 1, no 13 (29 June) and no. 14 (13 July 1981).

56. Zemke interviews.

57. Don't Bankrupt Washington, "Fact Sheet," fall 1981.

58. *Initiative News Report* 3, no. 14 (13 July 1981).

59. Ibid.

60. *Initiative News Report* 1, nos. 3 and 6 (22 September and 3 November 1980). John J. Fialka, "Property Tax Initiative Is Talk of California," *Washington Star,* 20 April 1978.

61. Charles Winner, quoted in Larry J. Sabato, *The Rise of Political Consultants* (New York: Basic Books, 1981), p. 27.

62. Zemke interviews.

63. Joel Connelly, "N-Forces Amass Election War Chest," *Seattle Post-Intelligencer,* 30 September 1981; Doug Underwood, "WPPSS: Contractors Donate to Defeat Bill," *Seattle Times,* 29 September 1981; Doug Underwood, "'Big Money' Plays Big Part in Initiative 394 Campaign," *Seattle Times,* 29 September 1981.

64. *Initiative News Report* 2, nos. 17, 19, 20, 21.

65. Ibid.

66. Shelby Scates, "Initiative Is Common Cents Measure," *Seattle Post-Intelligencer,* 27 September 1981.

67. Zemke interviews.

68. Washington State Public Disclosure Commission (hereafter "PDC"), *PDC News,* 28 September 1981.

69. Zemke interviews.

70. Don't Bankrupt Washington, "Summary of Survey Results," September 1981.

71. "Tony Schwartz: Radio's Responsive Chord," *Campaigns and Elections* 2, no. 1 (Spring 1981), pp. 18–26.

72. Zemke interviews.

73. Washington State PDC, *PDC News,* 22 October 1981.

74. Ibid.

75. Ibid.

76. Zemke interviews.

77. Washington State PDC, *PDC News,* 22 October 1981.

78. Tony Schwartz, interviewed in *Initiative News Report* 4, no. 11 (1 July 1983).

79. Ibid.

80. Zemke interviews.

81. Schwartz interview.

82. Zemke interviews.

83. Ibid.

84. Ibid.

85. Ibid.

86. Washington State PDC, *PDC News,* 30 November 1981.

87. *Initiative News Report* 2, no. 22 (16 November 1981).

88. Don't Bankrupt Washington Committee, news release, 4 November 1981.

89. Robert H. Keller, telephone interview with the author, 25 March 1985. A more detailed account of Keller's campaign is given in chap. 1 of William Rodgers, *Corporate Country* (Emmaus, PA: Rodale Press, 1973).

90. Washington Secretary of State, "History of State Initiative and Referendum Measures" (Olympia: State of Washington, 1977), p. 17.

91. Keller interview.

92. Ibid.

93. Washington Secretary of State, *History,* p. 20.

94. (Washington) Secretary of State, "Official Voters Pamphlet 1970" (Olympia: State of Washington, 1970), p. 6.

95. Peter Steinhart, "California's Bottle Initiative, If Passed, May Save More Than Bottles," *Los Angeles Times,* 28 March 1982.

96. Washington Secretary of State, *History,* p. 34.

97. Keller interview.

98. Ibid.

99. Ibid

100. Ibid.

101. See Rodgers, *Corporate Country.*

102. Keller interview.

103. Ibid.

104. General Accounting Office, *Report on Bottle Bills, 1980* (Washington, D.C.: Government Printing Office, 1980), quoted in *CAW Waste Watcher* (newsletter of Californians Against Waste, sponsor of 1982 California Bottle Bill Initiative), April 1981.

105. Earl Selby and Miriam Selby, "The Lobby That Battles Bottle Bills," *Reader's Digest,* May 1976, p. 242.

106. Field Institute, *The California Poll,* news release, September 1982.

107. William K. Shireman, "A How-to Guide for Defeating Popular Ballot Initiatives," testimony before the California State As-

sembly Committee on Elections and Reapportionment, 7 December 1983, distributed by Californians Against Waste, Sacramento.

108. Armando Acuna, "Anti–Bottle Bill Ads False, Say Boy Scout, Campfire Leaders," *San Jose Mercury,* 30 September 1982.

109. Tom McCall, quoted in Californians for Recycling and Litter Clean-up news release, mid-October 1982.

110. Mark Nelson, and Ed Pope, "Year of the Smear: Bottle Bill Proponents Attack Foes' Ad," *San Jose Mercury,* 30 October 1982.

111. Combination of statistics from *San Francisco Examiner,* 8 August 1982, and *Initiative News Report* 3, no. 10, and 4, no. 23.

112. Environmental Action Foundation, Washington, D.C.

113. "Campaign Close-Up: D.C. Bottle Bill," *Initiative and Referendum: The Power of the People!* (San Francisco: Initiative Resource Center, Winter 1988).

Chapter 5

1. Sources for this section are: telephone interviews with Martin Schiffenbauer, 31 December 1984, and David Mundstock, 4 February 1985; Martin Schiffenbauer, letter, 11 February 1985; "Co-Oper Hailed 'Super Citizen' by Mayor," *Berkeley Co-Op News,* 10 December 1984.

2. Patrick Quinn, telephone interview with the author, 21 May 1985.

3. Rena Wish Cohen, "The Quinn-tessential Political Watchdog," *Panorama* (section of the [Chicago] *Sunday Herald*), 18 January 1981, p. 7.

4. Quinn interview.

5. Ibid.

6. Ibid.

7. Ibid.

8. Coalition for Political Honesty, "Candidates Support Political Honesty," press release, fall 1976.

9. Michael J. Lennon, and Caroline A. Gherardini, eds., *Illinois Issues Special Report: The Cutback Amendment* (Springfield, Ill.: Sangamon State University, 1982), pp. 15–16.

10. Ibid.

11. Cohen, "Quinn-tessential."

12. Lennon and Gherardini, *Report,* p. 17.

13. Ibid, p. 14.

14. Charles W. Wiggins, and Janice Petty, "Cumulative Voting and Electoral Competition," *American Politics Quarterly* 7 (1979), pp. 345–46.

15. Quinn interview.

16. Lennon and Gherardini, *Report,* p. 18.

17. Ibid., pp. 19–20.

18. Ibid., pp. 20–22.

19. Quinn interview.

20. Lennon and Gherardini, *Report,* pp. 24–25.

21. Cohen, "Quinn-tessential."

22. Lennon and Gherardini, *Report,* p. 27.

23. Ibid., p. 33.

24. *Initiative News Report* 3, no. 16 (9 August 1982).

25. Ibid., 4, no. 8 (29 April 1983).

26. Quinn interview.

27. Ibid.

28. Ibid.

29. Ibid.

30. David D. Schmidt, "Cook County Judges Issue: Illinois Coalition Wins," *Initiative News Report,* 19 April 1985, p. 1; Quinn interview.

31. Quinn interview.

Chapter 6

1. Howard A. Jarvis, *I'm Mad as Hell* (New York: Times Books, 1979), p. 227.

2. Ibid., pp. 194, 205–6, 212–17.

3. Ibid., p. 5.

4. Ibid., pp. 235–77.

5. Ibid., p. 280.

6. Ibid., pp. 16, 25.

7. Ibid., p. 25.

8. Ibid., p. 32.

9. From the 1940s through 1970, not a single Initiative qualified for the state ballot without the aid of paid petition circulators. See Chapter 3.

10. Jarvis, *I'm Mad as Hell,* p. 33.

11. Ibid., p. 20.

12. Ibid., p. 21.

13. Ibid., p. 50. See also Roger Rapoport, *California Dreaming: The Political Odyssey of Pat and Jerry Brown* (Berkeley, Calif.: Nolo Press, 1982), 232.

14. Ibid., p. 20.

15. Ibid., p. 38.

16. Ibid., p. 39.

17. Lou Cannon, *Reagan* (New York: G. P. Putnam's Sons, 1982), pp. 189–90.

18. Jarvis, *I'm Mad as Hell,* pp. 40–43.

19. Ibid., pp. 43, 49.

20. Ibid., pp. 22, 51, 53.

21. James Ring Adams, *Secrets of the Tax Revolt* (San Diego: Harcourt, Brace, Jovanovich, 1984), p. 164.

22. Rapoport, *California Dreaming,* p. 234.

23. Jarvis, *I'm Mad as Hell,* p. 112.

24. Adams, *Secrets,* p. 165.

25. Rapoport, *California Dreaming,* p. 234.

26. Jarvis, *I'm Mad as Hell,* p. 118.

27. Ibid., pp. 69–70.

28. Ibid., pp. 89–90.

29. Rapoport, *California Dreaming,* p. 237.

30. Jarvis, *I'm Mad as Hell,* pp. 126–27.

31. Adams, *Secrets,* p. 166.

32. March Fong Eu, Secretary of State, *Statement of Vote and Supplement, Primary Election,* 6 June (Sacramento: Secretary of State, 1978), pp. 191–225.

33. Adams, *Secrets,* p. 167.

34. Rapoport, *California Dreaming,* p. 238.

35. Adams, *Secrets,* p. 167.

36. Jarvis, *I'm Mad as Hell,* p. 190.

37. David Magleby, *Direct Legislation: Voting on Ballot Propositions in the United States* (Baltimore: Johns Hopkins University Press, 1984), p. 64.

38. Jarvis, *I'm Mad as Hell,* p. 110.

39. David D. Schmidt, "California's 'Save Proposition 13' Sinks Local Bond Prices," *Initiative News Report* 5, no. 12, p. 1.

40. Ibid.

41. Joel Fox, aide to Howard Jarvis, telephone interview with the author, 8 May 1985.

42. Charles Burress, and Mark Barabak, "Howard Jarvis Dies," *San Francisco Chronicle,* 13 August 1986.

43. Daniel Rosenheim, "The Tax Rebellion Has Cooled Off," *San Francisco Chronicle,* 31 October 1985.

44. Diane Curtis, and Daniel Rosenheim, "Major Changes in School Financing," *San Francisco Chronicle,* 30 October 1985.

45. Jerry Roberts, "A Hidden Crisis in Public Works," *San Francisco Chronicle,* 29 October 1985.

46. Vick Gould, "Statement *for* Initiative Measure 251," in "Official Voters Pamphlet" (Olympia: Secretary of State, 1970), p. 4. See also Martin J. Durkan, "Statement *for* SJR 1," in "Official Voters Pamphlet" (Olympia: Secretary of State, 1972), p. 38.

47. *History of State Initiative and Referendum Measures* (Olympia: Secretary of State, 1977), p. 35.

48. The legislature's amendment was labeled "SJR 1."

49. Joseph Tuchinsky, executive director of the Michigan Citizens Lobby, telephone interview with the author, 15 April 1985.

50. Adams, *Secrets,* p. 321.

51. Ibid., p. 315.

52. Ibid., p. 323.

53. "Massachusetts Information for Voters 1976" (Boston: Secretary of the Commonwealth, 1976), p. 4.

54. Adams, *Secrets,* p. 324.

55. Ibid.

56. Ibid., p. 325.

57. "Massachusetts Information for Voters 1980" (Boston: Secretary of the Commonwealth, 1980), p. 6.

58. Adams, *Secrets,* 325.

59. Citizens for Limited Taxation, "Legislature Votes No on Prop. 2½, CLT Prepares Second Petition Drive," press release, 6 May 1980.

60. As Anderson told the author in a fall 1980 telephone interview. CLT's 1980 campaign literature emphasized this claim.

61. "Massachusetts Information for Voters 1980."

62. Poll by Research Analysis (a polling firm), 5–6 October 1980, published in *Initiative News Report* 1, no. 5.

63. David D. Schmidt, "Massachusetts," *Initiative News Report* 1, no. 8 (10 December 1980).

64. Adams, *Secrets,* p. 332; Chip Faulkner, spokesperson for CLT, telephone interview with the author, 29 February 1988.

65. "Argument *for* Question 2," in "Massachusetts Information for Voters, 1976," p. 7.

66. Adams, *Secrets,* p. 332.

67. "Tax Initiatives in Decline this Year," *Initiative News Report* 3, no. 6, pp. 5–6. (9 August 1982).

68. Quoted in Rosenheim, "Tax Rebellion Has Cooled Off."

69. *Initiative News Report* 1, no. 5 (22 October 1980), and 1, no. 7 (17 November 1980).

70. *Initiative News Report* 3, no. 16 (9 August 1982), and 4, no. 2 (28 January 1983).

71. "Tax Initiatives: A Different Story in Each State," *Initiative News Report* 5, no. 22 (16 November 1984).

72. George Brown Tindall, *America: A Narrative History* (New York: Norton, 1984), p. 261.

Chapter 7

1. Ernest C. Bolt, Jr., *Ballots Before Bullets: The War Referendum Approach to Peace in America, 1914–1941* (Charlottesville: University of Virginia Press, 1977), p. 44.

2. Ibid., p. 20.

3. Ibid., p. 63.

4. Ibid., p. 143.

5. Ibid., p. 158.

6. Ibid., p. 163.

7. Ibid., p. 173.

8. Ibid.

9. Ibid., p. 171.

10. Ibid., p. 181.

11. Ibid., p. 183.

12. Ibid., p. 189.

13. Lynn Ludlow, "The Groups Behind Battle to Pass Prop. P," *San Francisco Examiner,* 5 November 1967.

14. Ibid.

15. "Farley v. Healy (431 P.2d. 650): The Use of the Municipal Initiative as a polltaking Device on Non-municipal Issues," *California Western Law Review* 5 (1968), p. 148.

16. "No on P" (editorial), *San Francisco Chronicle,* 2 November 1967.

17. "Reagan Blasts Proposition P," *San Francisco Chronicle,* 1 November 1967.

18. "Yes on P" (advertisement), *San Francisco Examiner,* 5 November 1967; "The 'Far-Flung Friends of P,'" *San Francisco Chronicle,* 2 November 1967.

19. "Fulbright Won't Say Yes or No," *San Francisco Examiner,* 5 November 1967.

20. "Veterans Call for 'No' on Prop. P," *San Francisco Chronicle,* 3 November 1967; "Yes on P" (advertisement).

21. "U.S. Reaction to the Defeat of Prop. P," *San Francisco Chronicle,* 9 November 1967.

22. Thomas Kearney, registrar of voters, ed., *San Francisco Voter Information Pamphlet, General Election November 7, 1978* (San Francisco: Office of the Registrar of Voters, 1978), p. 105.

23. "Jobs With Peace Referendum Results" (Boston: Jobs With Peace Campaign, 1985).

24. Ibid.

25. Jill Nelson, executive director of Jobs With Peace Campaign, telephone interview with the author, 6 August 1985.

26. "Jobs With Peace Referendum Results."

27. Margaret Lane, "Baltimore Publishes Info on Military Uses of Local Taxes," *Jobs With Peace (National Network Newsletter),* November–December 1983, p. 7.

28. Philip McManus, "Bringing the Initiative Home," post-election memo to campaign workers, 1980.

29. Joel Kotkin, "Calif. County to Vote on Antinuclear Arms Measure," *Washington Post,* 2 June 1980; "Yes on A," pamphlet (Santa Cruz: Yes on A Committee, 1980).

30. McManus, "Bringing the Initiative Home."

31. John Keith, "Lockheed Up in Arms Over Measure 'A,'" *Santa Cruz Phoenix,* 1–14 May 1980.

32. McManus, "Bringing the Initiative Home."

33. Ibid.

34. "Santa Cruz," *New Abolitionist,* newsletter (Baltimore, Md.: Nuclear-Free America, February 1985).

35. Sen. "Mac" Mathias, "Garrett Park, Md., Is a Nuclear-Free Zone," *Congressional Record,* 6 May 1982.

36. "80 Nuclear Free Zones in U.S.A.," *New Abolitionist,* December 1984, p. 1.

37. "Nuclear Free Zones in America," *New Abolitionist,* December 1984, p. 10.

38. "Cambridge, Mass. Defeats Ban on Nuclear Arms Research," *Initiative News Report* 4, no. 22 (18 November 1983).

39. "80 Nuclear Free Zones."

40. "The Corporate Campaign," *New Abolitionist*, January–February 1984, p. 1.

41. Ibid.

42. Mark Fritz, "Nuke Ban Splits Ann Arbor," *Lansing State Journal*, 29 October 1983. See also "Ann Arbor: Victory in Defeat," *New Abolitionist*, December 1984, p. 5.

43. "80 Nuclear Free Zones."

44. Ibid.

45. "Nuclear Free Zones in America," insert, *New Abolitionist*, February 1985.

46. "Takoma Park—One Year Later," *New Abolitionist*, December 1984, p. 2.

47. Randall Kehler, telephone interview with the author, 30 July 1985.

48. Larry Liebert, "Behind the Anti-Nuclear Arms Initiative," *San Francisco Chronicle*, 23 November 1981.

49. Jay Matthews, "Less Bang for the Bucks: A Millionaire's Fight for the Nuclear Freeze," *Washington Post*, 6 June 1984.

50. Kehler interview.

51. Ibid.

52. Judith Scheckel, director, Traprock Peace Center, telephone interview with the author, 1 August 1985.

53. Randall Kehler and Judith Scheckel, "Yes: The People Decided," *Sojourners*, March 1981.

54. Robert Kaiser, "Sudden Ground Swell for a Nuclear Freeze," *San Francisco Chronicle*, 13 April 1982.

55. Institute for Defense and Disarmament Studies, Brookline, Mass., biographical sketch of Randall Forsberg.

56. Kehler interview.

57. Kehler and Scheckel, "Yes."

58. Kehler interview; see article in the *Nation*, 1 December 1980.

59. J. Seidita, interview with the author, 9 July 1982.

60. Ibid.

61. Matthews, "Less Bang."

62. "Initiative," *New Yorker*, 26 April 1982, p. 30.

63. Larry Liebert, "One Man's 'Obsession' to Halt Nuclear Arms Race," *San Francisco Chronicle,* 21 April 1982.

64. Matthews, "Less Bang."

65. "Nuclear Freeze Fundraising Bonanza," *Initiative News Report* 3, no. 11 (1 June 1982).

66. Matthews, "Less Bang."

67. Michael Betzold, "Michigan Puts Freeze on Ballot," memo circulated at National Freeze Referendum organizers conference, Fontbonne College, St. Louis, 9 July 1982.

68. Malik Edwards, interview with the author, 9 July 1982. See also Tom Sherwood, "Referendum on Nuclear Weapons Freeze Is Sought Here," *Washington Post,* 27 March 1982.

69. Karin Fierke, "The Freeze and the Fall Ballot," *Freeze Newsletter,* July 1982, p. 7.

70. Kaiser, "Sudden Ground Swell."

71. Fierke, "Freeze and the Fall Ballot"; Nancy Carroll, interview with the author, 9 July 1982.

72. "State of the Campaign," *Freeze Newsletter,* July 1982, p. 6.

73. Quoted in Adam Clymer, "The Nuclear Freeze: Politicians Find It Difficult to Predict Issue's Influence on Fall Elections," *New York Times,* 6 July 1982.

74. Robert Scheer, *With Enough Shovels: Reagan, Bush and Nuclear War* (New York: Random House, 1982); Caspar Weinberger, testimony before the U.S. Senate Foreign Relations Committee, 3 November 1981.

75. Mervin D. Field, "Majority Favors Nuclear Freeze," *San Francisco Chronicle,* 21 April 1982. See also nationwide poll by ABC News/Washington Post conducted 21–25 April 1982, and presentation of poll results by Louis Harris, 27 July 1982.

76. Randall Kehler, "Message from the National Coordinator," *Freeze Newsletter,* October 1982, p. 3.

77. Quoted in *New York Times,* 16 March 1982.

78. "Anti-Freeze Initiatives / Report #2," memorandum from *Interchange* (a peace activists' information clearinghouse), Washington, D.C., 20 January 1983.

79. American Security Council, "1982 Voting Index/Washington Report," September 1982, brochure.

80. Jerry Falwell, fundraising letter from Moral Majority, Inc., 17 June 1982; emphasis in original.

81. Quoted in "Responses to the Film 'Countdown for America,'" memo circulated by Nuclear Weapons Freeze Campaign.

82. Caspar Weinberger, testimony before the U.S. Senate Foreign Relations Committee, 29 April 1982.

83. John Barron, "The KGB's Magical War for 'Peace,'" *Reader's Digest,* October 1982, p. 235.

84. Ronald Reagan, speech in Columbus, Ohio, 4 October 1982.

85. Randall Kehler, statement to the news media, 5 October 1982.

86. Ben Senturia, "National Referendum on the Freeze to Occur," *Freeze Newsletter,* October 1982, p. 5.

87. Lee Dembart, "Foes of Nuclear Freeze Initiative Will Seek Free TV Time for Ads," *Los Angeles Times,* 19 October 1982.

88. "INR Campaign Spending Study," *Initiative News Report* 4, no. 23. (2 December 1983).

89. Julie Ingersoll, and Patrick McGuigan, "Freeze Gains Widespread Voter Support, Suffers Loss in Arizona," *Initiative and Referendum Report,* November 1982, p. 4.

90. "Nuclear Arms Freeze: Victorious, But Not Invulnerable," *Initiative News Report* 3, no. 22 (12 November 1982).

91. Randall Forsberg and Randall Kehler, press release, 19 November 1982.

92. Quoted in Robert Shogan, "Nuclear Freeze Movement Emerges as Political Test," *Los Angeles Times,* 17 April 1982.

93. "A-Freeze Leaders Seek 1 Million Volunteers," *San Francisco Chronicle,* 3 December 1983.

94. Kehler interview.

Chapter 8

1. Andreas Gross, Swiss Initiative expert, interview with the author, Zurich, Switzerland, 4 October 1987.

2. Geoffrey de Q. Walker, *Initiative and Referendum: The People's Law* (St. Leonard's, New South Wales, Australia: Centre for Independent Studies, 1987).

3. Gerald Häfner, interview with the author, Bonn, West Germany, 3 September 1987.

4. Jody H. Seaverson, memo to Sen. James Abourezk and Pete Stavrianos, 23 July 1975, "Re: the Anti-Bureaucracy Act."

5. John Forster, telephone interview with the author, 18 July 1985.

6. Sen. James Abourezk, statement in *Congressional Record,* 11 July 1977.

Under S. J. Res. 67, introduced by Sen. James Abourezk in 1977, and S. J. Res. 33, introduced by Sen. Mark Hatfield in 1979, the federal Constitution would have been amended to allow voters to propose and enact national laws by petition and popular vote. The petition requirement would be a number of signatures equal to 3 percent of the votes cast in the preceding presidential election—about 2.6 million signatures for 1988. Such Initiatives would be on ballots only in November of national election years. The Initiative process could *not* be used to pass amendments to the Constitution. Congress would have the power to amend or repeal an Initiative passed by the voters, but only (1) by two-thirds majority roll call vote of both houses during the first two years after the Initiative is approved, or (2) by simple majority vote of both Houses after two years.

7. Forster telephone interview.

8. The record book of that hearing, a hefty 647 pages, was printed by the U.S. Government Printing Office under the title *Voter Initiative Constitutional Amendment: Hearings Before the Subcommittee on the Constitution on S. J. Res. 67, December 13 and 14, 1977* (Washington, D.C.: Government Printing Office, 1978).

9. The Gallup poll was based on personal interviews with 1,536 adults in more than 300 scientifically selected localities during the period 6–9 January 1978. They were asked: "The U.S. Senate will consider a proposal that would require a national vote—that is, a referendum—on any issue when three percent of all voters who voted in the most recent presidential election sign petitions asking for such a nationwide vote. Do you favor or oppose such a plan?" Table 8-1 displays the results.

10. George Gallup, "National Initiative Favored," *San Francisco Chronicle,* 15 May 1978.

11. *Voter Initiative Constitutional Amendment,* pp. 85–89, 647.

12. Personal recollection of the author, who served on Senator Abourezk's staff from July through December 1978.

13. Anne Charles, "Grassroots Drive for a More Direct Democracy," *National Opinion Poll Quarterly,* Winter 1979, p. 14.

Table 8-1
Attitudes Toward a National Initiative (see n. 9)

	% Favor	% Oppose	% No Opinion
Nationwide	57	21	22
College graduates	58	30	11
High school graduates	59	19	22
Grade school education	46	11	43
Eastern U.S.	55	19	26
Midwestern U.S.	56	23	21
Southern U.S.	59	19	22
Western U.S.	57	23	20
Under 30 years old	59	19	22
30 to 49 years old	59	22	19
50 years and older	52	22	26
Republicans	56	25	19
Democrats	59	20	21
Independents	56	22	22

14. Sen. Mark Hatfield, statement in *Congressional Record,* 5 February 1979; news release, *Initiative America,* 5 February 1979.

15. Forster telephone interview.

16. Michael Nelson, "Power to the People: The Crusade for Direct Democracy," *Saturday Review,* 24 November 1979, p. 16.

17. The author has a confirmation copy of that telegram.

18. Roger Telschow, telephone interview with the author, 15 October 1984.

19. *Initiative News Report* 3, no. 18 (13 September 1982).

20. Benjamin Barber, *Strong Democracy: Participatory Politics for a New Age* (Berkeley and Los Angeles: University of California Press, 1984), pp. 281–89. The petition signature requirement of Barber's proposal ("two to three percent of the number of ballots cast in the previous presidential election") mirrors Abourezk's. Rather than "yes" or "no" votes on a proposal, however, Barber proposes giving voters five options: an unequivocal "yes," a "yes" with reservations, an unequivocal "no," a "no" on the specific proposal but not necessarily on the intent of the Initiative, and a "no" calling for postponement of a final decision until there has been more deliberation and debate. If the two "yes" options add up to a majority, the Initiative would go to a second popular vote six

months later for a final decision. If the three "no" options add up to a majority, however, the "nays" prevail with no further action. Barber suggests that civic education on national Initiatives be ensured by (1) sending voter information booklets, with pros and cons of each Initiative, to every voter (this is already done for Initiative elections in many states); (2) limiting campaign spending by interests supporting or opposing an Initiative; and (3) broadcasting town meetings, discussions, and debates at frequent intervals during the months prior to the election, giving all sides a chance to be heard at no cost to the speakers.

Chapter 9

1. Marc Caplan, *Ralph Nader Presents: A Citizen's Guide to Lobbying* (New York: Dembner Books, 1983). The paperback edition can be ordered from the publisher: Dembner Books, 80 Eighth Avenue, New York, NY 10011.

2. Gale Cook, "Initiative Process a Sacred Cow to GOP," *San Francisco Examiner and Chronicle,* 20 May 1984. Weinberger's plan was to prohibit circulation of Initiative petitions, requiring them to be signed only in offices of election officials.

3. Joan Flanagan, *The Grass Roots Fund Raising Book* (Chicago: Swallow Press, 1982).

4. *A Celebration of Volunteers* is available for $5.00 from the Northern Rockies Action Group, 9 Placer St., Helena, MT 59601.

5. *Talking Back* is available from the Public Media Center in San Francisco, which also gives expert advice on Fairness Doctrine strategy as well as designing and producing television, radio, and newspaper ads.

6. Larry J. Sabato, *The Rise of Political Consultants* (New York: Basic Books, 1981).

Index